# PRAISE FOR *MAKE LEARNING PERSONAL: THE WHAT, WHO, WOW, WHERE, AND WHY*

*"Many books claim to be about learning, few live up to the claim. This is one of the few. It addresses the key focus for changing classrooms: the culture and language. With many important and useful clarifications and distinctions, it helps the move from today's dominant depersonalized classrooms toward greater learner motivation, engagement, and achievement. It is packed with a rich range of examples from the United States and elsewhere, including teachers' stories, and a great model of the journey of change. The authors have considerable expertise in this territory; this book deserves to become a considerable resource for improving classrooms."*

**—Chris Watkins, Reader in Education, University of London, Institute of Education, United Kingdom**

*"Bray and McClaskey are pioneers in personalized learning. This book will provide the clarity and direction many are looking for to focus their classrooms on personalizing instruction."*

**—Kecia Ray, Executive Director of Learning Technology and Library Services, Metropolitan Nashville Public Schools, Tennessee**

*"In an age of educational upthrow, one of the major themes emerging is that of personalization. And while this concept can connote many different models of instruction, Bray and McClaskey do an excellent job of making the case for a framework that is pedagogically appropriate, research based, and theoretically sound. Make Learning Personal makes the case for a personalization pedagogy, replete with ideas and examples that paint a canvas of possibilities for today's classroom teacher. The graphics, charts, and support resources are well designed, helpfully structured, and ready for practical application in the classroom. Through this book, educators have a helpful companion that augments their experience and expertise in transforming their classroom to meet the needs of our children as they prepare for their roles in the global knowledge economy."*

**—Walter McKenzie, Educational Leader, Writer, and Speaker, Washington, DC**

*"Make Learning Personal should be on the top of every educator's professional reading list. From concept to conclusion, this book is a landmark resource that will inspire and support educators around the world to liberate school culture so that all learners can become self-directed, independent, expert learners. Bray and McClaskey provide compelling and comprehensive research-based rationale about why there needs to be a cultural shift to working in partnerships with all learners. What sets their work apart are the authentic examples and proven practical and*

*achievable processes that educators can implement to make the shift to success made through working in partnership. As such, this book is a resource that you will delve into over and over again as your transformational learning journey evolves."*

**—Greg Alchin, Learning Experience Designer,
Orange, New South Wales, Australia**

*"Too many in education believe that 'personalized' is a synonym for 'individualized' or 'differentiated,' thus enabling them to feel current while justifying outdated, teacher-centered approaches. After reading this book, educators will never look at their jobs the same way again."*

**—Fred Bramante, President, National Center
for Competency-Based Learning, New Hampshire**

*"Many schools acknowledge that personalizing learning is of the utmost importance; every child is an individual, so the learning we provide them should take this into account.* Make Learning Personal *demonstrates how to ensure a personalized learning approach can happen in your school. It draws on the experiences of many experienced educators from different parts of the world, and its authors have crafted a book that every school should go to for ideas and inspiration. Bray and McClaskey are passionate about personalizing learning, and this book will start you on that very same journey."*

**—Kevin McLaughlin, Primary Teacher, Old
Mill Primary School, Leicester, United Kingdom**

*"This book is on my mandatory reading list for educators who want to transform schools into learner-centered environments. Bray and McClaskey clear away the hype and buzzwords to focus on the crucial aspects of personalized learning. They provide a clear, research-supported rationale for why personalized learning is imperative, outline practical steps for implementation, and share examples of where personalized learning is already working. The book is simultaneously visionary, motivational, and practical. It is an excellent resource and I highly recommend it."*

**—Jon Tanner, Personalized Learning Initiative Task Force Leader,
Oregon School District, Oregon, Wisconsin**

*"In this book, Bray and McClaskey have performed a wonderful service to the future of personalized learning design—grounded in research, supported by real-world examples, and centered on the learner."*

**—Steve Nordmark, Chief Academic Officer,
KNOVATION Making Learning Personal, Cincinnati, Ohio**

*"This is a must-read for those embarking on a teaching career, those who are just starting out, and those experienced teachers who want to reflect on why they went into teaching and how they can improve the experience for themselves and their students. This book is my cup of tea: it is very well researched and replete with fabulous examples and great advice on how to give students a voice in their own learning. In this book every story matters because every student matters."*

**—Peter H. Reynolds,** *New York Times* **Bestselling Author and Illustrator,** *The Dot, Ish, Sky Color,* **and** *The North Star,* **Boston**

*"Personalizing learning is the key to reforming public education and is a hot topic nationwide. In the last two weeks I've spoken at a statewide conference and on two webinars, sharing experiences of over ten years in personalizing learning. At each event, I share the exciting news of this fabulous new book:* Make Learning Personal. *In it, Bray and McClaskey provide more than theoretical background, offering guidance for the requisite cultural change necessary to transform both teachers and students to become co-learners. Finally, someone has made clear the distinctions between personalization, differentiation, and individualization. Bray and McClaskey's chart has become the go-to resource for this critical understanding. Personalized learning shifts the responsibility for learning to the students; in my school we like to say, "The person who does the work is the person who does the learning." If the teacher is working harder than the student, something is out of kilter. Grounded in Universal Design for Learning and the belief that all learners can succeed, this book provides the structure and the moral courage to affect meaningful change in schools across the country."*

**—Lauren Kelley Parren, Innovation Coach, Bristol, Vermont**

*"The authors gather and interpret the many forms in which educators worldwide seek to 'personalize' the learner's experience. Over years of use, that term has taken on many meanings, and this guide helps users clarify their own."*

**—Kathleen Cushman, Author,**
***The Motivation Equation, Fires in the Mind,* and *Fires in the Bathroom,* New York**

*"Bray and McClaskey combine their long years of experience in this comprehensive publication, written from both their hearts and minds. They provide a thought-provoking way to reframe the conversation of personalized learning from the learner's point of view. At the same time they detail their unique '5 W's' scaffold for implementing personalized learning—including tools, case studies, and*

*reflective questions to ponder. I invite you to explore the personalized learning landscape in this book, so that we can inform ourselves and empower the learners we serve to take ownership of their own authentic learning."*

**Julie Duffield, Senior Research Associate,**
**WestEd, San Francisco**

*"How do we create a school culture where students own their learning? Where being a learner is more valuable than being a student? Personalizing learning for each student seems like a daunting task, but this book is filled with examples from multiple grade levels that will help any naysayer understand not only why we need to do this but how it can be done. This is not about adaptive learning but rather a sensible approach to teachers purposefully designing learning with each learner in mind, based on what we now know about how the brain works. Whether you are a classroom teacher, school administrator, or district leader, Bray and McClaskey have taken a complex process and broken it down into doable steps for you. You will learn about the Universal Design for Learning (UDL) process, which helps teachers to systematically 'reduce or eliminate the barriers that keep learners from learning.'*

*"Bray and McClaskey recognize that change is hard and provide a sensible three-tiered approach to help move any classroom, school, or district toward personalizing learning for each learner. Even for teachers in schools and districts that aren't ready to make this change, there are ideas and processes to start moving in this direction. The first step is recognizing that each learner is unique and learns in different ways and at different paces. This is a book written in easy-to-understand language that will provide educators with the justification for adopting a personalized approach to learning and provides the road map to get there. I will definitely purchase multiple copies to share with our district leaders and plan to lead a book study next year!"*

**—Nancy White, 21st-Century Learning & Innovation Specialist,**
**Academy School District 20, Colorado Springs, Colorado**

*"One of the biggest issues with personalized learning is the lack of common understanding about exactly what it means to personalize learning. While some are talking about personalization, what others are referring to is actually individualization or differentiation. This book is THE handbook for all educators, administrators, and community members as it provides the essential background and language needed to understand how to help learners take ownership of their own learning. Each section—the what, who, wow, where, and why—provides extensive research and examples that explain why learners need to be provided with authentic voice and choice. It's time to get the students off the 'stage' of school and help them to become lifetime motivated and engaged learners!"*

**—Laura Lindquist, Educational Technology Coordinator**
**and Personalized Learning Coach,**
**Verona Area School District, Verona, Wisconsin**

"Barbara and Kathleen do an outstanding job of really capturing what personalized learning can look like in your classroom. They take you step by step through a journey of how you can turn your classroom into an environment where all learners have a voice and choice."

—Rita A. Mortenson, Educational Technology Coordinator
and Personalized Learning Coach,
Verona Area High School, Verona, Wisconsin

"This is a book that should be read by every educator and should be a part of every teacher preparation program. Weaving learning theory, research, and practical strategies together to create a deep understanding of what it means to personalize learning, Bray and McClaskey are masterful in guiding educators as they create learner-centered environments. Sharing success stories and practical examples, this book provides exactly what is needed to help teachers create learning environments that motivate and engage ALL learners."

—Lisa Wilson, Programs/Services Administrator,
Grant Wood Area Education Agency, Cedar Rapids, Iowa

"If every educator could articulate what true 'personalized' learning looks like, our schools and classrooms would be much better places for students. It's time for us to stop talking about getting away from the factory model of schools and actually start doing it. This book is critically important reading for anyone who cares about empowering kids as learners."

—Dr. Scott McLeod, Founding Director, CASTLE, Storm Lake, Iowa

"As an educator for more than thirty years, I have seen a myriad of ideas to improve education, many of which have been met with mixed results. I believe that personalized learning could truly be the game-changer! Barbara and Kathleen have certainly done their homework in clearly defining what it means to personalize learning. They identify stages that can help teachers gradually adapt their role, moving from a teacher-centered classroom to a learner-driven environment that is truly transformational. This book will serve as a valuable handbook as educators make the decision to empower their learners!"

—Betty Wottreng, Director of Technology Services,
Verona Area School District, Verona, Wisconsin

"Bray and McClaskey have clarified what it means to truly personalize learning. They not only explain why this is such a powerful way to help learners of all ages learn, but they guide educators through the process of creating powerful personalized learning environments that work."

—Linda Ullah, Personalized Learning Coach, Charlotte, North Carolina

"Barbara and Kathleen have done an amazing job writing about personalized learning. I totally connected with both authors from the start of the book, where they openly share their own stories with deep emotion and raw honesty. Barbara and Kathleen both write from the heart, and I found their stories inspirational and touching.

"This book has given me a deeper insight into personalized learning in all areas, from the 5 W's—what, who, wow, where, and why—to 'me,' as the reader, and how I can personalize learning.

"There is a good balance between research; stories from teachers, leaders, and learners; and practical ideas that teachers can use in our own context. It is a comprehensive well of information, and I would highly recommend this book to any educator who wants a great starting point in personalized learning and wants to give their learners the best possible learning for the rest of their lives.

"Thank you for writing this much-needed book!"

**—Tina Photakis, Elementary Teacher,
Cowandilla Primary School, Adelaide, South Australia**

"The core or central theme of this book is having the leaner at the center of learning. This differs from the current educational paradigm and many educational publications in that often curriculum and instruction are the focus of the discussions rather than the learner. The book is nicely and strategically divided into what, who, wow, where, and why. Ideas are well supported by educational research, theories, and psychology with case studies that reinforce and exemplify the theoretical concepts covered. This is a great addition to the literature for this generation of learners and learning theory."

**—Jackie Gerstein, Adjunct Faculty, Boise State,
Walden, and Western Governors Universities, Santa Fe, New Mexico**

"Bray and McClaskey are pioneers in the field of personal learning communities, and their new book provides an overview of personalized learning: what it is and what it is not, scenarios from schools and districts who are already engaged in personalized learning, professional development to support changes in teaching to achieve effective personalized learning, and much more! Most importantly, perhaps, is the chapter on why personalized learning is a good idea, including its effects on student engagement, keeping students in school, and increasing the graduation rate. This book encourages educators to consider a variety of ways learning can be personalized for students from a variety of perspectives. Many thoughtful images suggest 'what is' compared to 'what could be' so that educators can reflect on their own practice and begin to move toward providing an *environment for more student voice and choice so that students take responsibility for their own learning and delve more deeply into subject matter, making it their own."*

**—Sara Armstrong, Co-author, *The Invent to Learn Guide to 3D Printers in the Classroom: Recipes for Success*, Berkeley, California**

*"Deep learning only occurs when it has meaning for the learner, and this book is a solid example of how this works. Bray and McClaskey provide a tour through learning opportunities that is spiced with personal learning stories told by both students and teachers. These narratives provide a sense of reality for pre-service teachers to envision and inservice teachers to acknowledge.*

*"Notably, the authors acknowledge that change is transitional and provide a process educators can use to evolve an 'ecology of learning' into a personalized learning environment. They introduce the Wow factor as the place in the transition where teacher and learner roles change. The resources in this book support reaching this significant point in personalizing learning.*

*"This book provides a useful framework for positive change in education."*

**—Leigh E. Zeitz, Associate Professor, Instructional Technology, University of Northern Iowa, Cedar Falls, Iowa**

# Make Learning Personal

# Make Learning Personal

## The What, Who, WOW, Where, and Why

**Barbara Bray**
**Kathleen McClaskey**
*Foreword by John H. Clarke*

CORWIN
A SAGE Company

**CORWIN**
A SAGE Company

FOR INFORMATION:

Corwin
A SAGE Company
2455 Teller Road
Thousand Oaks, California 91320
(800) 233-9936
www.corwin.com

SAGE Publications Ltd.
1 Oliver's Yard
55 City Road
London EC1Y 1SP
United Kingdom

SAGE Publications India Pvt. Ltd.
B 1/I 1 Mohan Cooperative Industrial Area
Mathura Road, New Delhi 110 044
India

SAGE Publications Asia-Pacific Pte. Ltd.
3 Church Street
#10-04 Samsung Hub
Singapore 049483

Acquisitions Editor:   Robin Najar
Associate Editor:   Desirée A. Bartlett
Editorial Assistants:   Ariel Price;
                        Andrew Olson
Production Editor:   Amy Schroller
Copy Editor:   Mark Bast
Typesetter:   C&M Digitals (P) Ltd.
Proofreader:   Dennis W. Webb
Indexer:   Pilar Wyman
Cover Designer:   Anupama Krishnan
Cover Photo:   Scot Allen
Marketing Manager:   Amanda Boudria

Printed in the United States of America

A catalog record of this book is available from the Library of Congress.

ISBN 978-1-4833-5297-8

MIX
Paper from
responsible sources
FSC® C014174

This book is printed on acid-free paper.

14 15 16 17 18 10 9 8 7 6 5 4 3 2 1

# Contents

# Foreword

The personal stories told by Barbara Bray and Kathleen McClaskey in their introduction reminded me how hard I found it to be promoted from first and second grade and, forty years later, how hard it was to persuade our high school that my children should design at least part of their high school program around personal interests. With our oldest daughter, our success was marginal. She was too early. At last, my youngest child got to be among the first in the school to design his senior year around a personal passion—for computer animation. Our high school, where the authors have visited, continues to develop personalized learning for all kids, using Barbara's and Kathleen's ideas in view.

All learning is personal. Barbara and Kathleen have used their personal experiences and years of teaching to present a comprehensive and coherent view of personalized learning, empowering both learners and teachers to take greater control over their own growth. Personalization, rather than large-scale test scores, belongs at the organizing center of education redesign, because the idea of diversity, rather than uniformity, now describes our learners, schools, and career opportunities, and the roads to the future are many.

In reading *Make Learning Personal*, I found myself reorganizing and reconsidering what I thought I understood about personalizing learning and teaching. Personalized learning is not one thing; it consists of many strategies and concepts, old and new, brought together to put each learner at the center of the learning experience—thereby challenging teachers to guide all their learners along unique paths of discovery. Barbara and Kathleen infuse their book with widely recognized ideas and strategies derived from 100 years of learner-centered innovation and thought, which now constitute a foundation for personalized learning. First, they compare Personalization vs. Differentiation vs. Individualization to clarify some of the confusion around the terminology. Then, they place personalized learning in the context of learning theory, from Dewey and Vygotsky to Dweck and Csíkszentmihályi.

They connect the need for adaptable teaching processes to changes in orientation to schooling, evolving from one generation to the next. They explain the heritage and practice of personalized learning broadly, giving teachers and administrators a specific definition that allows great flexibility. The authors use their own innovations to weave a cohesive framework, offering a multitude of options for teachers who decide to restructure their work with young people.

Although it is steeped in theory and research, *Make Learning Personal* is an eminently practical book. Adapting to diversity without clear guidelines could easily degenerate into wild flailing, but the process of personalization that Bray and McClaskey have designed is hardly chaotic. Instead, it is tightly organized around three stages that teachers experience as they move from teacher-designed classes to learner-driven planning. At each stage, the authors introduce real examples of teachers and learners plotting out transformational journeys, with techniques and processes that teachers can adopt at each stage to continue their own journeys. Practical suggestions, such as Personal Learner Profiles, the principles of Universal Design for Learning, and Personal Learning Backpacks, tie directly to the general framework they have so carefully described.

In the same way they explain a process for teachers to use in moving toward learner-driven practices, they also describe in detail "model" schools where personalized learning has been developed around the world. Like learners in a personalized setting, we as educators and readers are left with the impression that we have a dependable process within which we can redesign our work, with an enormous array of specific choices that may fit our plans as we proceed.

We are fortunate indeed that both Barbara and Kathleen have strong backgrounds in learning technology. With new technologies, school-aged children are already personalizing their explorations of the world they inhabit. Without new technologies, personalized learning would be almost impossible. Recent innovations in the use of technology are changing the way teachers work with learners, but, as Barbara and Kathleen show, technology also has the power to reduce "class size" to one independent learner at a time, each using unique talents, passions, and aspirations to drive personal inquiry and creative expression.

Advances in technology make personalized learning possible, opening avenues of inquiry wide enough to help learners manage the skills of inquiry and expression they will need as adults. Barbara and Kathleen show how learning technology, with professional guidance, gives learners control over what they know, how they know it, how they can learn more, and how they can present their work in ways that clearly demonstrate the competence they have achieved.

I am confident this book will open new windows for educators who see the importance of engaging each learner in deep, active learning. I admire the way Barbara and Kathleen present varieties of applicable techniques without losing track of generative ideas. At its heart, *Make Learning Personal* offers educators a way to work with learners that accentuates professionalism in education. Like doctors and lawyers, we need to use our understanding of how we learn to shape the experience of the unique young people we serve.

At a time when control over schools is still slipping toward government, business, and restrictive brands of "accountability," Barbara and Kathleen show how improved learning results not from compulsion but from engagement with issues that make a difference to learners. Managing freedom, rather than compliance, drives growth. I am grateful that these two people have had the courage to help pioneer learner-driven schools, providing all of us with refreshed access to satisfaction and joy in learning.

**John H. Clarke**
Starksboro, Vermont
April 26, 2014

# Preface

## WHY A BOOK ON PERSONALIZED LEARNING?

The term *personalized learning* is being used more and more today, but when you take a closer examination on what they are really saying, there is something else being talked about. The buzz is about personalized learning being used to describe a number of products and services offered in the educational marketplace, and there is very little talk about learning and the learner. When you look even closer at these programs, they contribute little to learning and to improving education. Companies are very good at framing their programs as personalized learning. However, personalizing learning is not something someone does to a learner. To really learn and understand what learners are to learn, learners need to own and take responsibility for their learning. When this happens, teaching and learning changes. This book provides the background and rationale for this to happen so learning starts with the learner. We need to change the perceptions about learning and realize every child is a learner.

**Focus of the book: Personalizing learning always starts with the learner!**

## HOW IS THE BOOK ORGANIZED?

The book follows the organization of the 5 W's of Personalized Learning eCourse we have been offering to educators since 2012. Each chapter expands on the *What*, *Who*, *Wow*, *Where*, and *Why* of Personalized Learning and can be used as a supplement for that eCourse. However, this book was written to stand on its own for anyone interested in personalized learning. The value of this book is in clear definitions with charts, details that expand on the charts, and additional stories and journeys of educators and learners who have personalized learning and share that they will never go back to traditional teaching environments.

## WHY BUY THIS BOOK?

There are publications that include information about personalized learning as something you do to learners. The primary focus of this book is around starting with the learner first. The text in this book is drawn from research and experts in the field along with stories from teachers, leaders, and learners. There are three main reasons to read this book.

1. *The definition of personalized learning that starts with the learner has to be clear for educators before they change their teaching practice.* This book is to help educators and anyone interested in learning to understand the importance in building a common language and shared meaning of personalized learning. When all the stakeholders in an educational community have this same understanding and what it means for teaching and learning, they can then develop a shared vision and a set of beliefs that guide the transformation of their schools. Readers will be able to make more informed decisions on how they want learners to learn and the meaning of school, teaching, and learning.

2. *Teachers need to know how learners learn best. Learners need to know how they learn best.* In order to design lessons and projects that include effective instructional strategies, it is critical for teachers to understand how learners may need or prefer to engage with the content. To make curriculum accessible to every learner, teachers can consider how a learner needs or prefers to access and interact with content so that materials are designed and available anytime, anywhere. To help assess learners and for them to reflect on their learning, it is important to know how learners need or prefer to express their knowledge and understanding. Once we understand who the learners are and how they learn best, designing the learning environment is key in supporting the ways learners need or prefer to learn. This book provides strategies and tools for teachers and learners to understand how they prefer and need to learn based on the Universal Design for Learning principles and learners' interests, aspirations, and talents.

3. *Teacher and learner roles change in a personalized learning environment.* There is a process in creating learner-centered and eventually learner-driven environments where learners can develop the skills and strategies to become self-directed expert learners. The goal in creating personalized learning environments is more than moving and grouping desks or putting technology in learners' hands.

Learners will need to acquire the skills to choose and use the appropriate tools and strategies to meet their learning goals. The teacher's role becomes more of a mentor and facilitator of the learning in guiding the process. Teachers only know what they know about teaching and learning from being a student themselves and how they were taught. When these roles change, the idea of students who are taught and receive information is different from an expert learner who drives their learning. They are now considered learners who learn anytime, anywhere. This book provides background, research, a process, and strategies to help learners become expert learners.

## WHAT IS IN THIS BOOK?

The *What, Who, Wow, Where,* and *Why* of personalized learning provides the rationale to personalize learning. This book was not designed to give the reader the *How* to personalize learning, but there are many examples and stories from teachers who show the reader how it can be done. From what we found, *personalized* means just that. Personalized learning looks different for each district, school, and classroom because all are unique with different teachers, learners, administrators, demographics, and available resources.

The *What* is about defining personalized learning. It is also about what is not personalized learning. It is apparent how easy it is to confuse the marketplace and frame terms so consumers believe they have to buy a product or service. This section on what is and what is not personalized learning will help readers clarify the position they want to take on personalized learning. There are programs and initiatives that support personalizing learning, but they do not personalize learning for the learner. This section helps the reader understand that there has to be a common language around the terms for teachers, learners, and all key stakeholders in the school community when they decide to personalize learning. A special feature in this section is the Personalization vs. Differentiation vs. Individualization chart.

The *Who* is about defining learners and how they learn best. The focus for too many years has been on instruction, curriculum, and standardized tests. The learner got lost in the equation. Teachers became responsible and accountable for learning instead of the learner. This section provides the research behind the neuroscience of learning and how Universal Design for Learning (UDL) is for all learners. When learners know how they learn best and work with their teacher as a partner in their learning, they take responsibility for their learning. This section provides the research and tools to understand how you learn best and then how your learners learn best. Special features in this section include strategies to build a Personal Learner Profile, a Personal Learning Backpack and a Class Learning Snapshot of four diverse learners.

The *Wow* is about teacher and learner roles changing. This chapter introduces the Stages of Personalized Learning Environments as a process educators take over time. When learners have a voice and choice in their learning, teachers are no longer lecturing and the only expert in the class. In a traditional teacher-centered class with direct instruction, teachers work harder than the learners. When learners take control of their learning, the dynamics of the classroom change. The learners are working harder because they are motivated and engaged in the learning process instead of being passive learners receiving information. The *Wow* is about how the roles change through the stages with scenarios, examples, and stories from educators and learners around the world. When they changed, the culture in the school changed, so this chapter discusses the culture shift and how to deal with change from experts in the field and a teacher's perspective. The special features in this section include the Stages of Personalized Learning Environments chart and stories from educators and learners.

The *Where* shares how personalized learning is happening now around the world. Teachers want to see what it looks like so the chapter gives the reader examples and models of personalized learning environments on a global perspective. The common theme of the school, district, and large-scale models is that learning starts with the learner. Each model, approach, or initiative shared in this chapter was chosen to tell a story as a journey. Some models have jumped right in and shaken up their system where others are dipping their toes in personalized learning a little at a time. Some are small schools within schools. Others are complete countries. Special features in this section include stories from people on this journey, the models, characteristics about the models, and criteria to use when researching any of these models.

The *Why* is about the rationale to personalize learning that readers need before they take any steps to develop personalized learning environments. This chapter opens with the rationale for creating expert learners and how Universal Design for Learning guides the process. This chapter introduces a continuum for learners to become self-directed, independent, expert learners. It provides concerning statistics that justify why our digital and connected learners also have to be prepared for their future as global citizens. The state of education is not working for most of today's learners. For educators to develop a shared vision, they need to have a clear understanding of where they are currently with teaching and learning. This section compares initiatives and programs in a fixed traditional system with how they could be in a flexible personalized learning environment. By this point in the book, teachers and administrators are ready to personalize learning in their classrooms. They need a good rationale to justify moving to a personalized learning environment, and this section summarizes key points to do that. The special features in this section are the continuum of expert learners and details of each section, information and statistics on declining engagement, charts comparing the traditional vs. flexible learning systems, the rationale to personalize learning, and examples of sixty-second speeches to personalize learning.

The last chapter, *Your Turn to Personalize Learning,* is about the culture shift that happens when you turn the learning over to your learners. You will understand why systemic change causes a culture shift, with specifics from experts on change; your readiness for culture shift; and why culture shift is important to connect the dots of initiatives and programs under the personalized learning umbrella. You will see why it is important to create a shared vision, belief system, and commitment to personalize learning by all stakeholders. Leaders can use the list to build their action plan. Teachers can build their own action plan and then follow strategies for how to make sense of learning. The special features in this section are the chart comparing traditional classrooms with learner-centered environments, the CBAM (Concerns-Based Adoption Model) adapted to include strategies on how to deal with concerns about personalizing learning, Fixen's Stages of Implementation adapted to relate to personalized learning, criteria to determine your readiness to personalize learning, and a graphic describing a self-sustainable personalized learning system. The last section shares information about making sense of learning and gives you predictions on what personalized learning environments will look like in the future. Today is the first day of your journey, and this list can be your road map.

## WHO WILL WANT TO READ THIS BOOK?

This book is for anyone interested in understanding what it means to personalize learning and how that learning impacts schools, educators, learners, parents, and the community. Teachers and administrators will want to read this book to transform the teaching and learning environment and to create a culture where learners take ownership of and responsibility for their learning. They will want to use this book as a study guide, for discussions in faculty meetings, for research, and for ideas to drive their design of personalized learning environments. Teachers will want to read this book so they understand their role in a personalized learning environment. Publishers and education solution providers will be interested in this book to create solutions that meet the needs of their clients who want to personalize learning. This book is required reading for teachers before they jump in and change their teaching strategies to personalize learning. It will guide them as they create learner-centered personalized learning environments so their learners are confident about who they are as learners and know how they learn best.

This book is required reading for administrators before they make purchasing decisions based on definitions of personalized learning that are not clear or right for their situation. This book will guide schools and districts that want to create a school culture built on trust with learners who are engaged and motivated to learn. The authors have provided video and web content throughout the book available to you through QR codes. To read a QR code, you must have a smartphone or tablet with a camera. We recommend you download a QR code reader app that is made specifically for your phone or tablet brand.

Parents will want to read this book to understand how a personalized learning environment can help their children become more self-directed in their learning. This book is designed to recognize and nurture their children's interests, talents, passions, and aspirations.

QR codes may provide access to videos and/or websites that are not maintained, sponsored, endorsed, or controlled by Corwin. Your use of these third-party websites is subject to the terms and conditions posted on such websites. Corwin takes no responsibility and assumes no liability for your use of any third-party website. Corwin does not approve, sponsor, endorse, verify, or certify information available at any third-party video or website.

# Acknowledgments

This book was born from our experiences as parents, teachers, administrators, school board members, graduate instructors, professional developers, and business owners. Over the last twenty-five to thirty years, these varying experiences in our careers have given us a broad and unique perspective on teaching and learning. These perspectives are from the wisdom of many people, especially the teachers whom we are privileged to work with and the learners who inspire us every day. We need to give a big thank you to all the teachers and learners who motivate us to want to learn and make a difference in teaching and learning. In writing this book, we also drew from our own experiences as teachers who were given the freedom to create learner-centered environments over twenty years ago. We also appreciate the administrators who supported us as we applied our versions of constructivism to our teaching practice and as professional developers supporting teachers.

In 2010, mutual friend and colleague Julie Duffield introduced us at the Computer Using Educators (CUE) Conference in Palm Springs, California. Julie thought if we put our educational experiences and passions together, we could "change the world." So we would especially like to thank Julie for her vision about what we could do together. Without her, this book would have never happened.

Early in our research, we read articles by John H. Clarke, a researcher from Brown University who focused on personalized learning at the high school level. John has been a source of encouragement and affirmation as we delved deeper into personalized learning. We want to thank John for his continued support, for introducing us to the inspirational staff and learners at Mt. Abraham Union Middle/High School in Bristol, Vermont, and for writing the foreword to our book.

As we continued our research on personalized learning, we came across a researcher from London who gave us a unique and in-depth perspective on learning. Chris Watkins, a reader and researcher at the University of London, showed us how to make sense of learning. His writings helped us clarify our own focus. Chris has been an inspiration to us on what type of learning environments need to be created for all learners. We want to thank Chris for continuing to share and write on the importance of learning about learning.

We would like to thank Lisa Fry Wilson and other Iowa educators who reached out to us to learn more about personalized learning. This is where we first developed the 5 W's of Personalized Learning eCourse in 2012, and we appreciate their direction and feedback as we started our journey. We also would like to thank some of our earliest supporters: Greg Alchin, Learning Experience Designer from New South Wales, Australia; Sandra Baker and Terri Stice from Green River Regional Education Cooperative (GRREC) in Kentucky; Larry Schaefer from the Connecticut Association of Public School Superintendents; and Madeline Heide, Assistant Superintendent of the American School in Mumbai, India. We need to thank Scot Allen, Director of Communications at Mid-Pacific Institute (MPI) in Hawaii for granting us permission to use pictures of their learners in our eCourse and on the cover of our book.

One of our first interviews for our website was with James Rickabaugh, the Executive Director of the Institute @ CESA #1 in Wisconsin who we thank for his dedication to personalizing learning for southeastern Wisconsin and beyond. From his interview, we learned about Lisa Welch and Wanda Richardson, K–1 co-teachers from the Kettle Moraine School District in Wisconsin. We have been following Lisa's and Wanda's journey for three years to where they are now, KM Explore, a K–5 charter school they helped design. We want to thank Lisa, Wanda, and the KM Explore staff for creating a national personalized learning model.

We want to thank Kevin McLaughlin, a primary-level teacher from the United Kingdom who redesigned his classroom into learning zones where his learners developed their weekly learning goals called PJs (Personal Journeys). When we first met Kevin, he was a Year 4 teacher and is now teaching and personalizing learning for kindergarteners. We use and share his perspective of what it means for teachers to shift the culture in their classrooms. We would also like to thank Chris Edwards, another inspirational teacher from the United Kingdom, who as a Year 2 teacher explained how he sees the learner in every child. He shared how he started his journey as a professional musician and moved to the classroom to design learning environments where learners self-direct their learning, what Chris considers "messy learning."

We want to thank two other educators for sharing their stories of why they are committed to making a difference for their learners: Shelley Wright, a high school educator and consultant in Moose Jaw, Saskatchewan, Canada, where her learners own and drive their learning and Sarah

Downing-Ford, a seventh-grade language arts teacher in Maine who shared how her learners assess their own work by unpacking the standards and how they assess each other.

We want to also thank the thought leaders who shared their journeys with us on how they are transforming education. David Truss, Vice Principal of the Inquiry Hub in Vancouver, Canada, talks and writes about learners following their passions to design projects they really care about; Greg Wilborn is Personalized Learning Coordinator at District 11 in Colorado Springs, Colorado, where learners have a wide choice of what they learn; Fred Bramante is coauthor of the book *Off the Clock* about competency-based learning and discusses the importance of redesigning public education; Keven Kroehler, founder of EdVisions Schools, explains why hope matters; Kathleen Cushman is an education journalist with a particular interest in the adolescent years who wrote the "8 Universal Secrets that Motivate Learners"; and Elliot Washor, co-founder of Big Picture Learning, explains the importance of the "person" in personalization and about personalized learning plans that start with each learner's voice, choice, and interests.

We keep learning what personalizing learning means with each story and journey from teachers and educational leaders and realize that it looks different everywhere. We are learning from Verona Area School District (VASD), who made a commitment to personalize learning. Betty Wottreng, Director of Technology Services, took the lead by designing a coaching program with their personalized learning coaches Rita Mortenson and Laura Lindquist, who amaze us with their dedication to support their colleagues. VASD teachers are redesigning their classrooms and encouraging learner voice and choice. People like Kayleen DeWerd, a third-grade teacher at Glacier Edge Elementary, took it a step further by involving learners in the design process. Betty mentioned the process to Jon Tanner, Director of Technology Services at Oregon School District, Wisconsin, who jumped in with his teachers, many of whom are already turning the responsibility for learning over to their learners. Jon's commitment to his teachers and their journeys drives us even more to share the importance of transforming teaching and learning. Henry County Schools in Georgia opened our eyes to why structures need to be in place to make learning work. Karen Perry, Program Director for Next Generation Systems Grant with a very forward-thinking team that includes Aaryn Schmuhl, Assistant Superintendent, and Brian Blanton, Instructional Technology Coordinator, has developed an effective personalized learning system that can be replicated around the country. Thank you Betty, Jon, Karen, and your teams for your commitment to personalizing learning in your districts!

We would like to thank two outstanding organizations, Students at the Center and the Nellie Mae Education Foundation, who continue to share their invaluable research on learner-centered environments with us and the world.

Thank you to the educators around the world who have taken our 5 W's of Personalized Learning eCourse. Your participation in and contribution to the discussions has given a whole new meaning to communities of practice. Your deep reflections and understanding of what personalized learning means to you and your learners continues to fuel our passion and expand our thinking about personalized learning. We have a special thank-you for Linda Ullah, coach, mentor, and friend, whose personal dedication to our work has been invaluable. A very big thank-you to Steve Nordmark, Chief Academic Officer of Knowvation, who used his understanding of personalized learning and Universal Design for Learning to carefully review each chapter and provide valuable feedback on the book's content. His input made a big difference.

We want to thank our husbands, Tom Bray and Jim McClaskey, who generously give their daily support in so many different ways so we can pursue our mission. We want to thank our wonderful children, Sara Zimmerman and Andrew Bray (Barbara's children), and Joshua McClaskey and Seth McClaskey (Kathleen's children) and our grandchildren who inspire us every day to work endless hours to make this a world where learners can follow their passions and realize their hopes and dreams.

**Barbara and Kathleen**

## PUBLISHER'S ACKNOWLEDGMENTS

Corwin gratefully acknowledges the contributions of the following reviewers:

Anthony Angelini
Seventh-Grade Social Studies + Language Arts Teacher
New Oxford Middle School
New Oxford, PA

Deidre Bothma
IT Curriculum Coordinator for Junior Schools
Elkanah House Preparatory
Sunningdale, South Africa

Janet Christy
Director of Student Learning and Staff Development
Northshore Christian Academy
Everett, WA

Julio César Contreras
Deputy Chief of Schools
Chicago Public School, Pershing Network
Chicago, IL

Tina Kuchinski
High School English Teacher
Gresham High School
Gresham, OR

Lyneille Meza
Coordinator of Data and Assessment
Denton Independent School District
Denton, TX

Dr. Carol Spencer
Educator/Director of Curriculum
Addison Northwest Supervisory Union
Vergennes, VT

Nancy White
21st-Century Learning and Innovation Specialist
Academy School District 20
Colorado Springs, CO

Andrea Golarz Ziemba
NBCT, Fifth-Grade Teacher
Morton Elementary School
Hammond, IN

# About the Authors

 **Barbara Bray** is Creative Learning Officer and co-founder of Personalize Learning, LLC, and Founder/Owner of My eCoach (my-ecoach.com). She posts on Rethinking Learning (barbarabray.net) and writes a regular column on professional development for OnCUE (Computer Using Educators). She is CUE Gold Disc winner (1998) and Platinum Disc winner (2009) for her contributions to educational technology for the advancement of teaching and learning and Micro Awardee for the Make Me a Million $ Competition in 2010.

Barbara is a teacher, writer, instructional designer, and creative learning strategist who connects people and ideas. As an educational technologist and professional developer, she has worked with schools, districts, individuals, businesses, and nonprofit organizations around the world to facilitate change, design new learning environments, and build online communities for teachers to connect and share teaching practice through action research. She builds coaching programs where teachers can become facilitators, advisors, and partners in learning. Barbara facilitates visioning sessions, assists with writing strategic plans, and researches and writes about personalizing learning so learners follow their passions to discover their purpose.

Barbara lives in the San Francisco Bay Area with her best friend and husband Tom, who she has been married to for forty-four years. She is very grateful for her sisters Sandy Ritz, Terry Leach, and Janet Ritz, for two creative children who are passionate about what they do and how they live, Sara Zimmerman and Andrew Bray, and for her amazing granddaughter, Cali—all who inspire her to follow her purpose to make learning personal for all learners.

 **Kathleen McClaskey** has been on a mission the last three decades to level the playing field for all learners. She has been a teacher, administrator, professional developer, innovative leader, visionary, and futurist who believes that everyone on the planet is a learner. As an educational technologist for over thirty years, graduate instructor, and a Universal Design for Learning consultant, she has worked worldwide in training thousands of teachers in using tools to instruct all learners in the classroom. In the last decade, Kathleen directed and designed the professional development in multiple technology-based projects in math, science, literacy, and autism to build twenty-first-century classrooms and sustainable learner-centered environments. She is passionate in empowering learners with skills and learning strategies so they can become self-directed learners who can realize their hopes and dreams and have choices in the postsecondary.

Kathleen is Co-Founder and Chief Executive Officer of Personalize Learning, LLC, Founder/Owner of EdTech Associates, Inc., and the advocacy chairperson for the New Hampshire Society for Technology in Education, an affiliate of ISTE. In 2010, she was a finalist for the Make Me a Million $ Competition. Kathleen was recognized for her advocacy work from ISTE (International Society for Technology in Education) by receiving the ISTE 2012 Public Policy Advocate of the Year Award.

Kathleen lives in New Hampshire with her husband Jim who she has been married to for forty-one years. She has two wonderful sons, Joshua and Seth, and two adorable grandsons, Austyn and Benny, who all continue to serve as her daily inspiration to personalize learning for every learner.

## BARBARA'S AND KATHLEEN'S JOURNEY

Since 2012, Barbara and Kathleen have talked and written about personalizing learning almost every day because they both are passionate about transforming teaching and learning. Each experience with teachers, learners, leaders, schools, and districts around the world gives them more opportunities to learn and grow. In 2014, they were finalists for the Trendsetter Award from *EdTech Digest* and believe this confirms that the conversations around personalizing learning are just the beginning of a complete transformation of the educational system.

# Introduction

Learning is personal. This is why we wanted to write this book. We have our own experiences with learning that impacted who we are and where we are now. We both have reasons why we are so passionate about personalizing learning for all learners. We also have children and grandchildren who have had experiences with learning that impacted who they are today.

This book includes stories from teachers and leaders with Wow moments and even disturbing moments that teachers had to share. Teachers told us that after they gave their learners a voice and choice in their learning, they would never go back to traditional teaching. Some are concerned that even if they change, other teachers resist changing because it is just too difficult with everything they are mandated to do. We hear stories every day from teachers passionate about teaching who are so frustrated with the system and the emphasis on testing. We are advocates for teachers who work harder than they should to dance around a broken system and still meet the needs of each of their learners. We believe in teachers and why they went into the profession. It was not for the money. It was because they wanted to make a difference.

For over a decade the focus has been on instruction, testing, and standards, which has impacted schools to a point where teachers and learners are leaving school. The dropout rate is too high. The burnout rate for teachers is growing. Kids are not sure what to do and what they want. Even if kids go to college, many drop out before they graduate. Learners that stay in the system learn how to be compliant and how to *do* school. Many learners told us that they learn more outside of school and just follow the rules so they can get out (or graduate) of school. They just want the grades and degree.

We decided now is the time to stop this madness and shake up the system. We need to put learning back in the learners' hands. We need to make learning personal so learners take responsibility for their learning.

Personalizing learning is all about the stories behind each learner. Since we are all learners, we need to start with our own stories about learning and why we wanted to write this book.

## BARBARA'S STORY

I was brought up in a house of artists in Maryland. My mother raised me with the idea that I could draw whatever I wanted and especially to draw outside the lines. I was brought up to be creative and come up with new ideas. I was able to read early and used to put on plays with my sisters. I used to laugh and giggle all the time. I was really good at pretending and dreaming about amazing things. I even wrote poetry before I was five. Then I started school and everything changed. I am left-handed and they wanted me to write with my right hand. My parents fought the school so I was able to continue writing left-handed. My handwriting is not the best, but it is with the hand that I'm supposed to write with. My parents were my advocates, but they could only do so much for me.

I asked questions in school and was told to be quiet. I didn't understand the tests and was told to just finish on time. It wasn't long before I realized that I might have been a good learner but needed to learn how to be a good student to make it in the system. In second grade, the teacher told my parents that I wasn't very smart and probably would have a tough time in school. She told them I would probably never go to college. I was labeled "stupid" in primary school.

I shut down fast and cried about school. I was embarrassed and became quiet and shy. Each year school became more oppressive and like a terrible weight on me. In tenth grade, they put me in a special reading class so I could answer the multiple-choice questions about each paragraph. Yet the paragraphs made no sense to me and there were several right answers, but I could only pick one. I got it that I needed to play the game to get out of school. I learned how to be a good student and graduated. Then I moved to California and went to a community college, Diablo Valley College.

It was there that I learned about me and how I learn. I had an English teacher that paid attention to my writing. He told me that I was an amazing writer and clever with words. No one had ever told me I was good at anything except my parents. He entered one of my poems in a national contest and it won first place. It took so long for me to realize that I have talents and passion about something that I love to do. I love to write. I love to share ideas. This was the beginning of me being a learner again, and it changed my life.

When I found out that I can learn what I want to learn, I realized that what happened to me happens all the time to learners of all ages. I became a teacher for a reason—to make a difference for learners. My son was identified as gifted at a very early age. He could read at three. He was musical and funny. When he started school, he had the same experiences as me. He learned how to do school and be compliant, but he had some learning challenges. At six, he needed everything to be perfect before he turned it in and, in some cases, erased the paper so much that there were holes in the paper. Teachers did not know what to do if he didn't finish his work. So we took him to a play therapist who tried to help him understand that failure is okay and being a little less than perfect is okay. This worked for some things but not for school. When I asked the school for help, they said since he was gifted he could figure it out. So they decided that if he was smart, he would make it just fine. His grades were good, but he wasn't motivated to learn. That is, until he took drama and music in high school. He now teaches music and theater workshops and is passionate about what he does for other learners because of his own story.

## KATHLEEN'S STORY

We all have a story to tell, and my story is about my oldest son who found school difficult, especially when it required reading and writing. As a toddler he was quite articulate, engaging many adults with the stories he would tell. His nursery school teacher remarked that she had never met a young boy who could tell stories in such detail and with such expression. Who was to know that he would enter first grade and not be able to learn to read?

In 1986, whole language was the method used to teach children how to read. I found out, years later, that this methodology was detrimental for a child with dyslexia. Yes, I never had any educator tell me that he was dyslexic as this was a medical diagnosis, one that educators could not address. In 1994, I located a professional evaluator who ascertained that the language difficulties my son had been having were due to a diagnosis of dyslexia. You see, my son was never taught to read or write in public school, and every word he seemed to know had been in printed form and was memorized. In seventh grade he could no longer memorize multisyllabic words, and he could no longer keep up with his classmates. He depended on teachers and paraprofessionals to support him at every level, gaining no independent learning skills for his entire educational experience. He tells me now, years later, that he felt "stupid" almost every day of his life in school; he always felt bad that he could not learn how to read.

As a consequence, he turned to activities that made him feel important, ones that would bring him into a different world than the one his father and I wanted for him.

In 1995, my son went to a private school for dyslexics in New York, where he was finally taught how to read. At sixteen years old, he went from a fourth-grade reading level to a ninth-grade reading level within a six-month period, based on the same evaluations by the independent evaluator. Graduating in 1998, he left a reader but had limited independent learning skills with equally limited choices in a postsecondary environment. (You need to understand that many learners who have difficulty learning become completely dependent on adults to support their learning.)

In 2003, I had a heart-to-heart talk with my son about his natural abilities to engage people in conversation and to crunch numbers mentally. He did not go to college, but he is using his natural abilities to make a living. Today, he is a successful car salesperson in Massachusetts.

My son is the reason I believe that personalizing learning will produce independent learners prepared for a lifetime of learning and prepare them for choices in college, a career, or entrepreneurial ventures. You see, there are millions of children just like my son in schools throughout this country and beyond. Like my son, these children have developed a poor self-perception as learners and do not possess independent learning skills necessary to have choices in postsecondary schools.

I ask that every educator reflect on the fact that the goal for educating our children is to create independent learners. With that in mind, consider how we can transform the learning environment so that every learner will gain the independent learning skills to be successful in school and in life.

How does this story end? Just recently my son and I had a conversation in which he said schools need to discover what kids are interested in and then give them opportunities to try their interests out in high school. He reflected that he would have liked the opportunity to do this, but he was never given the chance to share his hopes and dreams with anyone in school. What he said to me made me realize it was all about personalizing learning. That is why I do what I do and am so passionate about changing teaching and learning. It is all about the learner.

## EVERY STORY MATTERS
## BECAUSE EVERY LEARNER MATTERS

When we reflect on our own stories, we cry and think about our children and grandchildren's future. We think about the times we fought for ourselves and our children when, in fact, all of us as learners could have followed our dreams and hopes much earlier in our lives. Both of us are intrinsically motivated to make a difference so learners become self-directed toward what they are passionate about. This is our story, but know we are not alone and there are so many other stories. We believe children need to have opportunities to drive their learning and the system has to change.

We need every educator to see that every child is a learner first. We wrote this book because it had to be written.

*"If we teach as we taught yesterday, we rob our children of tomorrow."*

—John Dewey

# 1 What Is Personalized Learning?

*"The only thing that interferes with my learning is my education."*

—Albert Einstein

**A**n example of a learner-centered classroom might be one large room that combines two classrooms with two or more teachers co-teaching multiple grade levels. There are no walls that separate the two classrooms. You look around and do not see any desks. In fact, you might not even see any teacher desks. There are multiple areas with groups of tables, comfortable furniture, places to sit on the floor, ball chairs, and tall tables where learners stand or pace to learn. There is probably a lot of noise in one area where children are collaborating and building things at the creative station. In one corner, there is a child demonstrating to others at the showoff station using the interactive whiteboard. There is a quiet area with beanbag chairs where some children are reading quietly on their iPads. One teacher is sitting with a small group of children guiding questions and ideas between them. The other teacher is in a private corner meeting with one child checking for understanding.

This is only one picture of what personalizing learning might look like where teachers co-teach in a multi-age classroom. There are many examples of personalized learning shared throughout this book. Personalized learning looks different in different places because it is personalized for the teachers, the learners, and the community. This chapter is for you to start your journey in building your own understanding around what is and what is not personalized learning.

# DEFINING PERSONALIZED LEARNING

*Personalized learning* is a controversial term that means different things to different people depending on where and how it is referenced. Some educators believe it is the alternative to "one size fits all" instruction where others promote programs or tools that personalize learning for you and others emphasize that learning starts with the learner. The message is confusing.

Teachers have used multiple methods to personalize learning in their classrooms for years, but the opportunities to advance it are new. Consider personalized learning as a culture shift and transformational revolution shaking up teaching and learning.

Technology is moving the idea of "personalized" forward everywhere we look. Go into any store and you will see products personalized for you. When you order a book or movie online, you get "personalized" recommendations for books or movies similar to the one you just ordered. If you order multiple books and movies, you get even more focused selections of books, movies, and other products personalized just for you.

The idea around personalizing products for you involves data and performance based on previous selections. It is not about choosing what you believe is best for you. The technology is doing it for you. Because of social media, you are even getting products or services personalized for you based on others like you. This same concept is confusing educators about what they believe learners need to learn. One reason to start this book with the *What* of personalized learning is that the concept is confusing and needs clarification.

> **Pause/Think/Reflect**
>
> Is personalizing learning something that someone or something personalizes for you, or do you personalize your learning for yourself?

> *"Learning is personal."*

## National Education Technology Plan 2010

In 2010, the U.S. Department of Education defined the terms *personalization*, *differentiation*, and *individualization* in the National Education Technology Plan. In this plan, all three terms were interchangeable and focused on instruction.

> **Summary of the three terms from the 2010 National Education Technology Plan**
>
> **Individualization** refers to instruction paced to the learning needs of different learners. Learning goals are the same for all students, but students can progress through the material at different speeds according to their learning needs. For example, students might take longer to progress through a given topic, skip topics that cover information they already know, or repeat topics they need more help on.
>
> **Differentiation** refers to instruction tailored to the learning preferences of different learners. Learning goals are the same for all students, but the method or approach of instruction varies according to the preferences of each student or what research has found works best for students like them.
>
> **Personalization** refers to instruction paced to learning needs, tailored to learning preferences, and adapted to the specific interests of different learners. In an environment that is fully personalized, the learning objectives and content as well as the method and pace may all vary (so personalization encompasses differentiation and individualization) (USDOE, 2010).

## PERSONALIZATION VS. DIFFERENTIATION VS. INDIVIDUALIZATION (PDI)

Because the 2010 National Education Technology Plan compared the terms *personalization, differentiation,* and *individualization* as they relate to instruction, it was necessary to create a chart that compares these terms as they also relate to learning. The National Education Technology Plan defines personalization as instruction where teachers or the curriculum personalizes the learning for the learner. If learners want to learn something, it usually represents something personal to them. If a teacher or the curriculum decides what a learner is supposed to learn, it may not feel personal to the learner.

Since the first Personalization vs. Differentiation vs. Individualization (PDI) Chart was developed in 2012, it was important to reflect on the feedback and input from educators around the world to revise the chart to its current third version shown in Table 1.1.

*To read a QR code, you must have a smartphone or tablet with a camera. We recommend you download a QR code reader app made specifically for your phone or tablet brand.*

**Table 1.1** Personalization vs. Differentiation vs. Individualization Chart (v3)

| Personalization | Differentiation | Individualization |
|---|---|---|
| *The Learner . . .* | *The Teacher . . .* | *The Teacher . . .* |
| drives their own learning. | provides instruction to groups of learners. | provides instruction to an individual learner. |
| connects learning with interests, talents, passions, and aspirations. | adjusts learning needs for groups of learners. | accommodates learning needs for the individual learner. |
| actively participates in the design of their learning. | designs instruction based on the learning needs of different groups of learners. | customizes instruction based on the learning needs of the individual learner. |
| owns and is responsible for their learning that includes their voice and choice on how and what they learn. | is responsible for a variety of instruction for different groups of learners. | is responsible for modifying instruction based on the needs of the individual learner. |
| identifies goals for their learning plan and benchmarks as they progress along their learning path with guidance from teacher. | identifies the same objectives for different groups of learners as they do for the whole class. | identifies the same objectives for all learners with specific objectives for individuals who receive one-on-one support. |
| acquires the skills to select and use the appropriate technology and resources to support and enhance their learning. | selects technology and resources to support the learning needs of different groups of learners. | selects technology and resources to support the learning needs of the individual learner. |
| builds a network of peers, experts, and teachers to guide and support their learning. | supports groups of learners who are reliant on them for their learning. | understands the individual learner is dependent on them to support their learning. |
| demonstrates mastery of content in a competency-based system. | monitors learning based on Carnegie unit (seat time) and grade level. | monitors learning based on Carnegie unit (seat time) and grade level. |

*(Continued)*

**Table 1.1** (Continued)

| Personalization | Differentiation | Individualization |
|---|---|---|
| *The Learner . . .* | *The Teacher . . .* | *The Teacher . . .* |
| becomes a self-directed, expert learner who monitors progress and reflects on learning based on mastery of content and skills. | uses data and assessments to modify instruction for groups of learners and provides feedback to individual learners to advance learning. | uses data and assessments to measure progress of what the individual learner learned and did not learn to decide next steps in their learning. |
| Assessment **AS** and **FOR** Learning with minimal **OF** Learning | Assessment **OF** and **FOR** Learning | Assessment **OF** Learning |

**Personalization vs. Differentiation vs. Individualization Chart (v3),** (2013) by Barbara Bray & Kathleen McClaskey is licensed under a Creative Commons Attribution-NonCommercial-NoDerivs 3.0 Unported License.

## PDI CHART EXPLAINED

The positive feedback along with requests for the chart led to a report about the details of the chart. The report included the following questions with answers that help clarify the elements of the PDI chart and provide teachers, administrators, schools, and organizations with background information and resources to support discussions around the PDI chart.

- What do teaching and learning look like as they relate to these terms?
- How do we determine the learner's needs?
- How do learners participate in their learning?

**Pause/Think/Reflect**

Personalized learning requires the active direction of the learner; individualization lets the school tailor the curriculum to scaled assessments of interest and abilities. The difference between individualization and personalization lies in control. When a teacher differentiates instruction, the teacher is in control and working harder than the learners. Most traditional instruction actually depersonalizes how learners learn rather than encouraging learners to take responsibility for their learning. Pacing guides, grade levels, tests, and learners becoming compliant so they can "do" school are not personalized learning.

- How are goals and objectives determined for the learner?
- How do learners support their learning and each other?
- How do you know if learning is meaningful?
- How do you assess learning?

## What do teaching and learning look like as they relate to these terms?

**Table 1.2** What Teaching and Learning Look Like

| Personalization | Differentiation | Individualization |
|---|---|---|
| *The Learner . . .* | *The Teacher . . .* | *The Teacher . . .* |
| drives their own learning. | provides instruction to groups of learners. | provides instruction to an individual learner. |

*Source:* Personalize Learning, LLC

In a **personalized learning environment**, learning starts with the learner. Learners understand how they learn best so they can become active participants in designing their learning goals along with the teacher. Learners take responsibility for their learning. When they own and drive their learning, they are motivated and challenged as they learn so they work harder than their teacher.

When teachers differentiate instruction, learners are identified based on their challenges in a specific content area and skill levels. The teacher uses existing differentiated curriculum or adapts instruction to meet the needs of different groups of learners and select at-risk individual learners.

> **Pause/Think/Reflect**
>
> "When the teacher is directing the learning, the teacher tends to be the hardest-working person in the classroom."

When a teacher individualizes instruction, the teacher identifies learners' needs through evaluations based on their challenges or disabilities. The teacher reviews the findings and recommendations from the evaluations with other professionals to adapt materials and instruction for the individual learner who has cognitive or physical challenges.

**Figure 1.1** The Missing Piece

### The Missing Piece

In traditional classrooms, the focus is on instruction, standards, and tests. The missing piece (see Figure 1.1) in most of the conversations about teaching and curriculum is the learner. Consider the classroom as a puzzle and the learner is one piece of the puzzle. That piece too often gets left out of the discussions and decisions around teaching. The focus on teaching, data, and test scores tends to leave out the most important piece: the learner.

## How do we determine the learner's needs?

**Table 1.3** Determining the Learner's Needs

| Personalization | Differentiation | Individualization |
|---|---|---|
| *The Learner . . .* | *The Teacher . . .* | *The Teacher . . .* |
| connects learning with interests, talents, passions, and aspirations. | adjusts learning needs for groups of learners. | accommodates learning needs for the individual learner. |

*Source:* Personalize Learning, LLC

In a personalized learning environment, teachers can determine learners' needs and how they learn best. **Universal Design for Learning (UDL)** from CAST (Center for Applied Special Technology) is about understanding the variability of how each learner learns: their strengths, challenges, aptitudes, talents, and aspirations. Most important for teachers is to understand how learners can best access and engage with the content and how they can best express what they know and understand. This approach provides the foundation for all learners to take responsibility for their own learning.

With this information, the teacher and the learner become partners in learning. Learners have a voice in how they prefer

**Pause/Think/Reflect**

*"If you remove the veil of disability, you can see the learner."*

or need to acquire information, a choice in how they express what they know and how they prefer to engage with the content. When learners have ownership and take responsibility for their learning, they are more motivated to learn and more engaged in the learning process.

Differentiation is responsive teaching where teachers proactively plan varied approaches to what different groups of learners need to learn, how they will learn it, and how they will show what they have learned. In a differentiated classroom, the teacher is developing materials and resources to meet the needs of the different groups of learners. When a teacher designs materials for the needs of different learners with multiple resources for learners to choose from based on their needs, the teacher is working harder than ever before.

Individualized instruction usually involves learners with special needs who have an Individual Education Plan (IEP). These learners have been evaluated to determine their strengths and weaknesses in areas such as reading, math, writing, and other cognitive challenges. From these evaluations, a set of measurable goals is determined along with accommodations for the individual learner in an IEP. An agreement by the IEP team is needed to implement them. Implementation can include out-of-classroom one-to-one instruction and tutoring plus classroom accommodations by the teacher with frequent support by an instructional aide.

## How do learners participate in their learning?

**Table 1.4** How Learners Participate in Their Learning

| **Personalization** | **Differentiation** | **Individualization** |
|---|---|---|
| *The Learner . . .* | *The Teacher . . .* | *The Teacher . . .* |
| actively participates in the design of their learning. | designs instruction based on the learning needs of different groups of learners. | customizes instruction based on the learning needs of the individual learner. |
| owns and is responsible for their learning that includes their voice and choice on how and what they learn. | is responsible for a variety of instruction for different groups of learners. | is responsible for modifying instruction based on the needs of the individual learner. |

*Source:* Personalize Learning, LLC

In a personalized learning environment, learners actively participate in their learning. They have a voice in what they are learning based on how they learn best. Learners have a choice in how they demonstrate what they know and provide evidence of their learning. In a learner-centered environment, learners own and co-design their learning. The teacher is their guide on their personal journey. When learners have choices to interact with the content and discuss what they watched, read, and learned, they are actively participating as learners. Encouraging learner voice and choice is the key difference to the other terms: *differentiation* and *individualization*. When learners have a voice in how they learn and a choice in how they engage with content and express what they know, they are more motivated to want to learn and own their learning.

In a differentiated classroom, learners may be passive participants in their learning. Teachers may use direct instruction and other methods they differentiated based on the learning needs of individuals and different groups of learners in their classroom. Some teachers may set up learning stations or use multiple ways of showing the same content for different types of learners. If the teacher is designing the lesson and differentiating activities to meet different groups of learners, the teacher is directing how learners learn and learners tend to passively receive content and directions on what and how to learn.

When you individualize instruction, learning is passive even though the instruction is based on each learner's needs. Teachers or paraprofessionals deliver instruction to individual learners. Learners have no voice in the design of their instruction or choice in what they learn in this environment.

## How are goals and objectives determined for the learner?

**Table 1.5**  Goals and Objectives Determined for the Learner

| Personalization | Differentiation | Individualization |
|---|---|---|
| *The Learner . . .* | *The Teacher . . .* | *The Teacher . . .* |
| identifies goals for their learning plan and benchmarks as they progress along their learning path with guidance from the teacher. | identifies the same objectives for different groups of learners as they do for the whole class. | identifies the same objectives for all learners with specific objectives for individuals who receive one-on-one support. |

*Source:* Personalize Learning, LLC

To personalize learning, the teacher and learner co-design objectives based on the learner's learning goals. Goals are identified from learners' interests, aspirations, and talents and how they prefer and need to learn. Then the teacher works with learners to identify objectives that scaffold the skills they need to meet their learning goals. Learners follow these objectives, monitor their progress in meeting the objectives, and reflect on their progress. The teacher is the guide facilitating the learner's learning process.

When differentiating instruction, a teacher identifies the same objectives for different groups of learners. Teachers use and analyze data to identify and group the different learners in their classroom. From this data, they can use, adapt, or create different lessons and find resources on a concept around the same objectives they give to the whole class based on the different group of learners.

When you individualize instruction, learners may have the same objectives as all the other learners in the class. However, there can be specific objectives for learners who may need one-on-one support. Teachers or paraprofessionals then support and provide accommodations for individual learners to meet these specific objectives.

## How do learners support their learning and each other?

**Table 1.6**   Learners Support Their Learning and Each Other

| Personalization | Differentiation | Individualization |
|---|---|---|
| *The Learner . . .* | *The Teacher . . .* | *The Teacher . . .* |
| develops the skills to select and use the appropriate technology and resources to support and enhance their learning. | selects technology and resources to support the learning needs of different groups of learners. | selects technology and resources to support the learning needs of the individual learner. |
| builds a network of peers, experts, and teachers to guide and support their learning. | supports groups of learners who are reliant on the teacher for their learning. | understands the individual learner is dependent on the teacher to support their learning. |

*Source:* Personalize Learning, LLC

In a personalized learning environment, learners have acquired the skills to access appropriate and relevant tools and resources to support their learning. They have critical thinking skills so they can self-select the tools they need to support any learning task, whether at school or home. Digital literacy is an essential skill in a personalized learning environment. As twenty-first-century learners, they collaborate, share, and learn with their teachers, peers, experts, and other learners around the world. Being a connected learner is also an essential skill in a personalized learning environment. Each learner builds his or her personal learning network and connections based on the topic, resources, and skill level. In a personalized learning environment, everyone can be an independent and self-directed learner.

To differentiate instruction, the teacher selects the tools and resources for the groups of learners based on the needs of each group and the activities or products included in the lesson or project. The teacher also considers how appropriate a tool or resource is for the different groups of learners. Learners may be able to choose content or resources based on their reading or skill level.

> **Pause/Think/Reflect**
>
> *"Digital literacy is the ability to choose and use the appropriate technologies for the task."*

To individualize instruction, tools and resources are selected by the teacher and are sometimes recommended by an evaluator, special education professional, or consultant. The tools could include specialized software and hardware that supports the specific IEP (Individual Education Plan) goals agreed to by the IEP team. In the best cases, teachers or paraprofessionals learn how to use these specialized tools so that they can instruct learners in the use of these tools to support their learning. If these tools are used consistently, learners then adopt them as part of their toolkit. If the teacher works with individual learners in a Title I program, a Response to Intervention (RTI) program, or a one-to-one tutoring situation, the teacher chooses the tools based on the program used for the task at hand.

## How do you know if learning is meaningful?

**Table 1.7** How Learning Is Meaningful

| Personalization | Differentiation | Individualization |
|---|---|---|
| *The Learner . . .* | *The Teacher . . .* | *The Teacher . . .* |
| demonstrates mastery of content in a competency-based system. | monitors learning based on Carnegie unit (seat time) and grade level. | monitors learning based on Carnegie unit (seat time) and grade level. |

*Source:* Personalize Learning, LLC

In a personalized learning environment, learners demonstrate mastery based on a competency-based model, not on seat time. In this learning environment, teachers are expected to help all learners succeed in mastering skills. Competency-based pathways are a re-engineering of our education system around learning. It is a re-engineering designed for success where failure is no longer an option.

In individualized and differentiated environments, learners are awarded credit for classes based on the **Carnegie unit** (which measures seat time) that plays a powerful role in managing transactions within the education system. First, it provides a unit of exchange to allow different schools and institutions to relate to each other, especially the transition from high school to college. Second, the Carnegie unit is based on the amount of time a teacher is in front of a classroom and the time learners are in school. It doesn't take into account how effective the teacher is, how much time and effort the teacher contributes outside the classroom, or how much time and effort learners contribute.

> **Competency-based approaches build on standard reforms, offering a new value proposition:**
>
> "By aligning all of our resources (in schools, the community, and online) around student learning to enable students to progress upon mastery, our country can increase productivity in the education system, while simultaneously raising achievement levels overall and reducing the achievement gap."
>
> Sturgis, Patrick, & Pittenger, 2011

## How do you assess learning?

**Table 1.8**  How to Assess Learning

| Personalization | Differentiation | Individualization |
|---|---|---|
| *The Learner . . .* | *The Teacher . . .* | *The Teacher . . .* |
| becomes a self-directed, expert learner who monitors progress and reflects on learning based on mastery of content and skills. | uses data and assessments to modify teaching and provides feedback for groups of learners and individual learners to advance learning. | uses data and assessments to measure progress of what the individual learner learned and did not learn to decide the next steps in learning. |
| Assessment **AS** and **FOR** Learning with minimal **OF** Learning | Assessment **OF** and **FOR** Learning | Assessment **OF** Learning |

*Source:* Personalize Learning, LLC

**Assessment OF Learning** is summative and used to confirm what learners know and can do so teachers concentrate on ensuring that they have used assessment to provide accurate and sound statements of learners' proficiency.

**Assessment FOR Learning** provides information about what learners already know and can do so that teachers can design the most appropriate next steps in instruction so the teacher and peers can offer feedback to the learner throughout the learning process.

**Assessment AS Learning** is where learners reflect on their own learning, monitor their progress, and make adjustments to their learning so that they achieve deeper understanding.

Personalization involves assessment AS learning, FOR learning, and a minimum OF learning. This is where teachers develop capacity so learners become independent learners who set goals, monitor progress, and reflect on learning and assessments based on mastery.

Differentiation involves assessment FOR learning and OF learning. This assessment involves time-based testing where teachers provide feedback to advance learning.

Individualization involves assessment OF learning. This is where summative assessment is grade-based and involves time-based testing to confirm what learners know.

## RESEARCH AND RESOURCES SUPPORTING PERSONALIZED LEARNING

Personalized learning has been defined and illustrated through research, personal narratives, and school systems. All are contributing to this important dialogue that can help transform teaching and learning. The research is growing around this topic, yet we keep going back to the following resources because they illustrate and clarify what personalized learning is.

### Brown University

Educational researchers John H. Clarke and Edorah Frazer from Brown University set out to define personalized learning based on events occurring in a regular school day, aiming to assemble those events into categories that might explain how high schools can organize themselves to personalize learning for all students. They identified six categories of supportive interactions across all schools, each reflecting a developmental need of high school students that could be associated with a set of school practices organized to meet that need (Clarke & Frazer, 2003).

Figure 1.2 illustrates what they viewed as personal learning. It represents the six developmental needs, six areas of practice that respond to those

**Figure 1.2** Personal Learning

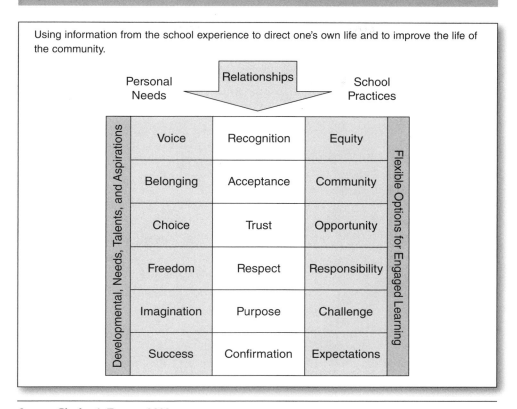

Using information from the school experience to direct one's own life and to improve the life of the community.

| | | |
|---|---|---|
| Voice | Recognition | Equity |
| Belonging | Acceptance | Community |
| Choice | Trust | Opportunity |
| Freedom | Respect | Responsibility |
| Imagination | Purpose | Challenge |
| Success | Confirmation | Expectations |

Personal Needs → Relationships → School Practices

Developmental, Needs, Talents, and Aspirations

Flexible Options for Engaged Learning

*Source:* Clarke & Frazer, 2003

needs, and six principles that describe the effect of interactions between the developmental needs of young adults and supportive school practices.

Figure 1.2 helps show that school is all about relationships between learners and how the school provides flexible options for learning. The left-hand column is about a learner's personal needs as a learner. The focus is on their talents, aspirations, and interests. Every learner needs his or her own voice and choice in an environment that encourages freedom and imagination. The school practices need to provide opportunities for engaged learning that encourage each and every learner to be challenged yet with reasonable expectations. Teachers, administrators, learners, and parents all need to trust and respect that learning opportunities are available for all learners and that teaching encourages each learner to be successful. Learners need to feel they are recognized, confirmed, and accepted as a valuable part of the community. Relationships are a key component of every community. When learners have a voice in their learning, the teacher and learner can work as partners in learning.

Chapter 10, "Making Learning Personal," of *Personalized Learning* (Clarke & Frazer, 2003) highlights teams of field researchers from Brown University visiting seven high schools in New England and shadowing twenty-one learners during their regular school days. One researcher observed Bart, who shared that he had been identified as learning disabled with clear limitations on his ability to decode symbolic forms. Bart had nine years of music training and played Beethoven, but no one knew it. He told the researcher how much he enjoyed media but was frustrated with some of the exercises. The observer noticed that Bart had no interaction with an adult or another learner throughout the day. Just putting yourself as the observer in a child's shoes gives you a feeling of what they experienced.

The study about school practices from Brown University demonstrates how learners' personal needs can be met as flexible options for engaged learning. The researchers determined that when you take into account how learners learn best based on their needs, talents, and aspirations and there is a learning environment that trusts and respects each learner, learners self-direct their learning to find their purpose and goals for learning.

> *Theresa Taylor, Principal, Glacier Edge Elementary School, Verona Area School District, Wisconsin, shared her reflection on Bart, being observed in school.*
>
> "Poor Bart! Of the six categories of supportive interactions indicated, I felt that recognition would have made the most impact for Bart, and for all children in our schools. I believe it is so important to know the child's story and greet them by name every time you have contact with them. By engaging in all six categories—recognition, trust, respect, acceptance, confirmation, and relevance—the learners and teachers engage in a relationship that will strengthen the framework and be a foundation necessary for personalized learning.
>
> "We continue to hear that we can't fit this new learning into our existing system. I agree. I am lucky that the staff I work with understand this and are willing to move towards personalized learning by building relationships and keeping student engagement, voice, and reflection as priority."

> *"Learning depends on a decision to engage information, not just to bring it in, but to move it around with other information so it makes sense. Choosing what information to manage increases the commitment to learn."*
>
> —John H. Clarke

In the 2004 NASSP report *Breaking Ranks II: Strategies for Leading High School Reform*, John H. Clarke in collaboration with the Education Alliance at Brown University and its Center for Secondary School Design elaborated on the definition of personalization, characterizing it as "a learning process in which schools help students assess their own talents and aspirations, plan a pathway toward their own purposes, work cooperatively with others on challenging tasks, maintain a record of their explorations, and demonstrate their learning against clear standards in a wide variety of media, all with the close support of adult mentors and guides" (NASSP, 2004).

> *"Historically, most classrooms have been `curriculum-centered' rather than `student-centered.' The core elements of the curriculum in most schools—textbooks and related print materials—are fixed, standardized, uniform, one-size-fits-all, but students on the other hand, are anything but uniform or standardized."*
>
> Rose & Gravel, 2012

## The Four Deeps and Nine Gateways to Personalize Learning

Dr. David H. Hargeaves and his colleagues identified the four "deeps" and nine "gateways" to personalize and improve learning in schools over time in their 2006 publication, "A New Shape for Schooling." The nine gateways are outlined and adapted here (Hargreaves, 2006).

1. Incorporate learner voice

2. Embed assessment for and as learning

3. Develop learning-to-learn strategies

4. Fully use new technologies

5. Offer a good choice of curriculum pathways

6. Routinely advise and guide learners through effective support structures

7. College and career readiness

8. Mentoring and coaching

9. The organization and design of the school

The four deeps of personalizing learning are the following:

1. Deep Learning

2. Deep Experience

3. Deep Support

4. Deep Leadership

The gateways are linked into clusters around the four deeps. These were adapted to include assessment *as* learning and refer to students as learners.

1. *Deep Learning* contains three gateways:
   - Learner voice
   - Assessment FOR and AS Learning.
   - Learning to learn is at the heart of personalization, for better learning is the purpose of personalization and its key outcome.

2. *Deep Experience* must ensure engagement as a precondition of learning.
   - The curriculum needs to be relevant.
   - It needs support by effective uses of technology.
   - It must engage learners with appropriate challenge.

3. *Deep Support* extends the advice and guidance and mentoring and coaching gateways and covers the broader well-being of individual learners—their health, general security, and freedom from poverty and disadvantage. Deep support also requires schools and teachers to collaborate with other institutions and individuals to secure deep learning for all learners.

4. High-quality, co-constructed *deep leadership* is required if a school is to understand the deeps and how they relate to each other and for creating the conditions in which they flourish. This does not involve introducing a new concept of leadership; it is more the exploration of leadership tasks around organization pathways, the workforce, and school design.

Hargreaves's perspective refers to "personalizing" learning rather than "personalized" learning, in order to emphasize that it is a process, not a product. It is a process that now asks educators, "How can I help create a real learner?"

## Learners Learning About Learning

Chris Watkins, reader at the Institute of Education, University of London, wrote an article for *INSI Research Matters* on the relation between learning and performance in schools. The evidence concludes that learning about learning is an educationally important strategy that improves performance. However, in the world of education, the culture of classrooms is one of teaching as telling and learning as listening (Watkins, 2006).

Effective learners understand how they learn with strengths identified as metacognition, self-monitoring, and self-regulation. Learners vary orientations between learning and performance where there is a concern for proving (performance) or improving (learning) orientation. We adapted and summarized key components in Watkins's research in Table 1.9 (Watkins, 2010).

### *Proving or Improving Orientation*

**Table 1.9** Performance Orientation vs. Learning Orientation

| Performance Orientation Classroom (PoC) | Learning Orientation Classroom (LoC) |
|---|---|
| Teacher-centered | Learner-centered |
| Learning is an individual process achieved by listening and following instructions. | Learning is an active process that requires student involvement and discussion. |
| Correct answer is the goal and following procedures is the method. | Understanding rather than memorization and replication is important. |
| Learners volunteer responses to teacher. | Participation generated by all where interaction is a key feature. |
| Whole-class lesson with little cooperation with learners working alone. | Learning happens in pairs, threes, and mixed groups. |
| Teacher generates and repeats rules and procedures to follow. | Class generates rules with freedom in way of working. |
| Praise if focused on behavior or for neatness. | Praise and feedback is informative and credible. |
| Teacher gives times available to answer questions. | Message is improvement and focusing on effort. |
| Learners focus on importance of tests and if every task is to be graded. | Performance in tests not linked to ability or prestige. |

*Source:* Watkins, 2010

The research concludes that a focus on learning can enhance performance, whereas a focus on performance alone can depress performance. With traditional instruction, the climate in the classroom becomes more performance oriented over years of schooling. A performance-oriented system focuses on looking good rather than learning well.

### Learners in the Driving Seat

Chris Watkins (2009) in "Learners in the Driving Seat" developed a metaphor of driving to better understand our learning. So what do we want for learners in our classes as well as for ourselves as learners? Here's where the metaphor of driving is valuable. When driving, we have an idea of a destination, perhaps a map of the area; we have our hands on the wheel, steering, making decisions as the journey unfolds. This is crucially related to the core process of noticing how it's going and how that relates to where we want to be. When it comes to learning, those core processes are the key to being an effective learner. They involve planning, monitoring, and reflecting. Plenty of research demonstrates that when learners drive their learning, it leads to greater engagement and **intrinsic motivation** for them to want to learn, learners setting a higher challenge for themselves, learners evaluating their own work, and better problem-solving skills (Watkins, 2009).

> It is about "metalearning," which means "learning about learning." Metalearning involves more than metacognition, learning about goals, feelings, social relations and context of learning. This research demonstrates effectiveness of the learner to have the ability to plan, monitor and review one's own learning. (Watkins, 2010)

*"The illiterate of the 21st century will not be those who cannot read and write, but those who cannot learn, unlearn, and relearn."*

—Alvin Toffler

## PERSONALIZED LEARNING OR NOT PERSONALIZED LEARNING

Why is the term *personalized learning* confusing? The word *personalized* is being used everywhere. Items are "personalized" just for you. Even coupons in the grocery store use the term to personalize your grocery list. Yet in education, some organizations are using the term for the technology or specific programs they use to personalize learning for you. Determine for yourself if the following terms, programs, or initiatives are or are not personalized learning.

- Adaptive Learning Systems
- Blended Learning
- Differentiated Instruction
- The Flipped Classroom

- 1:1 Programs
- Project-based Learning
- Individual Education Plans (IEPs)

## Adaptive Learning Systems

**Adaptive learning** is an educational method that uses computers as interactive teaching devices. Computers adapt the presentation of educational material according to students' learning needs, as indicated by their responses to questions and tasks. Both Knewton and Grockit are test prep companies that have developed adaptive learning systems. They offer online adaptive learning services that provide individualized learning experiences by applying mathematical modeling to students' studying. Their software is adaptive as the content it presents changes based on the students' performance—by their strengths and weaknesses. Algorithms dictate the most appropriate next question for students.

McGraw-Hill's LearnSmart methodology is simple. It determines the concepts learners don't know or understand and then teaches those concepts using personalized plans designed for each learner's success. The LearnSmart Advantage suite—LearnSmart, SmartBook, LearnSmart Achieve, LearnSmart Prep, and LearnSmart Labs—leverages years of data and advanced scientific algorithms to ensure that every minute a student spends studying with a LearnSmart Advantage product is the most efficient and productive minute possible.

Dreambox calls itself "intelligent adaptive learning" as technologically enabled personal tutoring. Its idea is to go beyond passively delivering previously recorded lessons, presenting digitized textbooks, or providing memorization drills. Dreambox involves assessments and levels of interactivity that approximate those of an experienced human tutor.

- Intelligent analysis of a student's solutions
- Interactive problem-solving support
- Curriculum sequencing
- Multiple learning experiences
- Customized presentation and pace

The Intelligent Adaptive Learning guides the learning experience and adjusts path and pace to stay within the learner's zone of optimized learning to accelerate understanding and critical thinking. The system also provides formative and summative data to the learner's teacher to enable more personalized instruction.

> "Practice math at your own pace with our adaptive assessment environment. You can start at 1 + 1 and work your way into calculus or jump right into whatever topic needs some brushing up." (Khan Academy, 2013)

Khan Academy provides interactive challenges and videos using their adaptive assessment environment. They have an extensive library of content that covers math, biology, chemistry, physics, humanities, finance, and history. Statistics are available on the learners' profiles instantly using at-a-glance information to see if learners hit their goals. Teachers and coaches also can access the learners' data on their dashboard.

## Blended Learning

**Blended learning** or hybrid learning combines online and on-site opportunities. There are different terms for blended learning, and opinions vary on what it means. In a report on the merits and potential of blended education, the Sloan Consortium defined hybrid courses as those that "integrate online with traditional face-to-face class activities in a planned, pedagogically valuable manner" (Sloan Consortium, 2005). According to Education Elements, which develops hybrid learning technologies, successful blended learning occurs when technology and teaching inform each other: material becomes dynamic when it reaches learners of varying learning styles. In other words, hybrid classrooms on the Internet can reach and engage learners in a truly customizable way.

Blended learning approaches use technology to:

- help learners master the content and skills they need,
- allow teachers to get the most out of their planning and instructional time, and
- streamline operations with costs similar to—or less than—traditional schooling.

A school can set up a blended learning model with on-site and online activities that use one or more of these models:

- Station Rotation Model
- Lab Rotation Model
- Flex Model
- Individual Rotation Model

*Station Rotation Model* is a program with a specific course or subject where learners rotate on a fixed schedule or as directed by the teacher.

KIPP LA Empower Academy is an example of this type of rotation model that includes small-group activities, whole-class instruction, pairs of learners working together, individual tutoring, and independent work.

Rocketship Education uses the *Lab Rotation Model* that differs from the Station Rotation Model in that learners rotate to another location in the school instead of staying in one classroom. Learners go to a learning lab for up to 100 minutes a day using predominantly online learning or adaptive software to track their progress.

San Francisco Flex Academy uses a *Flex Model* where teachers are facilitators in an online lab only. Learners move on an individually customized schedule with the teacher available on site to provide face-to-face support on a flexible and adaptive as-needed basis. SF Flex uses the K high school curriculum, which blends the company's patented learning environment with key features designed to make the high school experience successful, given the more complex content, skills, and time management requirements of high school learners.

Carpe Diem Collegiate High School uses the *Individual Rotation Model* where learners rotate on an individually customized fixed schedule that includes online learning. The teacher or the algorithm directs their learning. The Carpe Diem model blends individual digital curriculum with high-quality instruction. What sets Carpe Diem schools apart from the traditional classroom is that students work at their own pace informed by daily assessments based on their individualized learning plan. Their curriculum blends classroom instruction with digital coursework allowing for flexible scheduling.

There are blended learning models where teachers find or create online courses from places like Florida Virtual Schools, Coursera, or MIT as optional learning strategies to supplement coursework (Staker & Horn, 2012).

## Differentiated Instruction

The design and development of differentiated instruction as a model began in the general education classroom. The initial application came to practice for students considered gifted but who perhaps were not sufficiently challenged by the content provided in the general classroom setting. As classrooms have become more diverse, differentiated instruction has been applied at all levels for students of all abilities.

Differentiation is responsive teaching where teachers proactively plan varied approaches to what different groups of learners need to learn, how they will learn it, and/or how they will show what they have learned. In a differentiated learning environment, learners are identified based on their challenges in a specific content area and skill levels. The teacher uses existing differentiated curriculum or adapts instruction to meet the needs of different groups of learners.

According to Dr. Carol Tomlinson, differentiated instruction is both a philosophy and a way of teaching that respects the different learning needs of students and expects all students to experience success as learners. Learning activities may be differentiated on the basis of students' readiness for learning the specific content or skill, their interests, or their preferred ways of learning (Tomlinson, 2012).

To differentiate learning, a teacher identifies the same objectives for different groups of learners. Teachers use and analyze data to identify the different learners in their classroom. From this data, the teacher uses, adapts, or creates different lessons or resources on a concept around the same objectives based on the different group of learners.

The model of differentiated instruction requires teachers to be flexible in their approach to teaching and adjust the curriculum and presentation of information to learners rather than expecting students to modify themselves for the curriculum.

Differentiated instruction theory reinforces the importance of effective classroom management and reminds teachers of meeting the challenges of effective organizational and instructional practices. Engagement is a vital component of effective classroom management, organization, and instruction. Therefore teachers are encouraged to offer choices of tools, adjust the level of difficulty of the material, and provide varying levels of scaffolding to gain and maintain learner attention during the instructional episode.

## The Flipped Classroom

The **flipped classroom** enables learners to view lectures in video and other formats outside of the classroom. This allows learners to view and review the lecture and resources at their own pace and frees up more of the classroom time for collaborative problem solving, one-on-one support, and group work with the teacher and peers.

Jackie Gerstein (2011), EdD, online adjunct faculty for Boise State University, Western Governors University, and Walden University, created the graphic in Figure 1.3 as an overview of what can happen in a flipped classroom. The teacher can suggest out-of-class activities online, so learners need access to the Internet at home or somewhere they can use an Internet-abled device.

*The Flipped Classroom Flowchart*

**Figure 1.3**  The Flipped Classroom by Jackie Gerstein

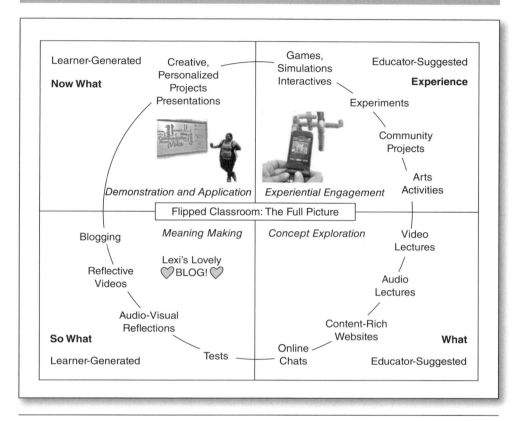

*Source:* Gerstein, 2011

Bergmann, Overmyer, and Wilie (2013) dispel some misunderstandings of a flipped classroom by describing what it is and is not. They emphasize that a flipped classroom is not an online course or where students work without structure or in isolation or where they spend their entire class staring at a computer screen. They point out that a flipped classroom includes an environment of greater interaction between students and teachers where students take responsibility for their learning. They emphasize "a blending of direct instruction and constructivist learning," "a class where content is permanently archived for review or remediation," and "a place where all students can get a personalized education" (Bergmann et al., June 2013).

In 2007, flipped-classroom pioneers Aaron Sams and Jon Bergmann defined the flipped classroom as a new model of instruction where "students watch recorded lectures for homework and complete their assignments, labs and tests in class." They point out that it is "the interaction and the meaningful learning activities that occur during the face-to-face time that is most important." (Bergmann & Sams, 2012)

In 2013, a group of educators from the Flipped Learning Network along with Pearson expanded on the definition of a flipped classroom by identifying the four pillars of F-L-I-P. This acronym represents Flexible Environment, Learning Culture, Intentional Content, and Professional Educator. What does this all mean? It means that the learning environment may change based on the lesson being taught and that learners may have flexible ways to learn the content in depth. Teachers may use intentional content to "maximize classroom time in order to adopt various methods of instruction" and they may need to know how and when to shift from direct instruction in a group to face-to-face time on an individualized basis (Hamdan, McKnight, McKnight, & Arfstrom, 2013).

Some teachers are using existing curriculum from Khan Academy and textbook companies like McGraw-Hill's Connect. Teachers are flipping their classrooms all over the country. Clintondale High School in Colorado flipped almost every class, and they call themselves the Flipped High School. One teacher in Montclair, California, Eric Marcos, started flipping his math classroom when his sixth graders decided it would be better if they did the flipping of the math concepts. They created hundreds of short tutorials themselves that are available online at MathTrain.tv.

A key feature of the flipped learning model is the opportunity to maximize learning opportunities in the classroom by deliberately shifting direct instruction to outside the group learning space. The emphasis on maximizing one-on-one interactions turns the focus to learners taking more control of their learning that more actively involves learners in the learning process.

## 1:1 Programs

**One-to-one programs** are also known as "anywhere, anytime" or "laptops for students" programs. Some schools are using tablets or iPads for their 1:1 program. These programs provide students with personal portable computers or mobile devices to enhance opportunities for learning. BYOD, or Bring Your Own Device, is a strategy schools and districts are using to bring the ratio to 1:1. Desktops, laptops, and mobile devices help schools engage the digital generation by nurturing individual (or one-to-one) learning experiences. The Maine Learning Technology Initiative (MLTI) is a model of 1:1 where they provide professional development and twenty-first-century tools to middle and high schools to support the attainment of the Maine state standards.

> MLTI made Maine the first state to seize the potential of technology to transform teaching and learning in classrooms statewide; first with a plan to equip all students and teachers in grades 7 to 12 with personal learning technology statewide; first to equip every 7th and 8th grade student and 7th through 12th grade teacher statewide with personal access to learning technology; first to empower every 7th through 12th grade teacher in every school statewide with professional development and support to fully tap the potential of computers and the Internet; and first to provide the option of home Internet access to every 7th and 8th grade student in every school statewide. (MLTI, 2009)

Anytime Anywhere Learning Foundation (AALF) was founded by Bruce Dixon in 2004. Dixon believes that the effective and contributing global citizens of tomorrow will be digitally fluent lifelong learners who participate fully in every aspect of social and economic life. These leaders must be granted an education that fosters their innate motivation to learn, encourages academic rigor through relevant application, and connects them with the world they will enter. They will be Anytime Anywhere Learners.

The challenge of anytime, anywhere learning is to support this investment by structuring education to provide students with meaningful tasks that require them to think about, construct, and share ideas in a connected world.

> **To take part in anytime, anywhere learning, learners must be provided with:**
>
> - A constructivist, international education where meaningful tasks subsume curriculum objectives.
> - A personal, portable computer with which to think about, construct and share ideas.
>
> Anytime Anywhere Learning Foundation, 2008

Project RED studied nearly 100 schools across the country with 1:1 ratios of students to mobile computing devices and showed that the proper integration of this technology leads to increased academic achievement for students. Schools with a 1:1 ratio reported increased graduation rates and student test scores as well as decreases in dropout rates and disciplinary action.

According to Project RED, schools with a 1:1 ratio reported increased graduation rates and student test scores as well as decreased dropout rates and disciplinary action. Yet a compilation of four new studies of one-to-one computing projects in K–12 schools identifies several factors key to the projects' success:

- Adequate planning
- Stakeholder buy-in, and
- Strong school or district leadership.

The researchers say the most important factor of all is the teaching practices of instructors—suggesting school laptop programs are only as effective as the teachers who apply them.

## Project-Based Learning

According to researchers (Barron & Darling-Hammond, 2008; Thomas, 2000), project-based learning essentially involves the following:

- Learners learning knowledge to tackle problems as they would be solved in the real world
- Increased learner control over his or her learning
- Teachers serving as coaches and facilitators of inquiry and reflection
- Learners (usually but not always) working in pairs or groups

Doing projects is not the same thing as project-based learning (PBL). Teachers may design one project that they expect all learners to do. Projects can be part of a lesson, and, in some cases, all learners are creating the same product. PBL is a dynamic approach to teaching in which learners explore real-world problems and challenges. With this type of active and engaged learning, learners are inspired to obtain a deeper knowledge of the subjects they are studying. Project-based learning hails from a tradition of pedagogy that asserts that learners learn best by experiencing and solving real-world problems.

In PBL you can plan rigorous and relevant standards-focused projects that engage students in authentic learning activities, teach twenty-first-century skills, and demand demonstration of mastery. Buck Institute for Education (BIE) has templates, rationale, and processes for PBL. BIE created PB-Online Edutopia to provide a step-by-step process.

Teachers can create real-world problem-solving situations by designing questions and tasks that correspond to two different frameworks of inquiry-based teaching:

- *Problem-based learning* tackles a problem but doesn't necessarily include a project.
- *Project-based learning* involves a complex task and some form of student presentation, and/or creating an actual product or artifact.

PBL can be personalized if learners have a voice and choice in how they obtain deeper knowledge and take control of their learning.

## Individual Education Plans (IEPs)

In the United States, the Individuals with Disabilities Education Act (IDEA) mandates an Individualized Education Program (IEP) to ensure FAPE (A Free and Appropriate Education) for students with disabilities. In Canada and the United Kingdom, an equivalent document is called an Individual Education Plan.

An **Individual Education Plan** defines the individualized objectives of a child who has been diagnosed with a disability, as defined by federal regulations. The IEP is intended to help children reach individual educational goals more easily than they otherwise would. In all cases the IEP must be specified to the individual learner's needs as identified by the IEP evaluation process and must especially help teachers and related service providers (such as paraprofessional educators, Speech and Language Pathologists, Occupational Therapists) understand the learner's strengths, weaknesses, and preferences and how the disability affects the learning process.

An IEP is meant to ensure that learners receive an appropriate placement and supports, which means the support of assistive technology not "only" in special education classrooms but also in regular education settings. It is meant to give the learner a chance to participate in "normal" school culture and academics as much as is possible. In this way, the learner is able to have specialized assistance only when such assistance is absolutely necessary and otherwise maintains the freedom to interact with and participate in the activities with school peers.

> In many cases, the learner does not necessarily gain independent learning skills. The IEP describes . . .
>
> - how the learner learns.
> - how the learner best demonstrates that learning.
> - what teachers and service providers will do to help the learner learn more effectively.

### *So what is and what is not personalized learning?*

After reading each of the preceding topics, you might still be confused as to whether they are or are not personalized learning. Project-based learning makes it sound like it can be personalized for the learner. It can be if the learner has a voice and choice in how the projects and activities are designed and implemented. Projects where all learners create the same product might not be really personalized. Flipped classrooms where learners watch videos of lectures might not be personalized. Blended learning environments where teachers direct what and when each learner learns might not be personalized. Consider how any of these topics support a personalized learning environment.

## BUILDING A COMMON LANGUAGE

It is crucial to build a common language around personalized learning so everyone in a school or district has a shared meaning and understanding of personalized learning with conversations around a similar vision, goals, and activities. With a common language around personalized learning, we can build a community of practice that grows with experiences and stories of what worked and didn't work. This is about transforming an entire system, which just does not happen overnight. A common language helps in creating the conversations that build and sustain a personalized learning system.

### *Personalized learning means learners . . .*

- know how they learn best.
- are co-designers of the curriculum and the learning environment.
- have flexible learning anytime and anywhere.
- have a voice in and choice about their learning.
- have quality teachers who are partners in learning.
- use a competency-based model to demonstrate mastery.
- self-direct their learning.
- design their learning path for college and career.

The previous bulleted list was pasted into Wordle and appears in Figure 1.4. Wordle is a program that captures the text from a document or website and displays the words most often used larger in a design of your choice. The main concept in this Wordle is apparent: learning!

**Figure 1.4** Wordle on Personalized Learning

*The focus of personalized learning is about learning that starts with the learner.*

*"Students, or more correctly called learners here, need to directly be in charge of their learning. They are recognized for their unique perspective and this is encouraged and welcomed. All learners have a voice (some will need to be encouraged to find theirs more so than others) and this needs to be recognized and heard. The structure of the school day needs to be rearranged to allow learners time to personalize their learning and work on meaningful, self-chosen tasks."*

—Ruth Hayward, teacher at the
Queanbeyan Distance Education Centre,
Queanbeyan Primary School, Australia

*"Shifting the focus from the teacher to the learner will take time and training, but it will also take the willingness to 'unlearn' what so many have been taught about student learning and teacher control. We can admire this dilemma for as long as we want, but the truth is, 'the train has left the station' and the learners are on it."*

—Jackie Johnston, Director of Alternative
and Community Education, District 112, Minnesota

## CHAPTER 1 REVIEW

1. Review the Personalization vs. Differentiation vs. Individualization (PDI) chart with your colleagues and how you see these three terms in your learning environment.

2. Reflect on what personalization means for you and your learners.

3. Discuss the section on research and resources supporting personalized learning with your colleagues.

4. Determine the common language of personalized learning.

## RESOURCES

- Center for Applied Special Technology: www.cast.org
- Knewton: www.knewton.com
- Grockit: http://grockit.com
- McGraw-Hill's LearnSmart: http://learnsmartadvantage.com
- Dreambox: www.dreambox.com
- Khan Academy: http://khanacademy.org
- Education Elements: http://educationelements.com
- Kipp LA Empower Academy: www.kippla.org
- Rocketship Education: www.rsed.org
- San Francisco Flex Academy: www.k12.com/sfflex/home
- Carpe Diem Collegiate High School: www.carpediemschools.com
- Clintondale High School, CO: www.flippedhighschool.com
- Eric Marcos 6th Grade Class MathTrain: http://mathtrain.tv
- Project RED: www.projectred.org

# 2 Who Are Your Learners?

*"Today you are You, that is truer than true.*
*There is no one alive who is Youer than You."*

—Dr. Seuss

## PERSONALIZED LEARNING IS NOT NEW: LET'S ASK THE LEARNING THEORISTS

In Plato's time (427–374 BC), the teaching and learning process was more about interpersonal interactions and fostering the individual ability to critically apply knowledge and cultivate individual passions for learning. Just imagine Plato teaching direct instruction to thirty learners at one time. It was all about personalizing the learning and not having everyone learn the same thing at the same time (Marquis, 2012).

Consider that if Plato personalized learning over 2,400 years ago, then maybe we need to rethink what it means for us today. To put a context and a more thorough background into the idea of personalized learning, we summarized the work of several key learning theorists along with learning approaches that support the idea that learners need to take responsibility for their own learning.

### Lev Vygotsky (1896–1934)

Russian psychologist Lev Vygotsky believed that mental tools extend our mental abilities, enabling us to solve problems and create solutions in the real world. This means that to successfully function in school and beyond, children need to learn more than a set of facts and skills. They need to master a set of mental tools—tools of the mind. After children

Vygotsky is the main influence of Universal Design for Learning (UDL). His theory emphasized a key point of UDL where when individuals become expert learners, the support they receive as they learn is gradually removed. This is very similar to the way training wheels are unnecessary once a person has successfully mastered bike riding.

master mental tools, they become in charge of their own learning, by attending and remembering in an intentional and purposeful way.

Vygotsky's theories stress the fundamental role of social interaction where community plays a central role in the process of "making meaning." Vygotsky's theory is one of the foundations of constructivism. It asserts three major themes:

1. **Social interaction** plays a fundamental role in the process of cognitive development. Vygotsky stated, "Every function in the child's cultural development appears twice: first, on the social level, and later, on the individual level" (Culatta, 2013).

2. The **More Knowledgeable Other (MKO)** refers to anyone who has a better understanding than the learner with respect to a particular task, process, or concept. The MKO could be a teacher, coach, or adult and could also be peers or technology.

3. The **Zone of Proximal Development (ZPD)**, shown in Figure 2.1, is the distance between a learner's ability to perform a task under adult guidance and/or with peer collaboration and the learner's ability to solve the problem independently. Learning occurs in this zone (McLeod, 2012).

**Figure 2.1**  Zone of Proximal Development

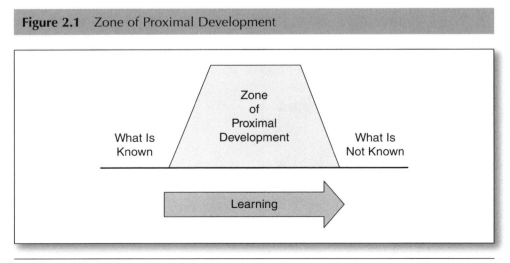

*Source:* Sincero, 2011

### *Why is Vygotsky's theory important in personalizing learning?*

Vygotsky's theory supports personalized learning because the purpose of education is for learners to become creative and innovative through analysis, conceptualizations, and synthesis of prior experience to create new knowledge. Learning is an active process in which learners construct new ideas or concepts based on their current and prior knowledge, social interactions, and motivation to learn. Vygotsky emphasized how important it is for learners to be in charge of their learning. He also was the first theorist to focus on making meaning and how being part of a community of learners supports each learner (Vygotsky, 1962).

> *"What a child can do in cooperation today, he can do alone tomorrow."*
>
> —Lev Vygotsky

## John Dewey (1859–1952)

John Dewey was way ahead of other theorists of his time. His ideas (1899) described in *The School and Society* have remarkable significance to the field of education as we now know it. Dewey believed that the development of curricula should be based on learner self-interests. He rejected the idea that children are primarily motivated by rewards and punishments; rather, children are motivated by what they are most interested in. He is often associated with child-centered education.

Dewey established the Chicago Laboratory School for the purpose of testing his educational theories and their sociological implications. His beliefs resulted in a curriculum based on learner interests designed to teach the social origins of knowledge and cooperation (Center for Dewey Studies, 2010).

### *Why is Dewey's theory important in personalizing learning?*

John Dewey's theory supports education's connection with society, the outside world, and real life. Dewey believed that what we learn should be meaningful and relevant. He also believed that the child is in the center just like the concept of personalized learning.

Dewey made the case that education needed to adopt new instructional approaches based on future societal needs. He claimed that twentieth-century schools should reorganize their curricula, emphasize freedom and individuality, and respond to changing employment requirements. Failure to do so would be detrimental to young people. Dewey would be rolling over in his grave knowing that in the twenty-first century we are still teaching as we taught yesterday.

> *"If we teach as we taught yesterday, we rob our children of tomorrow."*
>
> —John Dewey

### Jerome Bruner (1915–)

The outcome of cognitive development is thinking. The intelligent mind creates from experience generic coding systems that permit one to go beyond the data to new and possibly fruitful predictions.

#### Four features of Bruner's theory of instruction

1. *Predisposition to learn.* This feature specifically states the experiences that move the learner toward a love of learning in general or of learning something in particular. Motivational, cultural, and personal factors contribute to this. Bruner emphasized social factors and early teachers and parents' influence on this. He believed learning and problem solving emerged out of exploration. Part of the task of a teacher is to maintain and direct a child's spontaneous explorations.

2. *Structure of knowledge.* It is possible to structure knowledge in a way that enables the learner to most readily grasp the information. This is a relative feature, as there are many ways to structure a body of knowledge and many preferences among learners. Bruner offered considerable detail about structuring knowledge.

3. *Modes of representation.* Learners can access information using multiple modes of representation, such as visually, with words, or using symbols.

4. *Effective sequencing.* Sequencing, or lack of it, can make learning easier or more difficult (Bruner, 2013).

> *"Thinking about thinking has to be a principal ingredient of any empowering practice of education."*
>
> —Jerome Bruner

#### Why is Bruner's theory important in personalizing learning?

Bruner based his **Constructivist Theory** on Vygotsky's work. His theory is about important outcomes of learning that include not just the concepts, categories, and problem-solving procedures invented previously by the culture, but also the ability to invent these things for oneself. He introduced the ideas of readiness for learning and spiral curriculum. Bruner believed that any child can be taught at any stage of development in a way that fits the child's cognitive abilities. **Spiral curriculum** refers to the idea of revisiting basic ideas over and over, building on them, and elaborating to the level of full understanding and mastery.

## Mihaly Csíkszentmihályi (1934–)

Csíkszentmihályi is noted for his work in the study of happiness and creativity. Yet he is best known as the architect of the theory of **flow**. Flow is when people are fully immersed in what they are doing and there is a balance between the challenge of the task and the skill of the learner. Flow cannot occur if the task is too easy or too difficult.

When you are in flow, you are energized, focused, and completely involved and absorbed. If this occurs in a classroom, the process itself is a success. Csíkszentmihályi described flow as being completely involved in an activity for its own sake. The ego falls away. Time flies. Every action, movement, and thought follows inevitably from the previous one. Your whole being is involved, and you are using your skills to the utmost.

Mihaly Csíkszentmihályi published the graph in Figure 2.2 that depicts the relationship between the challenges of a task and skills. Flow only occurs when the activity is a higher-than-average challenge and requires above-average skills. Both skill level and challenge level must be matched and high; if skill and challenge are low and matched, then apathy results (Csíkszentmihályi, 1990).

> **Pause/Think/Reflect**
>
> When you are immersed in a task where you forget time and may even forget to eat, that is flow. When have you experienced flow?

### *Why is flow important for personalizing learning?*

Personalized learning environments offer flexibility and time so learners can get in the flow. If we can provide learning opportunities where learners find themselves in the flow, then they are more than motivated in the activity, they are so engaged they don't want to stop. That's what it means for learners to own and drive their learning their way.

> *"If you are interested in something, you will focus on it, and if you focus attention on anything, it is likely that you will become interested in it. Many of the things we find interesting are not so by nature, but because we took the trouble of paying attention to them."*
>
> —Mihaly Csíkszentmihályi

**Figure 2.2** Flow Based on Challenge and Skill

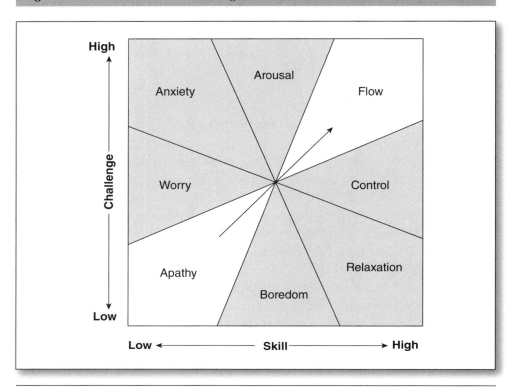

*Source:* Csíkszentmihályi, 1990

## Carol Dweck (1946–)

Carol Dweck (2006), a researcher at Stanford and author of *Mindset*, discovered in her research that belief guides a large part of your life. Much of what you think of as your personality actually grows out of this **"mindset"** and could prevent you from fulfilling your potential. You can have either a fixed mindset or a growth mindset. People are born with a love of learning, but the fixed mindset can undo it.

Think about a time you were enjoying a crossword puzzle, playing a sport, or learning a new dance when it started to become too difficult. You suddenly felt bored, or tired, or some other feeling that made you stop. The next time you did this activity, you now had a fixed mindset that you couldn't accomplish it. Now picture yourself in a growth mindset around this

**Pause/Think/Reflect**

Do you know people steeped in a fixed mindset? Think about how they are always trying to prove themselves and how they are supersensitive about being wrong or making mistakes. Did you ever wonder why they were this way? Are you this way?

activity. Picture your brain forming new connections as you meet the challenge and learn.

Just because some people can do something with little or no training, it doesn't mean that others can't do it if they get the training. Those with fixed mindsets think that someone's early performance is all you need to know about the person's talent and future. Whereas those with growth mindsets find success in doing their best in learning and improving. They learn from failure and find setbacks motivating. They keep trying and don't give up if they want to learn or do something (Dweck, 2010).

### Why is mindset important in personalizing learning?

Learners with fixed mindsets about learning may be resistant to learning. If they believe they cannot do a math problem or read at a certain level, then they give up easily. In a personalized learning environment, the teacher makes sure learners know the difference between a fixed and growth mindset. They help them identify if they have a fixed mindset about something and walk them through how to change it so they believe they can learn whatever is difficult for them.

> *"Picture your brain forming new connections as you meet the challenge and learn. Keep on going."*
>
> —Carol Dweck

## AS TIME GOES BY

Since we started with Plato and personalizing learning during his time, we thought we better look at what that means for our learners. Today's learners are different from those ten years ago—actually, even five years ago. The old saying "times are a-changing" is really true when it comes to how today's learners think and learn compared to previous generations. All of our brains work the same, but the latest generations are wired differently than their parents and almost foreign to their grandparents.

### Generation Y (1981–1996)

**Generation Y** is called the Millennials or the First Digitals. They prefer technology since they grew up in a digital environment. They have never known a world without computers. They access all of their information and content from the Internet.

Baby Boomers took to e-mail as soon as it became available so they could connect with family and friends. Then they joined Facebook; some quickly moved on to Twitter, Instagram, and other forms of digital communication. Now they are texting along with Gen Xers and later generations. Some Baby Boomers and Gen Xers are involved in social media to see what their children and grandchildren are up to.

This is when e-mail, texting, and instant messaging became big and people connected virtually with each other. Generation Y was the first to sign up for Facebook and Twitter because their friends matter most to them, and they are natural collaborators. They use technology at a higher rate than any previous generations. In fact, they cannot function socially without a mobile phone. Just watch them interact and multitask as they text, surf the Internet, and download music all at the same time. Gen Y may seem needy because they constantly seek feedback, responsibility, and involvement in decision making, but they really are adaptable and crave independence. Gen Ys tend to be optimistic about life.

They are the generation of entrepreneurs who don't want to work nine to five in one job or career. You can see many of them doing their work anywhere there is free Wi-Fi. They demand respect and expect to have a voice and be listened to. They have instant 24/7 access to information and tend to be assertive about what they know or can find on their own. Traditional school seems archaic to them. Their Baby Boomer parents told them over and over again that they were special. This resulted in Gen Ys expecting the world to treat them that way. They do not live to work; they prefer a more relaxed work environment with a lot of hand holding and accolades.

### Generation Z or the Net Generation (1997–Present)

Where Generation Ys tend to be optimistic, **Generation Z**s are realistic. They see how scary the world can be since they grew up post-9/11 and lived during the latest great recession. They hear and see reports of school shootings and are more aware of troubling times. Because of the economy, many of their parents lost their jobs. This impacted their lives by seeing and hearing how disturbing these times were first-hand. Since they are digital and mostly tech-savvy, they take problems on by wanting to understand them and confront them right away. They look for answers and tutorials on their tablet or mobile phone. Entertainment has changed.

**Pause/Think/Reflect**

Reflect on your generation and your impressions of Generations Y and Z. How does the time in which you were born impact how you prefer to learn?

The messages they view at earlier ages reflect their reality rather than depicting the perfect imaginary fairy tale life of previous generations. Movies such as *The Hunger Games* may depict characters they can relate to who face impossible scenarios but rise above them to create a better society. Some Gen Zs believe they have a responsibility to society. Many saw parents lose jobs and go into debt. They may use their digital skills to avoid debt and even reconsider if college is worth the cost if they can teach themselves. Gen Zs are globally aware and connected in social media at younger ages than ever before. They believe they can solve problems and make a difference. The world is smaller and information is instantaneous. Gen Zs know how to connect using social media and use digital tools. Since many Gen Z parents are entrepreneurial or have changed jobs multiple times, Gen Zs are watching and learning from them.

### What These New Generations Mean for Personalized Learning

Schools have not changed much in over one hundred years; someone from that time could walk into most schools today and feel right at home. Many Baby Boomers experienced traditional schools—some with desks bolted to the floor and knuckles slapped with a ruler.

Starting with Generation Y (1981–1996), education needed to change to keep children engaged. Since they grew up with technology, video games, and visuals that were coming at them faster with shorter segments, teachers found it difficult to keep their attention with traditional lectures. Many teachers became entertainers to keep their attention. It worked for some but not all. Schools tried different approaches like whole language, cooperative learning, project-based learning, and added technology. There were early adopters who integrated technology into their curriculum. Even with all of these approaches, too many kids were not paying attention and dropping out, especially those that lived in poverty and were considered high risk.

Personalized learning works for the latest generations because they want to control their learning. Since most of these learners use technology to connect and learn, they want to drive their learning using their mobile devices. When learners drive their learning, teachers' roles change. Even toddlers are being exposed to the latest technologies at younger and younger ages. This impacts what school means and what learning means.

## MEASURING AND DESCRIBING LEARNERS TODAY

Learners have been tested, labeled, and put in specific boxes based on different measurement tools. Many of these tools have been around for years and are not based on scientific research. Some tools limit learners in what they learn by believing they have limited learning styles, identified intelligences, or reading levels. Educators "bought in" to these theories even though there is no scientific evidence behind them, because they seemed to make more sense than IQ scores. This section explains why learning styles, multiple intelligences, reading levels, and standardized tests tend to cause a fixed mindset for teachers that are difficult to break.

## Learning Styles

For more than thirty years, the notion that teaching methods should match a learner's particular learning style has had a powerful influence on education. The seven learning styles most commonly used to describe how we learn best include the following:

- *Visual (spatial)*: prefer using pictures, images, and spatial understanding
- *Aural (auditory-musical)*: prefer using sound and music
- *Verbal (linguistic)*: prefer using words, both in speech and writing
- *Physical (kinesthetic)*: prefer using body, hands, and sense of touch
- *Logical (mathematical)*: prefer using logic, reasoning, and systems
- *Social (interpersonal)*: prefer to learn in groups or with other people
- *Solitary (intrapersonal)*: prefer to work alone and use self-study

A study published in the *Psychological Science in the Public Interest* challenged the concept of learning styles and their effect on performance. Four prominent cognitive psychologists found no evidence for validating educational applications of learning styles into general educational practice. They had ample evidence that children and adults will, if asked, express preferences about how they prefer information to be presented to them (Association for Psychological Sciences, 2009).

Research conducted over the last forty years has failed to show that individual attributes can be used to guide effective teaching practice. Rather than being a harmless fad, learning styles perpetuate stereotyping and harmful teaching practices they are supposed to fight. The learning styles theory ensures that the theory continues to survive despite the evidence against it (Scott, 2010).

The brain processes information with multiple sensory modalities such as visual and verbal. When we identify a learner as one learning style over another, it does not

> **Pause/Think/Reflect**
>
> If you identify with one learning style, will that keep you challenging yourself to do something that addresses a different learning style?

follow the research about how the brain works. Our brains are highly interconnected, so it is incorrect to think we can only be identified as having only one or even two learning styles. We use all of the modalities because that is how our brain works (Dekker, Howard-Jones, & Jolles, 2012).

What cognitive science has taught us is that children do differ in their abilities with different modalities, but teaching the child in his best modality doesn't affect his educational achievement. What does matter is whether the child is taught in the content's best modality. All learners learn more when content drives the choice of modality. Cognitive psychologists have used formal laboratory tasks to investigate the role of modality in memory. An important finding from that research is that memory is usually stored independent of any modality. You typically store memories in terms of meaning—not in terms of whether you saw, heard, or physically interacted with the information (Willingham, 2005).

Simply stated, the research has not revealed a compelling argument as to the impact of learning styles and their effect on predicting learning outcomes.

## Multiple Intelligences

In 1983, Howard Gardner proposed the theory of multiple intelligences in his book *Frames of Mind* with seven intelligences (Gardner, 1983). Later he added naturalist as the eighth intelligence. For many years, schools have been using these identifiers to describe learners and the types of instruction effective based on their specific intelligences. Recently, there are discussions that the idea of multiple intelligences has no evidence in science and that Gardner's theory is just a theory. Identifying yourself with one or more of the intelligences could label you as a learner. For example, if learners identify with the intrapersonal intelligence, they may take on that trait and not be open to the possibility that they can work collaboratively. Identifying as one or two intelligences could result in learners believing that is all they are and all they can do. Figure 2.3 shows Gardner's eight intelligences.

Although Gardner's claims have become popular with educators, very little research has been done to establish the validity of his theory. The few studies that have been done do not actually support the idea that there are many kinds of "intelligence" operating separately from each other. Among academic scholars who study intelligence there is very little acceptance of Gardner's theory due to a lack of empirical evidence for it. Even though Gardner first made his theory public in 1983, the first empirical study to test the theory was not published until twenty-three years later, and the results were not supportive (McGreal, 2013).

**Figure 2.3** Multiple Intelligences

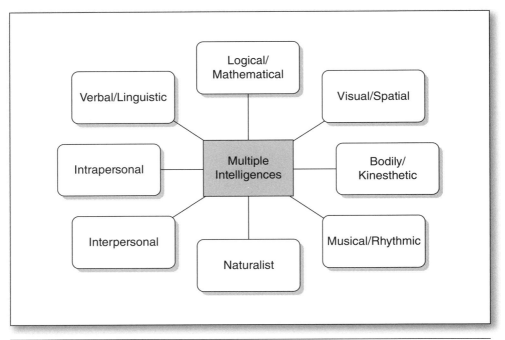

*Source:* Personalize Learning LLC

**Pause/Think/Reflect**

Which multiple intelligence have you identified with? Are you only this one or do you have multiple intelligences? Do the intelligences you identify describe how you learn? Have you used any of the intelligences to label yourself (e.g., I'm a spatial learner)? Use these questions to do more research on multiple intelligences before you use this tool to identify how your learners learn.

A critical review of the topic by Lynn Waterhouse (2006) found no published studies to support the validity of the theory. Multiple intelligences theory can hardly be described as scientifically sound.

Another issue with the theory of multiple intelligences is that too many of the categories correlate too highly with one another to be separate intelligences. Cognitive performance on skills related to verbal-linguistic, logical-mathematical, and visual-spatial tasks, as well as many memory tasks, tends to be highly related. In other words, it goes back to **"g"** or general intelligence.

The remaining intelligences have nothing to do with intelligence or cognitive skills but rather represent personal interests (e.g., musical represents an affinity for music; naturalistic, an affinity for biology or geology) or personality traits (interpersonal or intrapersonal skills, which correspond best to the related concept of emotional intelligence). And even those interest areas may be enhanced by "g." Only bodily-kinesthetic—the ability to manipulate one's own body with dexterity—may truly represent a separate cognitive ability, probably stemming from cerebellar activity involved in fine motor control. It may be better represented as a neurophysiological trait than as intelligence. Even for related activities—dancing, for instance—having at least a small amount of "g" is still going to be necessary to learn, say, complex dance choreography.

Finally, as Waterhouse noted in her exchange with Gardner, the theory of multiple intelligences has little value for clinical testing of intelligence or the prediction of future performance. "G" alone is highly predictive of both academic and work success. The other intelligences, or whatever they are, add very little (Ferguson, 2009).

## Lexile Scores

**Lexile scores** refer to a measurement of reading abilities based on the Lexile Framework for Reading, a nationally accepted scale designed to measure text and reading abilities. Lexile scores are used by educators not only to measure and track children's reading ability and progress but also to help them choose appropriate reading material for their abilities, allowing them to gain practice reading without becoming frustrated by the materials.

An individual's Lexile scores are determined by administering a test that measures both recognition and comprehension of text. The scale for Lexile scores ranges from 200L for beginning readers to 1700L for advanced readers. Once a child's Lexile score is determined, teachers and parents can reference a list of books that fall within the child's reading abilities based on Lexile score and grade level (MetaMetrics, 2013). Sample Lexile scores are shown in Table 2.1.

> **Pause/Think/Reflect**
>
> If you identify Lexile scores for children, will that limit the books you provide for them based on their Lexile range? Or will you let children challenge themselves to reach for books above their range?

**Table 2.1**  Sample Lexile Scores

| 400L | *Frog and Toad Are Friends* by Arnold Lobel | First Grade |
|------|------|------|
| 630L | *Sadako and the Thousand Paper Cranes* by Eleanor Coerr | Fourth Grade |
| 770L | *The Giver* by Lois Lowry | Fifth Grade |
| 1000L | *Black Beauty* by Anna Sewell | Seventh Grade |
| 1100L | *Pride and Prejudice* by Jane Austen | Ninth Grade |
| 1560L | The United States Constitution | Post High School |

*Source:* Personalize Learning, LLC, 2013

There are a few difficulties with using Lexile scores:

- Not all books have a Lexile score.
- Learners may feel that they cannot read outside of their Lexile range and will only choose books in that range.
- Teachers may provide books to learners only within a learner's Lexile range.
- Lexile does not consider the complexity of plot or writing style, which could affect comprehension.
- Lexile does not judge content, and some books are not appropriate for some ages. For example, *The Silence of the Lambs* by Thomas Harris is rated 770L, which is the same as *The Giver* by Lois Lowry.

Yet Lexile scores can support personalized learning if learners are learning to read. They may find that if they know their Lexile range, they can choose the books that may or may not challenge or frustrate them. If they are reading to learn, they still may want to know their Lexile scores and push themselves to go beyond their Lexile range.

### Standardized Tests

Standardized tests have been used as part of the American education system since the mid-1800s, but their use skyrocketed soon after the No Child Left Behind (NLCB) Act in 2002. Teachers and learners are both being put to the test, and many believe the system is failing. Less time is being spent on the sciences, social studies, and the arts to make way for preparing learners to take the tests in math, reading, and writing.

Learners are now tested starting in the third grade, and there is a push to start testing children even earlier—some skills even before starting kindergarten. Some test results are misleading.

Using test results to put learners into separate classes such as special education or accelerated classes does not seem like the best course of action. Teacher observations and feedback and formative assessment with self-reflection seem like a much better way to proceed.

Considering advancing a learner to the next grade or to graduate based on high-stakes testing is unfair to learners. There is no certainty that if learners have a bad test score one day that they would or would not test higher if given the same test on a different day. Multiple-choice questions on a test do not really test their creative processes or show that they know the material. On some tests the percentage needed to pass can be achieved by guessing and accidentally filling in the right bubbles (Concordia University, 2013).

**Pause/Think/Reflect**

Using these tests to determine if a school or teacher is "failing" or improving changes the focus from helping learners learn to using a false measure to determine school and teacher effectiveness. Some districts reward teachers with money for improved or high test scores.

*"Not everything that can be counted counts, and not everything that counts can be counted."*

—Albert Einstein

## HOW THE BRAIN LEARNS

The nervous system and the brain are the physical foundation of the human learning process. **Neuroscience** links our observations about cognitive behavior with the actual physical processes that support such behavior.

When we are exposed to new information from our senses, our brain needs to form an association between what we see and hear, which is encoded by different groups of neurons in various parts of our brain. Each time that input is repeated, sets of neurons fire simultaneously, strengthening the synaptic pathway that connects them, effectively creating memory (Johansen-Berg, 2011).

In scientific terms, learning is a neurobiological process indicated by the growth and strengthening of connections between neurons.

> *"Learning is not how the information gets in, it is what happens to the information once it is in your brain."*
>
> —Author unknown

Humans have three types of memory: sensory, short term, and long term. Learning can be defined as the moving of information from short-term memory, sometimes called working memory, to long-term memory.

**Sensory memory** is associated with the senses (e.g., seeing, hearing, touching) where information is stored briefly for processing. Information is stored for only a fraction of a second before the subconscious decision is made concerning how to process the information.

**Short-term memory** is the stage where further consciousness processing occurs, actively thinking about what has occurred. The primary purpose of short-term memory is

1. to purge or release the new information from memory.
2. to maintain the information in working memory via simple rehearsal.
3. to move (encode) the information from short-term/working memory into long-term memory for later recall.

**Working memory** holds limited information for a limited amount of time, by using cognitive learning strategies to transfer information from working memory to long-term memory.

Cognitive learning strategies are methods used to help learners link new information to prior knowledge to facilitate the transfer of learning through the systematic design of instruction. With respect to working memory, verbal/text memory and visual/spatial memory work together into a framework or schema of understanding. This requires learners to learn topics by scaffolding through a series of steps and chunking information into smaller units that are relevant and meaningful to them.

**Long-term memory** occurs when information is processed deeply, questions are asked repeatedly to retrieve information and followed by feedback, material is practiced often, and the study of material is spaced over days and weeks. When this happens more neurons are activated and retention is more likely improved (Johansen-Berg, 2011).

## Brain Research

The latest brain research involves some of the following discoveries that relate to how learners learn.

*The brain is adaptive and changing.* The brain is constantly changing, a concept referred to as neuroplasticity. **Neuroplasticity** means the brain can be improved and continues to adapt and learn through life, even after middle age and during old age. This also means that the brain can learn better and that the human potential for learning is limitless at any age (Doidge, 2007). Figures 2.4 and 2.5 are excerpts from the Brainy Approaches to Learning infographic by Students at the Center, a Jobs for the Future project. They depict the brain science behind student-centered approaches to learning.

This means when you learn something new, your brain makes new connections. Brain imaging technology has discovered how malleable the brain is and has refuted the idea that a person's mind is fixed or static (Groff, 2013).

*You learn when your brain is active.* Your brain is even active when you reflect on your learning. It is all about experiencing learning in an active role. It is about how we help learners develop questions about the information they read or hear, about inquiring minds that wonder, discover,

**Figure 2.4**   The Brain Is Adaptive

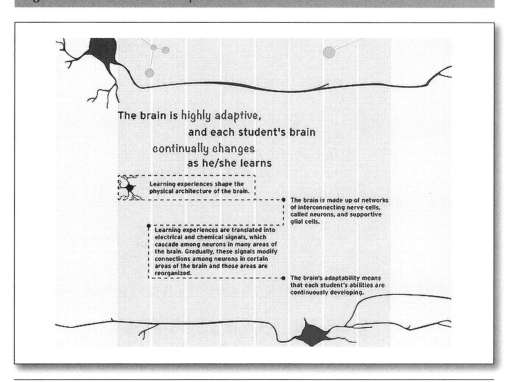

The brain is highly adaptive, and each student's brain continually changes as he/she learns

Learning experiences shape the physical architecture of the brain.

The brain is made up of networks of interconnecting nerve cells, called neurons, and supportive glial cells.

Learning experiences are translated into electrical and chemical signals, which cascade among neurons in many areas of the brain. Gradually, these signals modify connections among neurons in certain areas of the brain and those areas are reorganized.

The brain's adaptability means that each student's abilities are continuously developing.

*Source:* Hinton & Jobs for the Future, 2013

**Figure 2.5** Learning Is Active, Not Passive

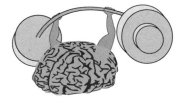

Learning is most likely to occur
when experiences are *active*, not passive

The changes in the brain's
neuronal connections that
underlie learning occur when
students are actively engaged in
learning relevant information.
Passive exposure to information,
on the other hand, does not
necessarily lead to learning.

In educational terms, this
suggests that "seat time" in a
classroom will not necessarily
lead to learning.

*Source:* Hinton & Jobs for the Future, 2013

question, and expand their thinking. An active mind with a growth mind-set is one that knows how to learn, unlearn, and relearn.

*Learners use most areas of the brain.* This runs contrary to the myth that individuals are using only 5 to 10 percent of their brain. Neuroscientists and neurologists have already presented evidence that refute this "10 percent" myth (Boyd, 2008).

*Cells that fire together, wire together.* In other words, the "use-it-or-lose-it" phenomenon, or simply put, if you want to retain new information, you have to use it constantly or else lose it. When you stop practicing a new skill or a new language, for instance, your brain will eventually prune or eliminate certain pathways. You'll eventually lose a new skill unless you keep on practicing (Luskin, 2013).

> *"Cells that fire together, wire together."*
>
> —Anonymous

## UNIVERSAL DESIGN FOR LEARNING (UDL)

The Center for Applied Special Technology (CAST) was founded in 1984 at the same time the educational report *A Nation at Risk* was released expressing the need to provide all individuals with full and equal educational opportunities. CAST envisioned new technologies as learning tools for learners, especially those with disabilities. Ann Meyers and David Rose from CAST (www.cast.org) developed **Universal Design for Learning (UDL).** The framework of Universal Design for Learning (UDL) is based on decades of brain research and the neuroscience of individual differences, human variability, and how we learn.

What they found in the early years at CAST is that UDL was not about learners overcoming their barriers; it was about reducing or eliminating the barriers that keep learners from learning. CAST started with digital books for those with reading challenges, offering linked definitions for those with limited vocabulary, large buttons that talked for those with low vision, and so on. In fact, each interface was customized for each learner. What they realized was that the curriculum, not the learner, was the problem.

UDL is a set of principles for curriculum development that gives all individuals equal opportunities to learn. UDL provides a blueprint for creating instructional goals, methods, materials, and assessments that work for everyone—not a single, one-size-fits-all solution but rather flexible approaches that can be customized and adjusted for individual needs.

> **Pause/Think/Reflect**
>
> UDL is an approach to curriculum that minimizes barriers and maximizes learning for all learners.

It is time to dispel the myth that UDL is only for special education. UDL provides an understanding about the why, what, and how of learning and tells us that there is variability in how learners learn—their strengths, challenges, aptitudes, talents, and yes, aspirations and passions. Universal Design for Learning is for *all* learners. CAST provided Figure 2.6 as an overview of the Why, What, and How of learning.

The **UDL guidelines** provide a lens for teachers to understand how learners learn best. With this understanding, teachers are better informed on how to universally design their instruction in order to reduce barriers to learning as well as optimize the levels of support and challenge to meet the needs and interests of all learners in the classroom.

> **Pause/Think/Reflect**
>
> Universal Design for Learning guides the design of a personalized learning environment.

## UDL Guidelines

The UDL guidelines (see appendix) can assist teachers in planning universally designed lessons that can reduce barriers to learning, as well as optimize levels of challenge and support, to meet the needs of all learners

**Figure 2.6**  Universal Design for Learning

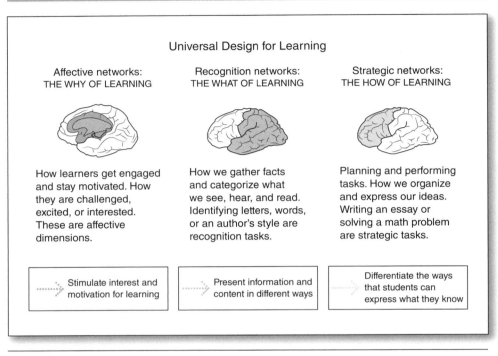

Universal Design for Learning

| Affective networks: THE WHY OF LEARNING | Recognition networks: THE WHAT OF LEARNING | Strategic networks: THE HOW OF LEARNING |
|---|---|---|
| How learners get engaged and stay motivated. How they are challenged, excited, or interested. These are affective dimensions. | How we gather facts and categorize what we see, hear, and read. Identifying letters, words, or an author's style are recognition tasks. | Planning and performing tasks. How we organize and express our ideas. Writing an essay or solving a math problem are strategic tasks. |
| Stimulate interest and motivation for learning | Present information and content in different ways | Differentiate the ways that students can express what they know |

from the start. They can also help educators identify the barriers found in existing curricula. UDL drew up neuroscience and educational research to design learning environments based on the UDL principles:

1. *Multiple Means of Representation* (perception, language, expressions, symbols, and comprehension)

2. *Multiple Means of Action and Expression* (physical action, expression and communication, and executive function)

3. *Multiple Means of Engagement* (recruiting interest, sustaining effort and persistence, and self-regulation)

The core beliefs of CAST are to develop the theory of self-efficacy for learners to believe in their own abilities and competence. UDL informs the design of the environment so that it is flexible enough to address variability. UDL happens both in the design of the learning environment and in the use of the design to facilitate the appropriate, dynamic interaction between the learner and context.

For so long the predominant instructional materials were printed textbooks and worksheets that were fixed and inflexible. Any learner that could not learn that way was labeled disabled, underachieving, or failing. Classrooms became textbook centered instead of learner centered. Since there were no obvious alternatives, learners had to learn how to adapt. Now that can change. In a well-designed learning environment, systematic variability is planned from the beginning based on the diversity of all learners.

> *"What we want are kids who are able to set good goals for themselves, to be able to regulate when things go wrong, to be able to sustain and handle frustration."*
>
> —David Rose

In recent years there has been heightened interest in Universal Design for Learning, particularly within the worlds of education policy and practice. UDL provides a powerful and comprehensive answer to the growing call for more "personalized" curricular materials that can accommodate the full diversity of learners and teachers within the education system.

## PERSONAL LEARNER PROFILE

A **Personal Learner Profile (PLP)** is created by learners with guidance from their teacher and possibly their parents. The PLP identifies how they learn best based on their strengths, challenges, interests, aspirations, talents, and passions. This is a very powerful tool because it validates learners and how they learn. Now they can actually have a conversation with their teacher about their learning. It will also help them in collaboration with their teacher to design their learning goals based on how they best access information, engage with content, and express what they know and understand.

### Access, Engage, and Express

The three principles of UDL guided the design of a Personal Learner Profile for each learner. The UDL principles were adapted to reflect how learners may access information, engage with content, and express what they know and understand. So, as shown in Figure 2.7, *Access* represents *Multiple Means of Representation*; *Engage* represents *Multiple Means of Engagement*; and *Express* represents *Multiple Means of Expression and Action*.

**Figure 2.7**   Access, Engage, and Express

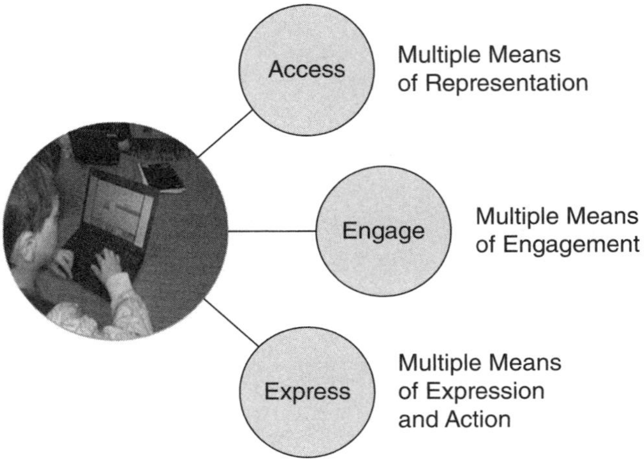

- Access — Multiple Means of Representation
- Engage — Multiple Means of Engagement
- Express — Multiple Means of Expression and Action

### How does each learner ACCESS information?

**Access** is about how a learner first processes information by accessing content through digital media, visual media, maybe through printed text, and sometimes through audio or touch. Learners have a preference on how they would like to access the content and sometimes a learner may have a specific need. Tables 2.2, 2.3, and 2.4 provide example statements of strengths and challenges in how learners might access information, engage with content, and express what they know.

**Table 2.2**   Access Strengths-and-Challenges Statements

| Strengths | Challenges |
|---|---|
| <ul><li>I am really good at explaining graphs and charts.</li><li>I have a great vocabulary.</li><li>I am an excellent reader.</li></ul> | <ul><li>I have a difficult time hearing.</li><li>I don't remember what is being said.</li><li>I have trouble reading text online.</li></ul> |

*Source:* Personalize Learning, LLC, 2013

For example, learners who may need to access digital files or media can use a reader, Speak Selection on the iPad, or maybe a translator. Once they access content, the important next step is how they process this information into useable knowledge and make connections with previous learning.

### *How does each learner need to ENGAGE with content and concepts?*

**Engage** describes how each learner engages with content and concepts using multiple strategies and tools that will keep his or her interest and encourage ownership of learning.

**Table 2.3**    Engage Strengths-and-Challenges Statements

| Strengths | Challenges |
|-----------|-----------|
| • I am great at teaching others.<br>• I am an excellent collaborator.<br>• I have outstanding leadership skills.<br>• I am very confident. | • I get distracted easily.<br>• I put things off.<br>• I am shy.<br>• I have difficulty working in groups. |

*Source:* Personalize Learning, LLC, 2013

Learners may prefer or need to have visuals, such as a video, to understand a concept. They continue to engage, to think deeper about the concept or content by problem solving or collaborating. Reflecting can help learners to think deeper or more critically on the content or concept. In the end it is about engagement that provides the motivation to learn.

As learners build their learner profile, you can also keep track of learners' aspirations, talents, and interests or passions. These can help define the learner when you develop specific assignments with voice and choice.

### *How do learners EXPRESS their knowledge and understanding of concepts, content, or ideas?*

**Express** is how each learner expresses what they know and understand through actions, such as writing, acting, presenting, building, drawing, or sharing. As with access and engage, learners have preferences or needs in how they express what they know and understand. In the end, expression is about giving learners voice and choice in how they demonstrate what they know and understand.

**Table 2.4**    Express Strengths-and-Challenges Statements

| Strengths | Challenges |
|-----------|-----------|
| • I am an outstanding speaker.<br>• I am very organized.<br>• I am a strong problem solver. | • I get anxious about presenting.<br>• I have a problem in organizing my writing.<br>• I have trouble remembering things. |

*Source:* Personalize Learning, LLC, 2013

## Criteria for Learner Qualities

Table 2.5 describes example statements of learner qualities from several learners based on their strengths and challenges. Strengths are listed as strong statements that learners believe they do well, present them positively, and show something they excel at. Challenges are where learners are having difficulty accessing information, trouble with how they engage with the content, and concerns with how they express what they know. The word *challenges* is used instead of *weaknesses* since weaknesses can be construed as barriers to their learning or labels about the learner.

**Table 2.5** Strengths-and-Challenges Statements Learners Can Use to Create Their Personal Learner Profile

| | Strengths | Challenges |
|---|---|---|
| **Access** | • I am really good at explaining graphs and charts.<br>• I have a great vocabulary.<br>• I am an excellent reader.<br>• I work well with others.<br>• I not only use tools and apps, I am good at explaining how to use them. | • I have a difficult time hearing.<br>• I don't remember what is being said.<br>• I have trouble reading text online.<br>• I cannot follow the sequence in a story.<br>• I have problems summarizing what I read. |
| **Engage** | • I am great at teaching others.<br>• I am an excellent collaborator.<br>• I have outstanding leadership skills.<br>• I am very confident.<br>• I know how to choose and use the right resources for tasks. | • I get distracted easily.<br>• I put things off.<br>• I am shy.<br>• I have difficulty working in groups.<br>• I get bored easily. |
| **Express** | • I am an outstanding speaker.<br>• I am very organized.<br>• I am a strong problem solver.<br>• I can construct effective arguments around problems. | • I get anxious about presenting.<br>• I have a problem in organizing my writing.<br>• I have trouble remembering things.<br>• I cannot figure out what to collect as evidence of my learning. |

*Source:* Personalize Learning, LLC, 2013

## Preferences and Needs About How We Learn

We all have preferences and needs about how we learn. What if kids don't know how to access, engage, and express? Have you ever asked them how they prefer to learn? Have you ever been asked how you prefer or need to learn? When kids have an opportunity to reflect on how they learn, this can be a way for them to explain who they are and how they learn and to have their learning validated. Table 2.6 provides you a few example statements of how learners prefer or need to access information, engage with content, and express what they know.

**Table 2.6** Preferences-and-Needs Statements

|  | **Preferences and Needs** |
|---|---|
| **Access** | • I need digital files with a reader.<br>• I prefer watching videos to understand concepts. |
| **Engage** | • I prefer to work with others on a project.<br>• I need feedback while working on activities instead of waiting until the end. |
| **Express** | • I prefer more time on projects.<br>• I need a checklist to keep me on task. |

*Source:* Personalize Learning, LLC, 2013

You will also want to consider *why* your learners will want to engage with the content. Learners want to learn more about something they are interested in. If they are aspiring to be an architect, they will want to do research about what architecture means and what skills are necessary so they are prepared for college. If learners are given an option to pursue an interest for a project, they want to learn more and show what they found out. If instruction taps into their talents, they are more motivated to use their talents to demonstrate what they know. Engagement is the affective side of learning. Table 2.7 gives you several examples of why learners may want to engage with content based on their aspirations, talents, and interests.

**Table 2.7** Why Learners Want to Engage With Content

| **Aspirations** | **Talents** | **Interests** |
|---|---|---|
| • Teacher<br>• Game designer<br>• Engineer<br>• Ballerina<br>• Journalist<br>• ? | • Athletic<br>• Musical<br>• Artistic<br>• Technological<br>• Gamer<br>• ? | • Poetry<br>• Rock climbing<br>• Snowboarding<br>• Painting<br>• Carpentry<br>• ? |

*Source:* Personalize Learning, LLC, 2013

Engagement is the affective side of learning. That includes what learners are interested in, have a talent in, or aspire to be. This can be what hooks them into wanting to learn something. As learners build their learner profile, you can also keep track of learners' aspirations, talents, interests, and passions. You can ask them what . . .

- they like to do and is fun for them.
- they like about school and their favorite subjects.
- types of hobbies and sports they enjoy.
- concerns them and what they could do that might make a difference.
- they want to learn.
- they don't like or want to learn.

Their answers can help define who they are as learners and how they learn best. This can help you develop specific instructional and learning strategies that can include their voice and choice. For example, learners who are artistic can draw a poster to demonstrate understanding of a concept instead of an essay.

### Jared's Personal Learner Profile

Jared is a typical learner in any classroom. Table 2.8 offers a Personal Learner Profile (PLP) for Jared based on his strengths and challenges in accessing information, engaging with content, and expressing what he knows and understands.

**Table 2.8**  Jared's Strengths, Interests, and Challenges

|  | Jared's Strengths, Interests | Jared's Challenges |
|---|---|---|
| **Access** | • I am really good at explaining graphs and charts.<br>• I am great at understanding math concepts. | • I have problems understanding directions when someone speaks them to me. |
| **Engage** | • I have a lot of energy when I work on something I am interested in.<br>• I am a great leader in group projects. | • I give up easily.<br>• Sometimes I don't pay attention.<br>• I clown around when I don't know something. |
| **Express** | • I am excellent at drawing.<br>• I am an outstanding singer and piano player. | • I never have enough time to finish my work.<br>• I have trouble setting goals. |

*Source:* Personalize Learning, LLC, 2013

Jared's profile could be any child in any grade level. He has a problem with auditory processing. He gets confused easily with oral instructions only. Yet he is very comfortable with visuals, especially interpreting graphs. If it was possible, Jared would love to listen to music while working. He's constantly tapping his fingers as if there's music in his head. Does this sound like anyone you know?

*Jared's interests and talents*: photography, piano, singing, and drawing

*Jared's aspirations*: to work at Pixar as an animator or be a video game designer

### Jared's Preferences and Needs

Most people can explain how they prefer or need to learn if they can identify how they access information, engage with content, and express what they know. Table 2.9 shows Jared's preferences and needs.

**Table 2.9** Jared's Preferences and Needs

|  | **Jared's Preferences and Needs** |
|---|---|
| **Access** | • *Prefers* information in visual form<br>• *Needs* images or screen captures that walk him through step-by-step instructions |
| **Engage** | • *Prefers* group projects<br>• *Needs* to check in with the teacher and use a checklist to stay on task<br>• *Prefers* to have music playing in the background while he studies or reads |
| **Express** | • *Prefers* to capture images for projects he creates<br>• *Prefers* to work with the group<br>• *Needs* to pull the content together to create a presentation or video |

*Source:* Personalize Learning, LLC, 2013

From Jared's preferences and needs, the teacher can sit with Jared to determine the best instructional and learning strategies to meet his needs.

The PLP is not a one-time exercise and needs to be used several times a year as learners change and grow. It may also be a great way to determine personal learning goals for learners to work on during the year. The information from the PLP and updated PLPs can help the learner and teacher monitor their progress toward

**Pause/Think/Reflect**

How do you prefer or need to access information, engage with content, and express what you know?

their learning goals. The PLP can be kept as a personal journal or a digital portfolio where the teacher can provide ongoing feedback.

## Personal Learning Backpack

A **Personal Learning Backpack (PLB)** contains resources, tools, and learning strategies identified for the learner. Jared's Personal Learning Backpack, shown in Figure 2.10, is personal to him and is based on how he understands how he learns best. Now that Jared knows how he prefers or needs to learn, he, with the support of his teacher, can determine the most appropriate resources and instructional and learning strategies to help him with the task at hand.

**Table 2.10**    Jared's Personal Learning Backpack

|  | Jared's Learning Strategies | Resources and Tools |
|---|---|---|
| **Access** | Jared uses video tutorials to walk him through step-by-step instructions. He demonstrates what he learned by helping teach another learner. | Educreations, Popplet |
| **Engage** | Jared creates a space to collect resources from the group. He wears headphones so he can listen to music while he is working on the project. | Dropbox, Google Drive |
| **Express** | Jared captures images for the presentation. He creates the logo and title. He checks in with the teacher to use a checklist to stay on task that he shares with his group. | iPad, digital camera, Toodledo, Draw Free, Prezi |

*Source:* Personalize Learning, LLC, 2013

### *How do you do this for your class?*

First, you have learners create their own Personal Learner Profile so they understand how they learn best. You probably know already that each learner in your class is different and unique. None are the same. There is no average learner. Each learner has a jagged learning profile or learning map. This jagged learning map profile, shown in Figure 2.8, is adapted from Dr. Todd Rose's Tedx Sonoma County talk "The Myth of Average" and his research on Project Variability. It is about the idea that no one person is average (Rose, 2013).

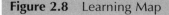

**Figure 2.8** Learning Map

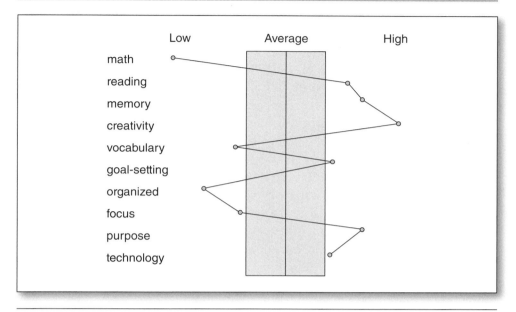

*Source:* Rose, 2013

Rose used the metaphor of how the size of air force pilots affects how they reach the airplane controls. The planes were created for the average pilot. Some pilots could not see the controls, and this caused some pilots to be confused and even planes to crash. The air force had to figure out how to fix this. Since each pilot was a different size and weight, it ended up designing flexible seats that could be adjusted for the different sizes of the pilots. Adjustable seats fixed the problem. It was not the pilot's error. The problem was that the seats were fixed. Rose used this as a metaphor about education. It is about understanding that all learners are different. The curriculum tends to be fixed to meet the average learner just like the seats in the plane were fixed to meet the average pilot.

Consider using the ideas from Dr. Todd Rose about the importance of looking at the extremes to design lessons

**Pause/Think/Reflect**

Think about yourself and where you are on your learning map. If you are all over the place like this map, and others have their own learning map, how do you learn in a class that teaches to the average?

**Pause/Think/Reflect**

If you design learning for the average, you design it for no one.

for all learners in your class. This idea of variability was adapted in the design of the Class Learning Snapshot.

## CLASS LEARNING SNAPSHOT

The **Class Learning Snapshot (CLS)** helps teachers universally design their lessons based on the learners in their class or classes. You start by looking at the extremes using four diverse learners in your class. Diverse means different than most of the other learners in the class. If you have multiple classes, choose four diverse learners from one of your classes. What you are doing is anticipating four diverse learners that you will have. This is called the **anticipatory set** and includes the strengths, interests, and challenges your four learners have in accessing information, engaging with content, and expressing what they know. Next, you include their preferences and needs based on these strengths, challenges, and interests. Instead of using their names, use initials for the four learners you choose. Table 2.11 shows a Class Learning Snapshot using four diverse learners

**Table 2.11**    Class Learning Snapshot of Four Diverse Learners

|  | Strengths, Interests | Challenges |
|---|---|---|
| **OB** | • Excellent team player<br>• Great at photography<br>• Strives for quality | • Long-term memory problems<br>• Trouble organizing<br>• Cannot sit still |
| **JT** | • Good sense of humor<br>• Very artistic<br>• Excellent social skills | • Reads two grades below grade level<br>• Difficulty planning tasks<br>• Trouble responding in writing |
| **SM** | • Strong reader<br>• Very creative<br>• Works well with others | • Anxious speaking in front of others<br>• Forgets sequence, message of story<br>• Uncomfortable voicing concerns |
| **JR** | • Questions for better understanding<br>• Persistent in completing tasks and projects | • Difficulty understanding text<br>• Not able to write descriptively<br>• Frustrated writing ideas on paper |

*Source:* Personalize Learning, LLC, 2013

Consider how the four learners you chose prefer or need to access information, engage with content, and express what they know or understand. The teacher needs to examine the possible barriers in the instruction and materials that each of these learners might have in any lesson. So if you look at OB, who has trouble organizing and long-term memory problems, he may not be able to manage files without someone helping him. One of his learning goals is to learn how to organize his information, and how he approaches this learning will vary from other learners. Since OB is a great team player, he finds someone to partner with who has good organization skills. The partner then can model organization skills for him, and it may be easier for OB to hear or see how to organize better from a peer than spending time working on this challenge.

**Table 2.12**    Preferences and Needs of Four Diverse Learners

|  | **Preferences and Needs** |
|---|---|
| *OB* | *Access*: prefers folder system for digital files<br>*Engage*: prefers to collects or creates images for group projects<br>*Express*: needs to present with visuals |
| *JT* | *Access*: prefers using digital files for all instructional materials and books, appropriate reading level, games and video<br>*Engage*: prefers to lead group activities, learns with video and music<br>*Express*: needs to create a game, illustrate a concept, and act in a video |
| *SM* | *Access*: prefers note taking and summarizing reading<br>*Engage*: needs to keep a reflective journal, illustrates story<br>*Express*: prefers to write a blog, draws pictures |
| *JR* | *Access*: needs visuals for textbooks and instructional materials, templates or graphic organizers for writing<br>*Engage*: prefers to design and build models<br>*Express*: prefers to present with video, sound, audio notes, and graphics |

*Source:* Personalize Learning, LLC, 2013

The preferences and needs of your four diverse learners (see Table 2.12) help you design the Class Learning Toolkit that includes instructional strategies you design, learning strategies where learners take responsibility for their learning, and resources, tools, and apps for your class.

## CLASS LEARNING TOOLKIT

The **Class Learning Toolkit (CLT)** helps teachers plan for the materials and methods learners use during their lessons and units. This toolkit gives teachers and learners an advantage in the design of projects. They have the resources and strategies at their fingertips when they need them. If you look at the four learners and their preferences and needs, you can collect apps and tools that will support how they learn best. Table 2.13 offers an example of a Class Learning Toolkit.

**Table 2.13**   Class Learning Toolkit

|  | Instructional Strategies | Learning Strategies |
|---|---|---|
| *OB* | The teacher models a file management system using Dropbox at the teacher station for the whole class. | OB works with a partner who helps him organize files and capture images digitally and demonstrates other art tools. |
| *JT* | The teacher demonstrates Voice Dream as the Text-to-Speech tool for reading comprehension with a small group. | JT uses his headphones and goes to a quiet area to read using the Text-to-Speech program. |
| *SM* | Teacher reviews note-taking skills and brings in Evernote as a tool to support writing. | SM works with partner to help her take notes using Evernote and uses the audio feature to play back for understanding. |
| *JR* | Teacher uses storyboarding and Popplet (graphic organizer) to demonstrate sequencing in a story. | JR brainstorms order of story using Popplet or drawing with markers on whiteboard with others in his group. |

*Source:* Personalize Learning, LLC, 2013

These are only a few apps and strategies to give you an example of what a Class Learning Toolkit could look like. There are so many new apps developed every day so this could be adapted by the teacher and the learners. The skills and learning strategies around these tools to support their learning are important for learners to independently use.

When you design a Class Learning Toolkit that includes methods and materials that meet four diverse learners, you can provide methods and materials for most, if not all, of the learners in your class. If you are a secondary teacher with multiple classes, choose four diverse learners from your classes to create a Class Learning Snapshot of your learners. There will be some learners who may need specific tools, apps, and instruction beyond your Class Learning Toolkit, but this provides you a better picture of your classroom than teaching to the average.

# LEARNERS *NOT* STUDENTS

You probably wonder why throughout this book the term *learner* is used instead of *student*. All of us are learners. Think about it. We were born curious and open to learning or we wouldn't walk or talk. It's just how each of us was made. Learning is part of us. We were not born students—we were born learners. Our first experiences of learning were through play and discovery.

If you consider anyone who is learning at any age and anywhere a "learner," then you give the responsibility for learning to the learner. The institution or anyone teaching students is accountable for the learning—not the learners. That means teachers are responsible for what the "students" learn. Doesn't this seem backward?

Where is the incentive and motivation to learn if all the responsibility is on the teacher? Students don't own what they are supposed to learn. If you change the thinking behind the terms, then using the term *learners* makes more sense.

Think about yourself as a learner in and outside of school. Are you a student or a learner? If you interact with people, go outside, or open a book, you might be learning something new. You are learning. You are self-directing that learning. You are a learner not a student. Let's compare the terms.

> **Pause/Think/Reflect**
>
> The next time you walk into any classroom, think of how every child is a learner first. Has your perception changed about the children in the class?

> **Use the Word *Learner* Not *Student***
>
> Acknowledging other learning environments, CAST (Center for Applied Special Technology) made the change from using the word *student* to *learner* in the UDL Guidelines 2.0, because the term *student* is too narrow. *Student* implies someone in the classroom. CAST realized that learning happens in many different environments where the term *student* might not be traditionally applied (e.g., museums, afterschool programs, adult learning). The word *learner* was therefore chosen because of the ranges of situations to which it could apply (CAST, 2013).

### Students . . .

- learn in a classroom.
- are assigned a task to do.
- follow required objectives.
- do the assignment designed by the teacher or curriculum.
- seek information for the assignment.

> **Pause/Think/Reflect**
>
> How do we create a school culture in which being a learner is more valuable than being a student?

- work individually or in a group depending on assignment.
- earn a grade to reflect meeting the objectives and standards.

### Learners . . .

- develop their own learning goals.
- monitor their progress in meeting their goals.
- have a purpose or interest to learn something.
- ask questions.
- seek information.
- find ways to collaborate with others.
- want to know something because they want to know it—not for a grade.
- are curious about life and never stop learning.

Lisa Welch is a K–1 teacher at KM Explore in Wisconsin. She wrote a comment about using *learners* not *students* that really makes this personal, so Lisa is letting us share it with you.

> *"I look at it as simple as when I was young. I was quite the 'student.' By this I mean I was given the task, given the materials to complete the task, and then was told the time frame to do it in.*
>
> *"I was VERY good at following directions, which made me an excellent student. Now if only I was a good learner! :-)*
>
> *"To be a learner, the goal/task needs to be initiated by the individual, the tools are sought out and either deemed appropriate or inappropriate for the task, and finally, the time frame is flexible for the learner since goals are achieved at different rates and new goals are inspired. A student waits for the teacher to direct. A learner directs their own learning."*
>
> —Lisa Welch, K–1 Co-Teacher, KM Explore,
> Kettle Moraine School District, Wisconsin

> *"The bottom line is, if you're not the one who's controlling your learning, you're not going to learn as well."*
>
> —Joel Voss, Neuroscientist, Northwestern University

## CHAPTER 2 REVIEW

1. Review the learning theorists, flow, and mindset as they relate to personalized learning.

2. Think about your generation and your impressions of the other generations and how they relate to personalized learning.

3. Review how schools have used learning styles, multiple intelligences, Lexile scores, and standardized tests to describe learners.

4. Research Universal Design for Learning (UDL), the UDL guidelines, and the UDL principles.

5. Think about every child as a learner first.

The idea of changing instructional strategies while you start personalizing learning may feel a bit overwhelming. We are going to share a process in the next chapter, along with examples and stories from teachers, so you can dip your toes into personalized learning.

## RESOURCES

### *Across the Generations*

- Multigenerational Characteristics
  www.brucemayhewconsulting.com/index.cfm?PAGEPATH=&
  ID=20209
- Generations in the Classroom
  http://adulted.about.com/od/andragogy/a/Generations-In-The-
  Classroom.htm

### *Describing Learners*

- Myth of Learning Styles
  www.changemag.org/Archives/Back%20Issues/September-Octo
  ber%202010/the-myth-of-learning-full.html
- Pros and Cons of Standardized Tests: Is the use of standardized tests improving education in America?
  http://standardizedtests.procon.org/view.answers.php?question
  ID=001747

### Learning Theorists

- Jerome Bruner's Theory
  www.simplypsychology.org/bruner.html

### Brain Research

- Brain Research Discoveries
  http://info.shiftelearning.com/blog/bid/324035/8-Brain-Research-Discoveries-Every-Instructional-Designer-Should-Know-About?
- Students at the Center, Brainy Approaches to Learning Infographic
  www.studentsatthecenter.org/brainy-approaches-learning

### Universal Design for Learning (UDL)

- CAST (Center for Applied Special Technology)
  www.cast.org
- What is UDL?
  www.udlcenter.org/aboutudl/whatisudl
- UDL 2.0 Guidelines
  www.udlcenter.org/aboutudl/udlguidelinesatch

# 3 Wow! Teacher and Learner Roles Are Changing

*"Tell me and I forget, teach me and I may remember, involve me and I learn."*

—Benjamin Franklin

When learners have a voice and choice in their learning, teachers change the way they teach. Learners take more ownership of their learning. Some teachers have expressed concern that personalizing learning the way they believe it is supposed to be implemented is such a big paradigm shift with all the other demands in their job. Several teachers were concerned that "it was just too big a change from how we teach." This led to the creation of the Stages of Personalized Learning (see Figure 3.1) as a realistic process to personalize learning.

## THE PROCESS THROUGH THE STAGES OF PERSONALIZED LEARNING ENVIRONMENTS

Ideally, all of us want to create learner-centered and eventually learner-driven environments so learners own and drive their learning. However, most schools have systems in place that support teacher-centered

**Figure 3.1** The Process Through the Stages of Personalized Learning Environments

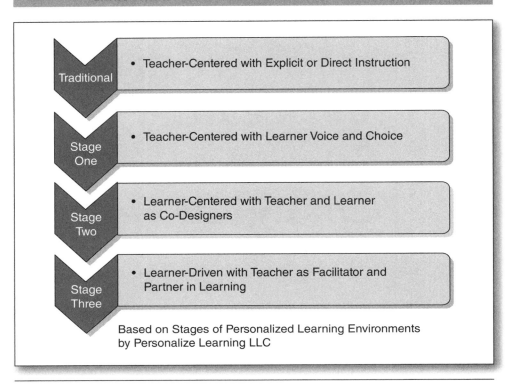

- Teacher-Centered with Explicit or Direct Instruction

Traditional

- Teacher-Centered with Learner Voice and Choice

Stage One

- Learner-Centered with Teacher and Learner as Co-Designers

Stage Two

- Learner-Driven with Teacher as Facilitator and Partner in Learning

Stage Three

Based on Stages of Personalized Learning Environments by Personalize Learning LLC

*Source:* Personalize Learning, LLC, 2013

**Consider This!** If the strategies that teachers learn are mostly lectures and explicit direct instruction, then it is not realistic to expect them to change the learning environment and how they teach right away. Change takes time.

environments that continue to put up barriers to changing teacher and learner roles. Yet teachers can start by dipping their toes into personalized learning using the stages as a process for teachers and administrators.

After several districts reviewed the Stages of Personalized Learning Environments, there was a big sigh of relief heard from the crowd along with a barrage of questions:

- You mean I don't have to do it all at once?
- How long can I be expected to stay in Stage One?
- Can I do Stage One with one lesson and Stage Two with another lesson?
- Where do project-based activities fit?

- How do we meet the demands of standards and accountability in a personalized learning environment?
- Do you have examples of teachers taking the first step toward personalized learning?
- If you include choice in some areas and voice in others but not all, is that still personalized learning?
- How do you personalize learning when you have a class with more than thirty learners?

## STAGES OF PERSONALIZED LEARNING ENVIRONMENTS

The Stages of Personalized Learning Environments are built on the framework of Universal Design for Learning (UDL) discussed in Chapter 2. UDL provides a foundation for transforming existing teaching strategies based on decades of brain research and the neuroscience of individual differences, human variability, and on how we learn. Personalizing learning for all learners means understanding how teacher and learner roles change through the Stages of Personalized Learning Environments (PLE).

**Stage One PLE:** The teacher understands how learners learn best and then universally designs instruction to teach and engage all learners. In these lessons and projects, they encourage learner voice and choice and design materials that are accessible to all learners.

**Stage Two PLE:** The learner and teacher are co-designers of lessons and projects. They both understand how the learner learns best and design a Personal Learner Profile that guides the learner on a learning path.

**Stage Three PLE:** Learners drive their learning with their teacher as a partner in learning. Learners are working toward becoming expert learners who can monitor their progress and reflect on their learning.

Progressing through the Stages of Personalized Learning Environments using UDL creates an "ecology of learning" where learners understand how to structure and take responsibility for their learning to achieve their learning goals and measure their progress toward those goals. When learners own their learning, they have a stake in what and how they learn. What this means is that learners are more empowered to self-regulate their learning. Learners are more motivated and engaged in learning when they have a voice and choice in how they learn.

The original Stages of Personalized Learning Environments chart in 2012 was created after the first version of the PDI (Personalization vs. Differentiation vs. Individualization) chart, mainly because teachers were concerned with how to personalize learning. Changes were made to the first version of the Stages in early 2013. Educators requested revisions and an update to version 2 for clarity and consistency. If Stage Two is learner-centered, there needed to be specific strategies for that stage. Version 3 in Table 3.1 now includes the tools created to guide the process, i.e., the Personal Learner Profile and Class Learning Snapshot. The wording was changed so Stage Two starts with both the learner and teacher as co-designers, because this is where the roles really start changing. Some teachers do jump right into Stage Two. Some schools were designed as Stage Three. Look for several stories and journeys from teachers throughout this chapter. However, *personalized learning* means that transforming teaching and learning to a personalized learning environment looks different in every district, every school, and every classroom. Each and every learner is unique. The culture and demographics of each school are different from other schools and impact how the stages are implemented.

**Table 3.1**  Stages of Personalized Learning Environments (v3)

| Stage One<br><br>*Teacher-Centered with Learner Voice and Choice* | Stage Two<br><br>*Learner-Centered with Teacher and Learner as Co-Designers* | Stage Three<br><br>*Learner-Driven with Teacher as Partner in Learning* |
|---|---|---|
| Teacher understands how each learner learns based on Personal Learner Profiles (PLP) and data. | Learner and teacher co-design and update the learner's PLP based on how they learn best. | Learner adjusts their PLP with teacher guidance by recognizing how their learning changes. |
| Teacher makes instructional decisions based on four diverse learners' PLPs to create a Class Learning Snapshot. | Learner identifies learning strategies and skills with teacher based on how they prefer or need to learn using PLP. | Learner is an expert learner who uses learning strategies and skills to support their learning goals. |
| Teacher redesigns the learning environment by changing the physical layout of the classroom. | Learner co-designs the learning environment with multiple learning zones with their teacher. | Learner expands their learning environment outside of school to include the larger community. |

| Stage One | Stage Two | Stage Three |
|---|---|---|
| **Teacher-Centered with Learner Voice and Choice** | **Learner-Centered with Teacher and Learner as Co-Designers** | **Learner-Driven with Teacher as Partner in Learning** |
| Teacher revises lessons and projects that encourage learner voice and choice. | Learner and teacher are transforming lessons and projects together to include learner voice and choice. | Learner designs challenging learning experiences based on their interests, passions, and talents. |
| Teacher universally designs instruction and materials to engage and guide learners in establishing learning goals. | Learner with teacher guidance decides how to access information, engage with content, and express what they know based on learning goals. | Learner self-directs how they access information, engage with content, and express what they know based on learning goals. |
| Teacher designs, adapts, or uses existing formative and summative assessment strategies and leads learner conferences with parents. | Learner contributes to the design of assessment strategies and reflects on their learning. Teacher and learner co-lead learner conferences with parents. | Learner designs assessment strategies and showcases evidence of learning through exhibitions that involve their parents, peers, teachers, and community. |
| Teacher is introduced to competency-based learning. Learning is still part of a standards-driven, time-based grade level system. | Learner demonstrates mastery of learning standards that may or may not be in a grade-level system as they and their teacher transition to a competency-based system. | Learner learns at their own pace by demonstrating mastery in a competency-based system. |
| Teacher or counselor suggests afterschool and extracurricular activities to learners based on learning goals. | Learner and teacher work together to determine extended learning opportunities based on learning goals and interests. | Learner selects extended and experiential learning opportunities based on goals, interests, and aspirations. |
| Teacher designs activities to include tools and strategies that instruct and engage all learners in the classroom. | Learner with teacher support acquires skills to choose and use the appropriate tools and strategies to access content and express what they know. | Learner chooses and uses the appropriate tools and strategies to engage in learning, to express what they know, and support them along their learning path. |

# STAGE ONE PLE: TEACHER-CENTERED WITH LEARNER VOICE AND CHOICE

A Stage One PLE lets teachers dip their toes into personalized learning. They are looking at how they teach now and the way they will change in how they understand each learner. This is where they invite learners to complete their Personal Learner Profile (PLP) to help them understand how they learn best. Teachers refer to the PLP to identify how each learner in their class prefers or needs to learn. With that information, teachers design a Class Learning Snapshot based on four diverse learners in their class or classes.

*In a Stage One Personalized Learning Environment, the teacher . . .*

- creates a Class Learning Snapshot based on Personal Learner Profiles (PLP) and data.
- makes instructional decisions based on learners' strengths, challenges, interests, and how they prefer or need to learn.
- redesigns the learning environment by changing the physical layout of the classroom.
- transforms lessons and projects that encourage learner voice and choice.
- universally designs instruction and materials to engage and guide learners in establishing learning goals.
- designs or uses existing formative and summative assessment strategies and leads learner conferences with parents.
- is introduced to competency-based learning. Learning is still part of a standards-driven, time-based grade level system.
- suggests afterschool and extracurricular activities to learners based on their learning goals.
- designs the Class Learning Toolkit to include tools and strategies that instruct all learners in the classroom. (Refer to Chapter 2 for more information on the Class Learning Toolkit.)

*The teacher understands how each learner learns based on Personal Learner Profiles (PLP) and data.*

The teacher invites learners to fill out or assists them in filling out their Personal Learner Profile and how they prefer or need to learn. Their PLP changes as learners grow and change throughout the year. The teacher reviews their PLP and other data in monitoring how their learning is changing.

*The teacher makes instructional decisions based on
four diverse learners' PLPs to create a Class Learning Snapshot.*

Teachers choose four diverse learners that are at the extremes instead of the average learner to help them guide instructional design. When teachers design a Class Learning Snapshot (refer to Chapter 2, Who Are Your Learners?), they have a better idea how learners learn and prefer to participate in their class. They may find certain children need more time to work independently where others work better in pairs or groups. With this new lens, teachers review and revise their lessons to include voice and choice.

*The teacher redesigns the learning environment
by changing the physical layout of the classroom.*

As teachers refer to the Class Learning Snapshot, they realize how diverse their learners actually are and how important it is to have flexible learning spaces. If learners have a voice in how they learn, then the teacher is not just standing in front of the class delivering instruction, and the room changes. There may be tables instead of desks, places to pace, places to create, and even places to show off. There may be areas to collaborate and work online. There is more noise in the classroom because learners are talking to each other and sharing more. Learners have more choice in how they prefer or need to learn so they will need spaces for independent and group work.

*The teacher revises lessons and
projects that encourage learner voice and choice.*

When teachers really understand how their learners learn best, they also realize it is important to transform lessons so more learners have a voice and choice in their learning. Teachers can include learner voice by involving learners in unpacking the standards. They can include choice when they provide multiple options for the tools or resources they use in the lesson and how learners demonstrate what they learned.

*The teacher universally designs instruction and
materials to engage and guide learners in establishing learning goals.*

Teachers review and revise existing lessons to include methods and materials that provide a hook or strategies to engage the diverse learners in their class. They refer to the Class Learning Snapshot and provide multiple options that motivate learners to plan their own learning goals. **Universally designed** implies concerns about accessibility so possible barriers identified for your diverse learners are removed and solutions are developed to support those learners.

*The teacher designs, adapts, or uses existing formative and summative assessment strategies and leads learner conferences with parents.*

The teacher directs assessment that is OF and FOR learning. The teacher uses existing data from test scores, quizzes, and grades and can include formative assessments such as rubrics, journals, and other strategies to collect evidence of learning. The teacher is responsible for monitoring learners' progress and discussing that progress with learners and their parents.

*The teacher is introduced to competency-based learning.*
*Learning is still part of a standards-driven,*
*time-based grade level system.*

Competency-based systems mean learners learn at their own pace and demonstrate evidence of learning instead of grades. When teachers first learn about competency-based systems, they cannot picture what it will look like in a classroom, especially in their school. Stage One is the place to start introducing and demonstrating competency-based learning. This also means that teachers moving to Stage One need to be realistic about their situation so they do not become frustrated and give up. There are teachers ready to jump in and personalize learning, but the system can put obstacles in their way. This is a systemic issue where schools are tied to bell schedules and grade levels. Stage One is where teachers are becoming aware of competency-based learning and what that could mean for their learners.

*The teacher or counselor suggests afterschool and*
*extracurricular activities to learners to meet learning goals.*

Teachers expand their relationship with their learners in Stage One. In getting to know how they learn, teachers also realize that some topics, activities, and courses are not available during the school day. Teachers can take on the role of advisor or involve a counselor to point to other opportunities that can support their learning goals beyond the school day.

*The teacher designs activities to include tools and*
*strategies that instruct and engage all learners in the classroom.*

Teacher use the Class Learning Snapshot and how their learners prefer or need to learn to guide them in the design of the Class Learning Toolkit (CLT). The CLT is used to universally design instruction that supports and engages all learners in the classroom. Technology expands opportunities for learners to access digital resources. Yet as teachers are used to direct instruction, it is a big leap to turn over all the learning to their learners. Most technology supports instruction in Stage One. The minimum technology to personalize learning in a Stage One PLE is a wireless infrastructure with at least a ratio of 5:1 learners per device, a projection system, and digital cameras with video capabilities. When teachers redesign the learning environment with multiple learning zones, they also find that the CLT guides the tools and resources that best support learning at the different zones.

## Teacher and Learner Roles Change in a Stage One PLE

Table 3.2 gives an overview of how teacher and learner roles change as they move to a Stage One Personalized Learning Environment. The teacher understands how learners learn and creates opportunities for learners to have a voice and choice in their learning.

**Table 3.2** Teacher and Learner Roles in a Stage One PLE

| The Teacher . . . | The Learner . . . |
|---|---|
| understands how each learner learns based on Personal Learner Profiles (PLP) and data. | works with the teacher to establish learning goals based on how they learn best. |
| makes instructional decisions based on four diverse learners' PLPs to create a Class Learning Snapshot. | creates a learning plan based on their personal learning goals. |
| redesigns the learning environment by changing the physical layout of the classroom for individual work and group projects. | chooses a learning environment for individual or group work. |
| revises lessons and projects to encourage voice and choice. | has more opportunities to have a voice in what they learn and choice in how they express what they know. |
| universally designs instruction and materials to engage and guide learners in establishing their learning goals. | has more choices in how they access content and engage in the activities so they are motivated to meet their learning goals. |
| designs, adapts, and uses existing assessment strategies and leads learner conferences. | has a voice and choice in how they express what they know and understand. |
| designs activities to include tools and strategies that instruct and engage all learners in the classroom. | has more options for tools and strategies to support their learning. |
| suggests afterschool and extracurricular opportunities based on their learning goals. | has more options for afterschool and extracurricular activities to meet their learning goals. |

*Source:* Personalize Learning, LLC, 2014

> *"Education is the kindling of a flame, not the filling of a vessel."*
>
> —Socrates

## What Does a Stage One Lesson Look Like?

Let's take a third-grade English/language arts lesson using the book *Miss Rumphius* by Barbara Cooney. The book tells the story of Alice, a young girl who lives in a little city by the sea. It describes Alice's life and how she makes the world more beautiful. Her grandfather is an artist who tells Alice stories of faraway places that have a deep influence on her. Alice admires her grandfather and keeps his words to her in mind: to make the world more beautiful. When Alice grows up, she becomes Miss Rumphius, the librarian attracted to books about faraway places who decides to travel the world. Accidentally, she finds a way to make the world more beautiful by spreading lupine seeds wherever she is. Before long, beautiful flowers blossom everywhere. That's how Alice becomes the Lupine Lady.

The teacher chose the Common Core English/Language Arts standard ELA-RL.3.2 for learners to meet: recount stories, including fables, folktales, and myths from diverse cultures; determine the central message, lesson, or moral and explain how it is conveyed through key details in the text.

*A traditional lesson for **Miss Rumphius** that meets this standard might look like this*

> The teacher reads the story to the class and then talks about morals and messages of stories. The teacher then discusses with the whole class the moral of the story about making the world more beautiful. She asks learners to reread the book for silent reading and take notes about what the moral means to them. She directs learners to write a book report explaining details in the text that convey the moral. Learners may use a worksheet or follow website links to follow the questions and prompts for a book report.

*Transforming this lesson on **Miss Rumphius** to include learner voice and choice*

> The teacher offers multiple ways to read, watch, or listen to the story at different learning zones. Some learners like to use the quiet corner with beanbag

chairs to read whereas others use their computer to listen to the audio file or e-book.

The teacher invites questions from the class about the story behind the story with prompts on the driving question "What makes the world more beautiful?" Learners then work in pairs to design and choose supporting questions that meet CCSS standard ELA-RL.3.1 about asking and answering questions.

The teacher asks learners to pair with another learner to propose how they will answer their question that explores the moral of the story by focusing on a supporting question. An example might be "How can we make the school more beautiful?" One pair of learners may research around the school and come up with the supporting question "How can we build a school garden that would make the school more beautiful?"

Learners work together and independently to research and present their findings that then meet additional ELA standards. The teacher can extend the lesson with learners writing or illustrating a proposal on how they would make the world a better place and then presenting their findings to the class or school site council to see if they can get the proposal funded. If the teacher wants to extend it further, each pair can pursue their project if their proposal is approved.

## What Does a Stage One Project Look Like?

*Let's start with an example of a traditional project for sixth-grade social studies*

In sixth grade, ancient Egypt can be taught using a world history textbook around ancient civilizations. Some social studies teachers flip the classroom and create a website with links to resources. Others provide a worksheet with questions for learners to use as prompts for research online. One activity is about the location of Egypt and meets several geography standards around mapping.

The teacher asks learners to find Egypt on a world map and then to locate the Nile River. They use a calculator on a website to calculate the distance between where they live and Egypt. Then learners write directions to get to Egypt by land, air, and sea. Using the websites found by the teacher, learners draw a map of ancient Egypt and add the locations of pyramids on their maps.

The teacher determines prior knowledge by asking learners what they know about the pyramids. What items were found or believed to be inside the ancient Egyptian pyramids? Learners keep a running tally of items that could be found inside a pyramid on the worksheet.

*Now let's transform this lesson
into a project with learner voice and choice*

The teacher didn't want to continue teaching the same lesson and wanted to find a way for her learners to have a voice in a project about ancient Egypt. Most of her lessons have learners work alone. She wasn't sure how to group the very diverse group of learners in her class. She created a Class Learning Snapshot (CLS) of four diverse learners so she could design activities that met most of her learners. She referred to the CLS to assign learners to the groups she believed would be more compatible and supportive of each other. She really wanted them to have ownership of the project because she was having trouble motivating them. She designed a project where learners were in groups of four as ancient Egypt travel agents. Learners had a voice in the types of roles they would play in their groups: manager, graphic organizer, facilitator, and MC.

Each group chose a name and logo for their travel agency and created business cards or a brochure, a poster, and a presentation promoting a specific city from ancient Egypt. The groups had a voice in the types of presentation they did, and some even designed and created costumes to represent the time period. Their agency made a presentation to the class and at a showcase for the school community.

It usually takes about six weeks to "cover" ancient Egypt in a core ELA/history classroom. This project can meet multiple Common Core State Standards in ELA and history and additional geography standards applicable to the same time period. Since the teacher allowed groups to choose different ways to present their findings, learners also can meet several of the National Education Technology Standards for Students (NETS-S).

## Transformational Journeys in a Stage One PLE

Teachers and leaders around the world want to share their stories. They have wow moments and want to talk about them. These are real stories from teachers that have taken risks and turned the learning over to their learners. They realized how changing their role so they are not controlling all the learning is exciting and fun. They also realize that their new role is rewarding and makes them less accountable for what learners are learning. They share that kids want to learn and are showing us the way. Some of these teachers are at Stage One. A few reach beyond. This section gives you a glimpse inside some exciting classrooms.

> *"The key to the future of the world is finding optimistic stories and letting them be known."*
>
> —Pete Seeger

### Kevin's Personal Journey and PJs

Kevin McLaughlin

Kevin McLaughlin was a Year 4 teacher when he shared his journey in 2012. Now he is a kindergarten teacher at Old Mill Primary School in Leicestershire, England. He shared why he adopted personalized learning for his learners.

Kevin explained that if you are going to consider personalized learning as an approach in your classroom then you should first understand that every learner is unique. Learners may appear to be similar, and at times we can indeed teach learners in the same fashion. But

*"I came up with the design after trial and error. I knew the traditional classroom layout would deter a personalized learning approach so it had to be changed. This requires a good understanding of your learners, how they interact with each other, and the development of trust and respect from the start of the academic year as a personalized learning approach will be daunting for any teacher at first.*

*"You need to be prepared to allow the learners to move around, to interact with their peers, to sit anywhere with anyone, to use the floor space as well as a table and not to use groupings of any sort unless there is a specific reason for it."*

—Kevin McLaughlin, Kindergarten Teacher, United Kingdom

to use this whole-class approach for every lesson you teach you run the risk of leaving learners behind. Learning requires more than a teaching plan that focuses on teaching. Kevin emphasized that educators need to focus on the learning that is going to occur and the learning that is to come. And that is why he is using a personalized learning approach. Check out Figure 3.2 to see how Kevin rearranged the furniture to create different zones for learning.

### The Learning Zone is divided into five areas

1. *Discussion and Thinking Zone.* Learners can drop in whenever they wish to talk about their learning, find solutions, help each other, or just think and chill out. It's also still the area where Kevin's class gathers for a whole-group focus or an additional Creation/Show-Off Zone.

**Figure 3.3** Five Zones for Learning

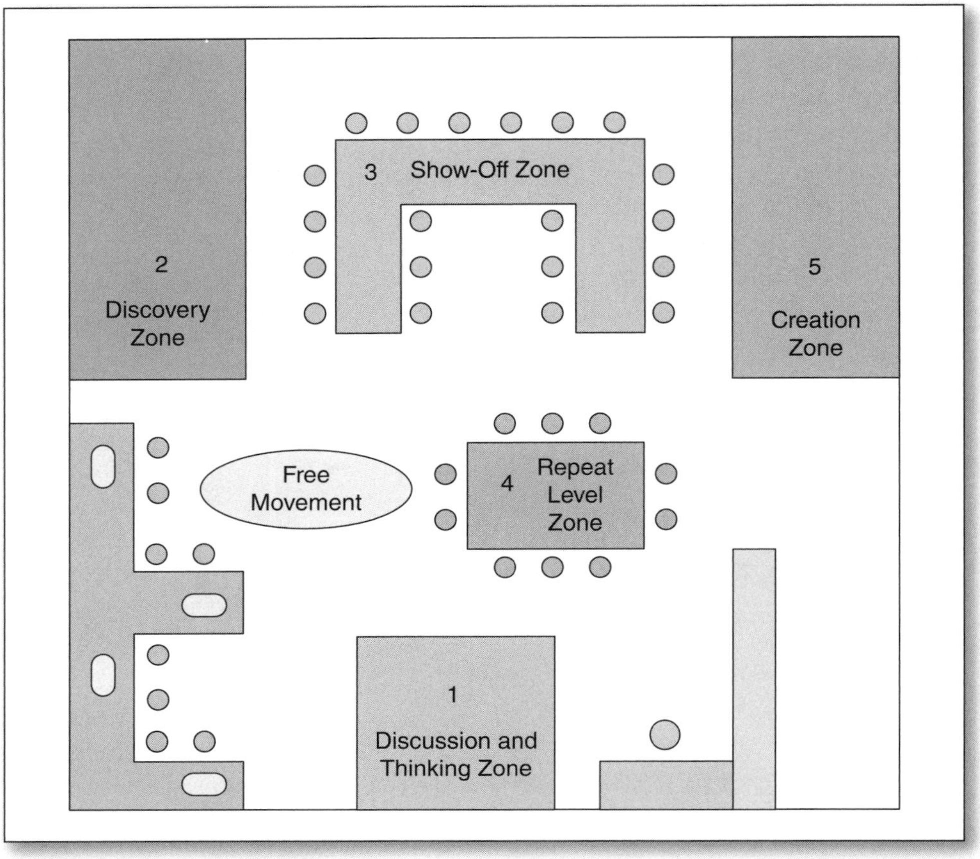

*Source:* Bray & McClaskey, 2013

2. *Discovery Zone*. There are two of these, although one is cut off the top of the image. These contain laptops and other technology learners can use to guide them on their learning, discover answers, investigate and solve problems, collaborate on projects, and create presentations.

3. *Show-Off Zone*. This is where learners focus on discoveries they have made and demonstrate their understanding through whatever medium they wish: writing, presentation, artwork, or display.

4. *Repeat Level Zone*. This has evolved from Kevin's use of gamification of learning and is an approach his class enjoys. Whenever learners

require help, advice, or explanations and are "stuck," this is the area they come to in order to repeat the learning so they can move to the next level.

5. *Creation Zone.* When learners created content for use in their learning, they also created presentations for a professional musician. During that time, the musician occasionally worked with children, teaching music.

Kevin showed how learners, even very young learners, can drive their learning in a flexible learning environment. The classroom layout allows his class the freedom to explore their learning in a way that would not be possible if they were grouped by ability and had specified seating arranged for them.

### Kevin's WOW moment about PJs

When the room changed, it changed his teaching. Kevin developed Personal Journeys that his learners call their PJs. Learners in his class use their own PJ, which is a mix of teacher-set targets and their own. He gives his children time to sit quietly to read through their PJ, adding their own ideas on how they will achieve the targets set for them. Every child has control over his or her learning and quickly sets off to achieve it. Some do math, while others continue with project work they devised for themselves. At any one time, there could be two or three subject areas on the go. Yet there is no chaos, no panic, and no behavior issues. Kevin shared that now he has time to see each and every child, assess his or her learning on the spot, and help learners revise their learning targets using their PJs.

Personalizing the curriculum for every child in his class has been an inspiring journey for Kevin. He shared that he watched in awe as children worked their way through their learning, solving problems in pairs, discussing and thinking, coming up with solutions, and offering suggestions and advice to their peers. It confirmed his belief that if we give learners opportunities to follow a personalized approach, they will fly. After the very first week of using PJs in his class he found the following outcomes:

> **Consider This!** Kevin jumped in on his own to add voice and choice. With some activities, his room is a Stage One PLE, and with other activities, his learners co-design the environment and create their own Personal Journeys.

- All children preferred this approach to their learning.
- All children were on task every day without having to be told.

•All children made progress in numeracy and achieved at least two learning targets set for them.
•All children achieved at least one of their own targets.
•All children told Kevin they were looking forward to the next week of learning in their Personal Journeys. (McLaughlin, 2012a)

> *"Bring your passions to the school setting."*
>
> —Kevin McLaughlin

### Laura's story as a Personalize Learning Coach

Moving to Stage One impacts how teachers teach and the support they receive from their school or district. Laura Lindquist is an Educational Technology Specialist for several elementary schools in Verona Area School District in Wisconsin. Laura is also a Personalize Learning Coach for the teachers in these schools. Laura shared her impressions of how teachers are transforming their teaching practice and impacting how learners are learning.

Laura Lindquist

When reviewing the three stages of personalized learning and looking specifically at Stage One, I see this stage as being a small step away from what many of the teachers in the building where I work are already doing. While for many, their defined goal is not exactly personalization but instead meeting the needs of all of their learners, these teachers could have a very easy time taking the one part that is missing— learner voice and choice.

In Stage One of personalized learning, the classroom is still teacher centered. The teacher designs the lessons, assessments, and classroom structure and she identifies how each learner learns best based on data. She also makes decisions for the learners based on their individual strengths and challenges. The teacher is still very involved in the assessment process with the creation of both formative and summative assessments and is responsible for guiding conferences with parents. The learning that takes place is also standards driven, based on grade levels and technology, and integrated into the curriculum to instruct all learners. All of the above are things that I see happening in many of the classrooms at the school where I work—personalized or not.

The differences between the traditional classroom and a personalized learning classroom really start to occur when you think about the role of the learner herself. In the personalized learning environment, the learner is no longer just a receptacle for knowledge, instead she starts to take an active role in the learning process. The classroom teacher in this environment allows for learner voice and choice. While the teacher is still at the forefront of the learning, she does work to begin acting as a support for learning and not just the sole decision maker. This is especially seen with things such as the creation of individual learning goals. In a personalized learning classroom, the teacher also begins to explore competency-based learning.

### Laura's WOW moment

Laura shares her WOW moment.

Personalization may indeed be the answer to help learners become more connected with, more interested in, and more excited about school. And of course all of this at the same time that they are learning key concepts tied to strong academic standards.

I have seen this firsthand with two different personalized learning experiences I have been a part of at the elementary school where I work. In one fourth-grade classroom, the teacher and I were both amazed by how some of the lowest functioning learners in the classroom truly stood out when provided with the opportunity for choice and voice. Two learners in particular who have struggled getting any work done on their own were able to choose and research their topic, plan a project, and put the entire thing together with minimal support from the teacher.

Both of the finished projects were exceptional in both their final presentation and in the learning that they showcased. And both the learners found success by meeting the high academic expectations and through the new sense of acceptance and recognition they found within the classroom community.

### Kayleen's WOW moment about the Personal Learner Profile

Teachers in Verona Area Schools learned about the Personal Learner Profile (PLP) as part of the Six Steps to Personalize Learning workshop in

Kayleen DeWerd

November 2013. Teachers were using multiple tools such as learning styles and multiple intelligences to determine how their learners learn. The PLP was new to them.

Kayleen DeWerd teaches third grade at Glacier Edge Elementary in the Verona Area School District and was intrigued about the idea of a Personal Learner Profile. She redesigned the PLP so it was in "kidspeak." *Access* was changed to *Getting*; *Engage* was changed to *Doing*; and *Express* was changed to *Showing*. Each of the statements was written so a third grader could understand and relate to them. She asked her kids to check the statements that sounded the most like them. Then she asked them to reflect on their answers and write a short summary about what they thought about their answers and themselves as learners now.

Kayleen showed up the next day so excited with examples of the kids' PLPs. She said she never saw her third graders more animated and excited. She said this was because she asked them about their learning. They loved talking about themselves, their interests, their goals, and how they prefer and need to learn.

She reflected on why her learners were so excited to share how they learned. She realized that this experience helped validate each child as a learner, something we rarely do. It also opened the door for children to have a conversation about their learning with their teacher: the first step in personalizing learning.

### Pause/Think/Reflect

"One statement that continues to replay over and over in my head is 'Get out of their way.' I know that the children that walk into my classroom are learners and are eager to discover new and interesting information."

—Kayleen DeWerd

*"I am not a teacher, but an awakener."*

—Robert Frost

## STAGE TWO PLE: LEARNER-CENTERED WITH TEACHER AND LEARNER AS CO-DESIGNERS

In a Stage Two PLE, the teacher and learners are co-designers of their lessons and projects. The learners and teacher both understand how the learner learns best. Learners design their Personal Learner Profile with guidance from their teacher who supports them as they meet their learning goals. Teachers are no longer the expert on content nor need to have all the answers. They involve learners in decisions and design of rules, lessons, activities, and assessments.

*In a Stage Two PLE, learners with their teacher . . .*

- co-design and update their PLP based on how they learn best.
- identify learning strategies based on how the learner prefers or needs to learn. The teacher designs instructional strategies based on a Class Learning Snapshot.
- co-design the learning environment with multiple learning zones.
- transform lessons and projects that include learner voice and choice.
- decide on the multiple ways to access and engage information and to express what they know based on each learner's learning goals.
- contribute to the design of assessment strategies and reflect on their learning. The teacher and learner co-lead learner conferences with parents.
- begin to demonstrate mastery of learning standards that may or may not be in a grade-level system as they transition to a competency-based system.
- are offered extended learning opportunities after school and, for some projects, during the school year.
- know how to choose and use the appropriate tool to access content and express what they know and understand. The teacher uses tools to engage and motivate learners.

### Learners and teachers co-design and update the learners' PLPs based on how they learn best.

Teachers work with learners to design their Personal Learner Profile. As the year goes by, they revisit their PLPs and learners' learning goals to identify any changes in how they learn best.

### Learners identify learning strategies and skills with their teacher based on how they prefer or need to learn using their PLP.

The teacher meets with learners to review their PLP to determine the best learning strategies for learners to support their learning and the skills they may need to become more independent in their learning based on how they learn best. Then teachers have a better idea of the instructional strategies to implement based on the Class Learning Snapshot by choosing four diverse learners in their class.

*Learners co-design the learning environment*
*with multiple learning zones with their teacher.*

Teachers identify the types of learning zones to make available in their class from information in the Class Learning Snapshot. After learners identify how they learn best with their PLP and the tasks they are to do in the lesson or project, they suggest ideas for the redesign of the learning environment for the task at hand. Furniture may look different: mobile, rolling, and flexible. In fact, there may be areas where there is no furniture or places to stand or pace.

*The learners and teacher are transforming lessons*
*and projects together to include learner voice and choice.*

After learners learn about learning, they also will want a say in what and how they learn. This is a great opportunity for teachers to present a lesson and invite learners to give their ideas on how and where in the lesson to include voice and choice. Even in the process of lesson design, learners can have a voice in unpacking standards, choice in the learning targets to meet, and choice in how to express what they understand.

*Learners with teacher guidance decide how to access*
*information, engage with content, and express*
*what they know based on learning goals.*

After learners build their Personal Learning Profile, they work together in groups or as a whole class to review what tools are best for them to access content. They learn about universally designed lessons and why some resources might work better for them. Consider this as an opportunity to have learners learn about learning and what that means for each learner. They need to discuss what motivates them, what helps them want to learn and engage in the learning process, and how they best can express what they know and understand. They also are learning about the skills they need to acquire to use different tools.

*Learners contribute to the design of assessment*
*strategies and reflect on their learning. The teacher*
*and learner co-lead learner conferences with parents.*

Learners use assessment for learning to monitor their progress. Teachers invite learners to help them design rubrics and checklists for projects. The teacher and learner co-lead their learner conferences with parents where learners demonstrate what they know and understand about the content up to that point. They also reflect on their learning and share what they learned about their learning.

*Learners demonstrate mastery of learning standards that may or may not be in a grade-level system as they and their teacher transition to a competency-based system.*

Learners collect evidence of learning, demonstrating mastery as they meet their learning goals and the standards. They create reflections about the evidence to include in their ePortfolio. Teachers align the competencies with standards and share those with learners for feedback.

*The learners and teacher work together to determine extended learning opportunities based on learning goals and interests.*

Extended learning opportunities involve online courses, internships, and community service learning projects. This is the beginning of an advisory program and competency-based system that encourages learners to pursue what they need when they need it. Teachers, advisors, and counselors are more aware of learners' goals and interests.

*Learners with teacher support acquire skills to choose and use the appropriate tools and strategies to access content and express what they know.*

Learners are acquiring the skills to know which tools are appropriate for the task and how to use them effectively. Teachers are building experience with multiple tools that are more accessible for different learners and creating a Class Learning Toolkit based on access, engage, and express. In Stage Two, it is necessary to have enough broadband and a fast wireless infrastructure in every area of the campus with 1:1 laptops or mobile devices.

## Teacher and Learner Roles Change in a Stage Two PLE

Table 3.3 shows how the teacher is now co-designing lessons and the environment with the learner. Learners are taking more responsibility for their learning by Stage Two PLE.

**Table 3.3**  Teacher and Learner Roles in a Stage Two PLE

| Teacher With Learner . . . | Learner With Support From Teacher . . . |
|---|---|
| co-designs and updates the learners' PLP based on how they learn best. | provides input and co-designs their PLP based on how they learn best. |
| identifies learning strategies and skills based on how learner prefers or needs to learn. | acquires skills to use the learning strategies based on how they prefer or need to learn. |

*(Continued)*

| Table 3.3 (Continued) | |
|---|---|
| **Teacher With Learner . . .** | **Learner With Support From Teacher . . .** |
| co-designs the learning environment with multiple learning zones. | chooses appropriate learning environment for the activity. |
| transforms lessons and projects to include learner voice and choice. | has a voice in the design of lessons and projects and choice in the types of activities included. |
| decides how to access information, engage with content, and express what they know. | researches multiple ways to access information, engage with content, and express what they know based on their learning goals. |
| co-designs assessment strategies and co-leads learner conferences. | reflects on their learning and monitors their progress. |
| provides options for competency-based learning. | has some opportunities to demonstrate mastery in transitioning to a competency-based system. |
| determines extended learning opportunities based on learning goals and interests. | chooses interests to have experiences that enhance their learning goals. |
| provides opportunities to learn skills on how and when to choose and use the appropriate tools and strategies. | acquires the skills to choose and use the appropriate tools to access content and express what they know. |

*Source:* Personalize Learning, LLC, 2014

## What Does a Lesson or Project Look Like in a Stage Two PLE?

The learner and teacher use the UDL lens to personalize learning and co-design the lesson. So what does that look like?

For U. S. history, eighth graders study the Civil War. Since there is so much information on the Civil War, the teacher and learners decided to start with one essential or anchor standard. In this case, they determined that the main issue learners had problems with was analyzing text and making connections to a concept.

### Essential or Anchor Standard

*Key Ideas and Details (Informational Text)*

**RI.8.3.** Analyze how a text makes connections among and distinctions between individuals, ideas, or events (e.g., through comparisons, analogies, or categories).

After determining the essential standard, the teacher and learners identified supporting standards for the history topic the Civil War. The power of using historical information such as primary and secondary sources is that learners can use visual information in multiple forms to understand the concept. They also chose one subtopic on which to do a short project.

### Supporting Standards

*Integration of Knowledge and Ideas (Integration of History)*
**RH.6–8.7.** Integrate visual information (e.g., in charts, graphs, photographs, videos, or maps) with other information in print and digital texts.

*Comprehension and Collaboration (Speaking and Listening)*
**SL.8.1.** Engage effectively in a range of collaborative discussions (one on one, in groups, and teacher led) with diverse partners on Grade 8 topics, texts, and issues, building on others' ideas and expressing their own clearly.

*Research to Build and Present Knowledge (Writing)*
**W.8.7.** Conduct short research projects to answer a question (including a self-generated question), drawing on several sources and generating additional related, focused questions that allow for multiple avenues of exploration.

*Presentation of Knowledge and Ideas (Speaking and Listening)*
**SL.8.5.** Integrate multimedia and visual displays into presentations to clarify information, strengthen claims and evidence, and add interest.

After the teacher and learners chose the standards, they brainstormed questions about the Civil War. They worked in pairs to prioritize questions until the whole class chose one essential question.

*Essential Question: What are the causes of the Civil War?*
Learners then paired with another learner to come up with supporting questions. The pairs prioritized those questions until they came up with one question to research and answer for their project.

*Supporting Questions*

- Why did Southern states secede from the union?
- What events or publications sparked the start of the Civil War?

- Was slavery the main issue for the war's beginning?
- What other factors contributed to the civil war beginning?
- If slavery began in 1619, why did it take 200 years for it to become an issue?
- Why did the South believe that they needed to continue slavery?

Table 3.4 shows two eighth-grade learners and sections of their Personal Learner Profiles to see how they would use their strengths and challenges to work together.

### Example Personal Learner Profiles

**Table 3.4**    Personal Learner Profiles of Susan and Justin

| Susan | Justin |
|---|---|
| • is an avid reader, likes to write descriptively, and enjoys drawing.<br>• is anxious when she speaks in front of others.<br>• forgets the sequence, moral, and message of the story.<br>• wants to ask questions but is uncomfortable voicing her concerns.<br>• works better individually or in a small group. | • reads and writes at a third-grade level.<br>• requires projects to be broken down into smaller segments.<br>• has a difficult time organizing and little ability to interpret concepts.<br>• needs to know the purpose behind reading assignments.<br>• loves to draw and is interested in multimedia. |

*Source:* Personalize Learning, LLC, 2014

### Instructional and Learning Strategies
### Aligned to Common Core State Standards

Table 3.5 shows the learning strategies Susan and Justin used that were based on their learner profiles to help them meet the Common Core and demonstrate what they know and understand. Because Susan and Justin understand how they learn best through their UDL lens, they were able to make choices for themselves. Those choices included how they access information, how they are engaged with information, and how they like to express what they know. Susan and Justin chose the supporting question "Was slavery the main issue for the war's beginning?"

**Table 3.5**  Strategies Aligned to Common Core State Standards

| Instructional and Learning Strategies | Common Core State Standards |
|---|---|
| The teacher demonstrates how to create an action plan using a mind-mapping program. Susan starts the project action plan with "who does what by when" with input from Justin. | SL8.1. Engage effectively in a range of collaborative discussions (one on one, in groups, and teacher led) with diverse partners on Grade 8 topics, texts, and issues, building on others' ideas and expressing their own clearly. |
| Justin and Susan view Ken Burns's *The Civil War* on PBS on the laptop. Justin uses an accessibility feature on the iPad (Speak Selection) to independently read the causes of the Civil War at the EyeWitness to History website. | W.8.7. Conduct short research projects to answer a question (including a self-generated question), drawing on several sources and generating additional related, focused questions that allow for multiple avenues of exploration. |
| Susan uses SweetSearch to research slavery before the Civil War with her laptop to collect images, text, and audio files to put in Dropbox. Justin collects bookmarks, PDF files, and other resources and sends them to Susan. | RH.6–8.7. Integrate with visual information (e.g., in charts, graphs, photographs, videos, or maps) with other information in print and digital texts. |
| They review, select, and organize the resources to answer their question to put in the correct order for their presentation. They create an outline with presentation notes and include proper citations for all resources. | RI.8.3. Analyze how a text makes connections among and distinctions between individuals, ideas, or events (e.g., through comparisons, analogies, or categories). |
| Susan and Justin work together to draw the title graphic using paper and pens and scan it into their files. They pull all of their resources and media files together to create a presentation using Prezi. | SL.8.5. Integrate multimedia and visual displays into presentations to clarify information, strengthen claims and evidence, and add interest. |

*Source:* Personalize Learning, LLC, 2014

Personalizing a unit of study like the Civil War is more than just memorizing battles, events, people, places, and times. The essential and supporting questions push the investigation of history further. This project encourages diverse learners to own and direct their own learning about  the Civil War. Susan and Justin have diverse learning challenges, yet both of them have a passion for drawing. Because they were able to choose how they would respond to the question, they were more motivated to design a title graphic and a Prezi presentation that used their creative talents.

Justin and Susan were responsible for their learning by choosing the question, the direction of their presentation, and which one of them did each of the tasks to complete their project.

### Transformational Journeys in a Stage Two PLE

Stage Two PLE is a huge step for many teachers. Some are ready to give learners more control of their learning, whereas others are transforming one lesson or project at a time. Some teachers find they need to introduce content with a lecture and then after the concept is introduced turn the learning over so it is more learner-centered. Because teachers are moving at different levels, examples of Stage Two PLEs are not as clear-cut as Stage One PLEs. In this section, several teachers share that after they gave more responsibility of learning to their learners, they would never go back to traditional direct instruction. Stage Two is where the Wow moments keep happening and teachers realize their role really has changed. These are just a few examples of transformational journeys several teachers have shared from their Wow moments. We begin with Sarah Downing-Ford, shown in Figure 3.6.

Sarah Downing-Ford

#### *Sarah's Journey*

Sarah Downing-Ford is a seventh-grade teacher at Massabesic Middle School in Waterboro, Maine. As part of a 1:1 program, her learners were taking more control of their learning. She realized that traditional lecture-based teaching was not going to work anymore.

Sarah shared that personalized learning does not mean eliminating the teacher. Some learners do not want to, and are not ready to, manage their own learning; they want to be told how to meet the targets. Others may be eager to charge through the targets and ascend levels like rungs on a ladder. The balance on the beam is determining if learners are driven by intrinsic or extrinsic motivation. The expression "You can lead a horse to water . . ." is an understatement when it comes to personalized learning. The key for teachers is to lay a framework, create a community of learners who don't throw in the towel when they are stuck, and make classroom expectations clear.

New learning is tackled as a whole group. If learners are willing and able to move faster, they may. If learners need to slow down, look from a different point of view, or practice, they may. Again, with this paradigm shift comes the change in tools to access learning and progress. Learners refer to progress charts posted in the room as a visual reminder of what they have completed and what they have not. Also, each learner has a checklist of measurement topics and levels on which they track their progress.

> **Pause/Think/Reflect**
>
> "If you asked my learners three years ago what our class looked like in September and compared it to what it looked like in June, they would probably say that it transformed from organized chaos to unorganized responsibility."
> Sarah Downing-Ford

Sarah listed the top ten things she learned about personalizing learning in her class:

10. Don't underestimate the abilities/flexibility of learners.

9. Never assume the abilities/flexibility of learners.

8. Share struggles, successes, and questions with colleagues and students.

7. Don't scrap the old stuff; as long as it meets a target, it is worthy.

6. Communicate with parents and learners a lot; you cannot communicate too much.

5. Find ways to create a bridge between the old system and the new system.

4. Stay organized.

3. Work with your team of teachers to create interdisciplinary units.

2. Nothing works as a canned program, modify as needed.

1. Have fun!

### Every Day Is a Wow for Sarah

Sixteen years into her career, Sarah would not choose to do anything else. She walks into school thinking about what she will teach and leaves thinking about what she has learned. Her learners are her world. Sarah has taught fifth grade to high school, including ELA, social studies, and music appreciation. Every position she has held has taught her volumes about herself and teaching as an art. One of her learners interviewed her for a research project on how people learn and asked her for a piece of advice to a college student studying to be a teacher.

> *"I affirm to be true to yourself, be true to your learners, and don't listen to the negativity that the public says about our profession. We do change lives one learner at a time."*
>
> —Sarah Downing-Ford

Shelley Wright

### *Shelley's Journey to WOW*

Shelley Wright is a high school chemistry teacher and consultant in Saskatchewan, Canada. Shelley tells her story and journey as a high school teacher and now consultant, coaching other teachers. Shelley played around with what it was like to have her learners teach each other using feedback loops. They discussed what worked, what didn't work, and what they would do differently next time. She describes how her learners loved doing case studies such as trying to solve a real medical problem. Why? They had ownership of their learning because they chose the problem, selected the resources to find solutions, and collaborated on how to solve the problem.

> *"Technology opens up learning. Inquiry opens up minds."*

As her learners worked with her to invent their own version of learner-centered learning, they realized that the three questions every learner in her classroom had to answer were

*What are you going to learn?*

*How are you going to learn it?*

*How are you going to show me your learning?*

This became their mantra—their framework for learning. This is what it means to give learners control over their education. Shelley facilitated discussions on how their brains work and how they learn best so they could drive their learning. What they found is that they had to go through a process of unlearning so they could understand this new way of teaching and learning.

Shelley realized she was the only teacher in the school whose learners were in charge of their learning. When they went to other classes, they were back to traditional teaching methods. This is when Shelley was asked to coach other teachers and started working with seven teachers through a process like this:

> **Pause/Think/Reflect**
>
> "I used to think that compliant, well-behaved students were the ideal; now I'm afraid for them. I'm afraid for the kids who think that scoring 90% actually means something in the real world. I'm afraid for the kids who believe the academic hoops they jump through so effortlessly guarantee that they will be successful at life. I've come to believe that being good at school might mean you'd make a decent academic, but it isn't a guarantee of much else."
>
> —Shelley Wright

- Sit down with the curriculum.
- Choose outcomes and the entire unit.
- Determine how learners are going to learn it and how to assess what they learned.

Shelley shared that every learner she's taught could learn, just often not the same thing or in the same way. And when she asked her learners about it, she always found they love to learn; they just don't like school. She asked them, "If you designed school, what would you do?"

- Start with the negative—what don't you like?
- What would the opposite look like?

> *"The process is really messy. Everything falls apart. When it falls apart, these are the most important teaching moments."*
>
> —Shelley Wright

> *"Self-education is, I firmly believe, the only kind of education there is."*
>
> —Isaac Asimov

## STAGE THREE PLE: LEARNER-DRIVEN WITH TEACHER AS PARTNER IN LEARNING

A Stage Three PLE puts the learning in learners' hands. Learners know how they learn best in this stage. They understand that learning changes as they learn so they revise their Personal Learner Profile on a regular basis. They realize that what they prefer or need to learn will change as they change.

In a Stage Three PLE, learners own and drive their learning. They monitor their progress as they learn and reflect on their learning. They have the skills now to choose and use the appropriate tools and strategies to learn what and when they want to learn. They enjoy learning and pursue topics they are interested in and are passionate about. Since they can self-regulate their learning, they know how to address any standards or graduation requirements as they design all their learning experiences.

*In a Stage Three PLE, learners . . .*

- adjust their PLP with teacher guidance by recognizing how their learning changes.
- are expert learners motivated and self-directed with support from their teacher, peers, family, and community.
- expand their learning environment in and outside of school to include the larger community.
- design challenging learning experiences based on their interests, passions, and talents.
- self-direct how they access information, engage with content, and express what they know based on learning goals.
- design assessment strategies and showcase evidence of learning through exhibitions that involve their parents, peers, teachers, and community.
- learn at their own pace and move on by demonstrating mastery of competencies.
- select extended and experiential learning opportunities based on goals, interests, and aspirations.
- choose and use the appropriate tools and strategies to engage in learning, express what they know, and support them along their learning path.

*Learners adjust their PLP with teacher guidance by recognizing how their learning changes.*

Learners monitor their own progress of their learning and adjust their Personal Learner Profile as they learn, unlearn, and relearn.

*Learners are expert learners who use
learning strategies and skills to support their learning goals.*

Learners are taking more responsibility for their learning and becoming more resourceful and strategic in how they learn. They really know how to tackle learning to get consistently good results.

*Learners expand their learning environment in
and outside of school to include the larger community.*

Learners know that learning can happen anytime and anywhere. They address their learning goals and know that meeting them might mean taking classes online, traveling overseas for a global project, participating for several months in a community project, or being an intern at a local company.

*Learners design challenging learning experiences
based on their interests, passions, and talents.*

Learners know how they learn best and address what they are interested in. They love to be challenged around something they are passionate about. This could be a senior project, a community garden, or an apprenticeship with a master craftsman.

*Learners self-direct how they access information, engage
with content, and express what they know based on learning goals.*

Learners review their learning goals and choose learning opportunities that help them meet those learning goals. They have a network of peers and advisors who point them to exciting learning opportunities that stretch and challenge them.

*Learners design assessment strategies and showcase
evidence of learning through exhibitions
that involve their parents, peers, teachers, and community.*

Learners select the evidence that best showcases how they demonstrate mastery. Learning is deeper and assessment is an essential part of their learning.

*Learners learn at their own pace by
demonstrating mastery in a competency-based system.*

Grades or tests are not learners' focus. Learners progress when they master a concept and reflect on their learning as they learn.

*Learners select extended and experiential learning opportunities based on
goals, interests, and aspirations.*

Learners review their learning plan and choose the best opportunities that will challenge them to meet their learning goals no matter if they are in or out of school.

*Learners choose and use the appropriate tools and strategies to engage in learning, express what they know, and support them along their learning path.*

Learners have acquired the skills to choose and know how to use the appropriate tools for any task. They also know what types of learning strategies work best for them based on how they learn best. This is the stage where most learners have their own device and there is wireless and enough bandwidth to do whatever they need to do to learn. Learners have access wherever and whenever they want to learn.

### Teacher and Learner Roles Change in a Stage Three PLE

Table 3.6 shows that the teacher is now a partner in learning with learners, and learners become expert learners who self-regulate and drive their learning.

**Table 3.6** Teacher and Learner Roles in Stage Three PLE

| Teacher as a Partner in Learning . . . | Learner as Driver of Their Learning . . . |
|---|---|
| guides the learner as they navigate the learning environment. | adjusts PLP with teacher guidance as their learning changes. |
| suggests learning strategies and skills to support learning goals. | is an expert learner who uses learning strategies and skills to support their learning goals. |
| looks for and develops partnerships in the community that can support learning goals. | identifies learning opportunities outside of school and in the larger community. |
| mentors the learner as they work on challenging learning experiences. | designs challenging learning experiences based on their interests, passions, and talents. |
| provides feedback to the learner about how they are meeting their learning goals. | self-directs how they access information, engage with content, and express what they know based on learning goals. |
| gives input on the design of assessment strategies. | designs assessment strategies and showcases evidence of learning through exhibitions that involve their parents, peers, teachers, and community. |
| facilitates moving to a competency-based system. | learns at their own pace by demonstrating mastery in a competency-based system. |

| Teacher as a Partner in Learning . . . | Learner as Driver of Their Learning . . . |
|---|---|
| connects the learner to extended and experiential learning opportunities that support their learning goals. | selects extended and experiential learning opportunities based on goals, interests, and aspirations. |
| uses a feedback loop about the learner's selection of tools and strategies that support them along their learning path. | chooses and uses the appropriate tools and strategies that supports them along their learning path. |

*Source:* Personalize Learning, LLC, 2014

### Transformational Journeys in a Stage Three PLE

Stage Three is where learners take control of their own learning. They are driving their learning, and that can happen at any age. Consider a thirteen-year-old who demonstrates mastery of math at a much higher level. She also understands that she needs assistance with her reading that is below grade level. As part of her Personal Learning Backpack, she chooses a text-to-speech tool to make the content accessible. She acquired the skills to know what tools and strategies work best for her even if she is learning something outside of school. She investigates something she is interested in and wants to learn about.

#### *Robin's WOW Story About His Pathways*

Robin was an eleventh grader at Mt. Abraham Union Middle/High School in Bristol, Vermont, who was in a webinar with John H. Clarke, Lauren Parren, Caroline Camara, and Josie Jordan as part of the Personalize Learning webinar series. Robin eloquently presented to a global audience as he shared his story about finding mentors to help him on his journey.

> "Pathways isn't just a program, it's a lifestyle."
>
> —Robin K., eleventh grade, Mt. Abraham Union Middle/ High School, Vermont

In Pathways, it is our job to go out and find people in the community to be our mentors. I went out and asked my uncle if he would teach me how to program robots. Before long we were showing off around the state our robot doing the hokey pokey. My uncle has been our mentor for the past three years for STEM-related topics. Also I have a mentor, Gabe, who is a blacksmith and another student at Mt. Abe.

He is a year younger than me.

I like that I can find mentors who are or are not related to me or someone even younger who has the skills I am interested in to be my mentor. Anyone you ask is willing to share what they know with you. I learned how to smith knives in my forge and also got to play with casting aluminum. I made a plasma speaker for my STEM topic that was 250,000 volts that played music.

I take pictures of all my work and even the notes in class. I needed to learn more about physics so I took an advanced physics class with help from my uncle from MIT's Open Courseware, 801 Classical Mechanics class. Everything was problem-based and we worked on a problem around the Nautilus X concept spaceship from NASA. My problem was what would a ramp look like from the center of the rotating space capsule to the outside so that you could walk on it comfortably. We worked together to derive equations and formulas and came up with the Fibonacci Spiral given the dimensions of the space capsule and desired force on the perimeter.

I chose the way I want to demonstrate what I learned and used photos of the notes and diagrams we used to come up with the answer. I like that I have not only mentors, but I have advisors and community contacts who check in with me to see what evidence I collected that meet the five competencies: Independent Learning, Critical Thinking and Problem-Solving, Global Citizenship and Collaboration, Communication, and Exhibition.

### Chris's Journey Through Messy Learning

Chris Edwards is a Year 2–Class2CE teacher at Chad Varah Primary School, Addison Drive, Lincoln, England. The school is for children in Years

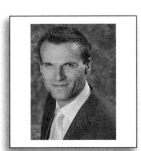

F (four years old) to 6 (eleven years old) with nearly 500 children in the school. Before Chris became a teacher, he was a professional musician. During that time he occasionally worked with children, teaching music. Chris loved it so much that he decided to become a teacher. As a musician, artist, and education technologist, Chris just couldn't see teaching like he was taught. His first design followed Kevin's learning zones.

Chris's kids have iPads and different learning zones to create, design, and engage in the learning process. With kids moving from zone to zone, Chris noticed the children taking more responsibility for their learning, and learning became messy. He calls it "Messy Learning."

Messy Learning is about all children learning and working toward success individually from the outside looking in. So it may look "messy" to others looking in. Chris calls the process iCreate. The different learning zones may involve problem solving, design, fine motor activities, reciprocity, and engagement.

Chris shared how he is confident that he now has a system in place that doesn't kill creativity but rather encourages and engages children in learning. Most importantly, he is also confident that they are developing an environment in which all children can begin to realize and reach their full potential.

### *Year 2 Self-Directed Learners—WOW!*

Chris told a story about being observed by his head teacher. The focus for the observation was "engagement and progress." He has twenty-nine Year 2 children in his class with sixteen iPads. Now why is this messy? Chris wanted to demonstrate how his children can be engaged and self-directed in their learning even without him.

In order for the "engagement" aspect of this lesson to work, Chris spent the first two hours of the day hidden in his closet. His assistant welcomed the class, took the register, and started the day—the children had no idea where he was. Chris was watching on a monitor from the confines of his hiding place. At 9:30 a.m. his head teacher entered the classroom to observe Chris, unaware of where he was.

Everyone was asking, "Have you seen Mr Edwards?"

Then Chris appeared on the interactive whiteboard (IWB) using his iPad's camera and airserver app. He had hung a big white sheet behind him to disguise where he was. The children only saw him on the whiteboard and became very excited.

Using the app, Chris then said over the speaker so all his learners and the headmaster could hear:

> I got so excited about your work on the North Pole that I decided to go. However, I got lost. I think I'm somewhere in Greenland, and I really need your help. I have to whisper as I can hear some animals nearby. I don't know what animals they have here, so if some of you could find out, e-mail me a list. It's really cold here. Could

you e-mail me a list of warm clothes to wear please? There's lots of snow here. I've heard of a shelter called an igloo, but I have no idea what they look like or how to make one. Could some of you find out what an igloo looks like and then have a go at building one using materials around the classroom? Perhaps you could video yourselves making it to help me out. Finally, I don't actually know where Greenland is! Can some of you have a look on the maps app and e-mail me a screenshot? I'd really appreciate your help all! Speak soon.

With this, they were off! Within five minutes, Chris was receiving e-mails from his class with screenshots of maps and lists of arctic animals and warm clothing. It was working! Chris could see on his monitor that all children were engaged and were completing the "tasks" with excitement. He could also see small groups of children collaborating to build igloos using Legos, blocks, and boxes. Every so often Chris would reappear on the screen to thank the children and show examples of what had been e-mailed. To close the lesson, Chris appeared on the screen to explain that a rescue helicopter had found him and was bringing him back to school. As the children went out for play, Chris emerged from the closet and the class exploded with excitement that he made it home (Edwards, 2012).

Chris realized this was just the beginning of Messy Learning. He changed the way he teaches because he learned that he did not even have to be in the room for his young learners to learn. Chris is in charge but has now changed the activities and strategies he uses with his learners.

## MOVING TO WOW!

This chapter includes just a few examples and models of teachers who let go and got out of the way of learning. Figure 3.3 is an overview of the process using the Stages of Personalized Learning Environments to encourage learner voice and choice, but not every lesson or project is only a Stage One or Stage Two. Stage Three means learners are driving their own learning.

Personalizing learning looks different in every setting, be it in school or outside of school, formal or informal learning. All teachers who shared their stories about turning learning over to learners mentioned that they would never go back to a traditional classroom. Teachers are also sharing that learners are talking more, wanting more, and learning more.

**Figure 3.3** Stages of PLE Overview

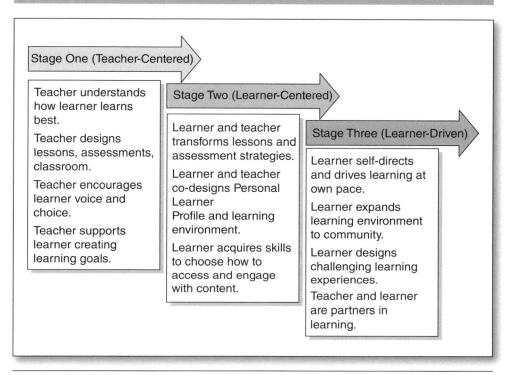

*Source:* Personalize Learning, LLC, 2014

The next chapter expands on these journeys by offering snapshots of both transformational large-scale models and models of personalized learning in schools and districts.

## CHAPTER 3 REVIEW

1. Determine why it is better to have a process that starts with dipping your toes in personalized learning.

2. Review the Stages of Personalized Learning Environments and the elements in Table 3.1.

3. Review the overview of the Stages of PLE and reflect on how this could change your role.

4. Read several of the Wow stories and find one to share with a colleague.

5. Consider the questions Shelley Wright asked her learners and ask your learners:

- What are you going to learn?
- How are you going to learn it?
- How are you going to show me your learning?

6. All of us are learners. Do you have a Wow moment that got you excited about learning as a learner yourself where you wanted to learn more?

- What activity or activities were occurring when that happened?
- What did you see and feel?
- What did you notice about your learning?

7. Now recall a Wow moment as a teacher with your learners. Share what was happening in the classroom when you realized it was a Wow moment where learners were engaged, motivated, and took charge of their learning.

- What tools were you using?
- What did you see and hear?
- What did your learners say to each other?

# 4 Where Is Personalized Learning Happening?

*"In times of drastic change, it is the learners who inherit the future. The learned usually find themselves equipped to live in a world that no longer exists."*

—Eric Hoffer

Wherever personalized learning is happening, each model looks different from every other model. The idea of "personalized" means that each school or district is taking into account the needs of its learners and teachers, the culture of its school, and community demographics. That also means that there is no standardized personalized learning model. This chapter is about the variability of the models, learning approaches, and stories around personalized learning. It is important to start with the key enablers and policy efforts that allow personalized learning to bloom. Personalizing learning is happening around the world, so we want to make sure you have an overview with multiple perspectives.

## GLOBAL, REGIONAL, AND STATE PERSPECTIVES OF SYSTEMIC CHANGE

### Finland's Educational System

> *"Finland's top goal for education—a better individual learning path."*
>
> —Pasi Sahlberg, Director General of CIMO
> (Centre for International Mobility and Cooperation)

Finland realized it needed to transform its educational system in the 1980s. The country was testing and teaching to prescribed standards by grade level. It realized its system was mediocre and creating a population of people who did not know how to think on their own. So it changed everything. It threw out the tests and changed teaching so it became the most valued profession. Teachers compete to get into the teaching master's two-year program. If they are accepted to become a teacher in Finland, they attend for free—and they work very hard. They then intern in a teaching hospital where they are given a mentor and learners as part of a lab environment.

Teachers are professionals selected from the top 10 percent of the nation's graduates to earn a required master's degree in education. Many schools are small enough so that teachers know every learner. If one method fails, teachers consult with colleagues to try something else. They seem to relish the challenges. Nearly 30 percent of Finland's children receive some kind of special help during their first nine years of school. Finland has vastly improved in reading, math, and science literacy over the past decade in large part because its teachers are trusted to do *whatever it takes* to turn young lives around.

> *"The teacher matters. Learners matter and learning is different. Learning is personalized."*

Finland has taken steps to better serve all learners and educators, including the following:

- Improving teacher recruitment and training at colleges of education
- Offering a high-quality curriculum with pathways to high-quality vocational training at younger grades
- Emphasizing play and the arts in education

There are no mandated standardized tests in Finland, apart from one exam at the end of learners' senior year in high school. There are no rankings and no comparisons or competition between learners, schools, or regions. Finland's schools are

**Pause/Think/Reflect**

What are your thoughts on Finland's approach for teachers?

publicly funded. The people in the government agencies running them, from national officials to local authorities, are educators, not businesspeople, military leaders, or career politicians. Every school has the same national goals and draws from the same pool of university-trained educators. The result is that a Finnish child has a good shot at getting the same quality education no matter whether the child lives in a rural village or a university town. Finland values good teachers, expects them to be highly trained (master's degrees), pays them what they are worth, and provides them ongoing support. Children start school at seven and stay with the same teacher for at least six years. All teachers are mentored and coached. No one is allowed to be left behind.

At the end of his book *Finnish Lessons*, Pasi Sahlberg (2011) shares his personal vision for Finnish education, a dream he hopes will animate a new and even more productive round of fundamental reform of Finnish education. He wants an education system that constitutes a "community

**Pause/Think/Reflect**

How can we adopt or adapt some of these strategies from Finland so schools in the United States do "whatever it takes"?

of learners that provides the conditions that allow all young people to discover their talents" (Tucker, 2012).

## British Columbia, Canada

Personalized learning for each learner in British Columbia means a shift from delivering a set of broad, uniform learning outcomes and courses throughout the pre-K–12 program, to learning that is increasingly learner initiated, self-directed, and interdisciplinary and facilitated by the teacher and co-planned with learners, parents, and teachers.

British Columbia's Interactive Discussion Guide involves the entire province. The Minister of Education invites teachers, learners, and parents to give their input on personalized learning. The guide interacts with the reader by letting learners describe what they like about school: "learning about bugs . . . playing outside . . . following their interests." Table 4.1 summarizes learner stages in British Columbia's Personalized Learning Plan.

| | Learners | Teachers |
|---|---|---|
| **Early Years** | Young learners may say they are learning through play from their teachers and other learners. | Young learners may ask the teacher to guide them and their family in planning their learning. |
| **Middle Years** | In the middle school years, learners may be exploring things in which they are interested. | Middle school learners may ask the teacher to guide them in applying their reading, writing, and math skills to a variety of projects. |
| **High School Years** | High school learners may want to work by themselves and with others in inquiry and project-based learning situations. | High school learners may ask their teacher to facilitate their learning opportunities or directly teach them what they need to know. |

**Table 4.1**   British Columbia's Personalized Learning Plan

*Source:* Interactive Discussion Guide, 2011

> "**Learner agency** is characterized by a pedagogy that builds on the passions of learners and also has real world relevance. We are seeing numerous examples of this in our schools, and the school structure is also beginning to change to accommodate this transition. Schools are adopting more flexible schedules, new and more personalized methods of reporting are being adopted, and examples of hands-on experiences from outdoor learning to community business partnerships are flourishing. Many do see learner agency as being key to the future of schooling."
>
> —Chris Kennedy (2013), Superintendent of Schools in West Vancouver, British Columbia

Personalized learning combines the How and What of learning. A personalized approach recognizes that there are still core requirements and expectations. There are still required skills—reading, writing, oral language, numeracy—and required knowledge in various subjects or disciplines. However, with personalized learning, there is an increased emphasis on the following competencies:

- Social responsibility
- Global and cultural understanding
- Environmental stewardship
- Healthy living
- Ethics collaboration
- Creativity
- Innovation
- Critical thinking and problem solving
- Digital literacy

## State of Maryland

In 2010, the legislators in Maryland took the unprecedented action of passing a bill to establish a task force to explore the principles of

Universal Design for Learning (UDL) to be included in education systems in that state.

For several months following, the twenty-two-member UDL Task Force chaired by Denise C. DeCoste, EdD, gathered broad support by all stakeholders and began researching UDL. In March 2011, the UDL Task Force published its report, *A Route for Every Learner: Universal Design for Learning (UDL) as a Framework for Supporting Learning and Improving Achievement for All Learners in Maryland, Pre-kindergarten Through Higher Education.*

It made recommendations on the steps that could be taken by the Maryland Board of Education, the Maryland State Department, the institution of higher education, and local school systems to lay the foundation for increased implementation of the application of **UDL principles** in the coming years. The task force strongly stated that "UDL serves as a framework that needs to be integrated into the design and implementation of curriculum, instruction, and assessment" (Maryland State Department of Education, 2011).

One year later in March 2012, the Maryland State Board of Education took the bold step of passing regulations that would require local school systems to apply UDL principles and guidelines in the development of curriculum, instruction, instructional materials, professional development, and assessments for all learners.

Since UDL is the framework for personalized learning, Maryland's journey will be crucial to follow and share results from the schools around the state.

## POLICIES AND INITIATIVES IMPACTING SYSTEM CHANGE

### Course Credit Policies

When educational policies are changed across a state or country, it is big. It impacts school communities and changes systems. In fact, policies are being developed to move to **competency-based systems** in a majority of states according to the report *50 States Scan Course Credit Policies,* by the Carnegie Foundation (2013).

As part of the Carnegie Foundation's reevaluation of the Carnegie Unit, K–12 credit policies were explored in all 50 states and the District of Columbia to better understand which states define credit based solely on seat time and which allow districts to define credit more flexibly. The Carnegie Foundation's (2013) report concluded the following:

Based on a scan of state policy language (code, regulation board policy, etc.) and conversations with officials from state departments of educations, findings were organized into five informational categories:

*Category 1)* The Carnegie Unit was abolished as primary measure of student learning. Credits must be awarded based on learners' mastery of content and skills rather than on seat time (1 state: New Hampshire).

*Category 2)* Districts define credits and may use seat time OR another measure, e.g., proficiency or competency, to award credit in core courses (29 states).

*Category 3)* Districts may apply for special-status or waivers to use measures other than seat time to award credit for core courses (4 states).

*Category 4)* Districts do not have any flexibility and must use time-based credits (11 states).

*Category 5)* Districts have some flexibility, but it is limited to special circumstances, such as credit-recovery programs or out-of-school learning, and may require approval from the state (6 states).

The Scan Report is a working draft that represents the most up-to-date research on each state's definition of course credit (Carnegie Foundation, 2013). Consider that twenty-nine states may use another measure or competencies to award credits. That means more than half the states are ready to move past course credit based on seat time. By the time the final report is released, there will probably be more states abolishing the Carnegie Unit.

## Council of Chief State School Officers and Innovation Lab Network

In November 2009, the Council of Chief State School Officers (CCSSO) and the Stupski Foundation established the Partnership for Next Generation Learning to create the innovation environments and flexibility that school, district, and state education leaders need in order to design systems that can deliver excellent learner outcomes on a broad scale. The Innovation Lab Network (ILN) is a group of states taking action to identify, test, and implement learner-centered approaches to learning that will transform our public education system. The goal of the ILN is to spur system-level change by scaling locally led innovation to widespread implementation, both within and across states, with a constant focus on learner outcomes. Current states in the ILN include California, Iowa, Kentucky, Maine, New Hampshire, Ohio, Oregon, West Virginia, and Wisconsin, including the Institute @ CESA #1. Schools and districts within these states have been given the opportunity to act as pressure testers of new and innovative ways to address the needs of their learners, with backing and support from their state departments of education. In the context of the ILN, CCSSO acts as a centralizing entity that facilitates collaboration and communication among ILN states and provides leadership as states move forward with their innovative efforts.

These innovations are grounded in shared principles, known as the *six critical attributes:*

1. Fostering world-class knowledge and skills

2. Learner agency

3. Personalized learning

4. Performance-based learning

5. Anytime/anywhere opportunities

6. Providing comprehensive systems of learner support

The ILN works to encourage states to operationalize these principles through collaboration, transparency, and mutual support. States are encouraged to work closely with key players at the local, district, and state levels, as well as with outside stakeholder groups, including the business and higher education communities (Council of Chief State School Officers, 2014).

## Nellie Mae Foundation

The Nellie Mae Foundation's (2014) vision is for "all New England learners to graduate high school ready to thrive in college, work and in our communities." Since 1990, the foundation has focused on systems change and funding learner-centered programs and schools. It is working to reshape public education across New England to be more equitable

> **Pause/Think/Reflect**
>
> How do you remove the barriers and shape state and federal policy to promote deeper learning?

and more effective—so every learner graduates from high school prepared for success. With new approaches expanding learning beyond the school calendar and walls, all learners can develop skills and knowledge for life in our changing world.

The Nellie Mae Foundation's District-Level Systems Change initiative supports the needed shift in high school–level education to prepare learners to thrive in a global, complex, and fast-changing society based on these priorities:

- *Developing school and district designs and practices* that enable all learners to achieve high standards through student-centered approaches
- *Creating sustainable policy change* to support these new approaches
- *Generating public will and increasing demand* for changes in practice

The foundation's State-Level Systems Change (SLSC) initiative works to remove barriers and shape state and federal policies that promote deeper learning through learner-centered approaches based on these priorities:

- *Identifying public policy changes*, particularly at the state and federal level, needed to promote equitable learner-centered learning
- *Adopting and effectively implementing public policy changes* in New England states and districts and at the federal level
- *Applying public resources* equitably and effectively to implement these policies (Nellie Mae Foundation, 2014)

## The Institute @ CESA #1 Personalized Learning Initiative

The Institute @ CESA #1, a division of Cooperative Educational Service Agency #1, was established in 2010 to work with member school districts on a unique regional approach to transform public education in southeastern Wisconsin into a system that is learner-centered and personalized for each learner.

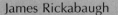

James Rickabaugh

Jim Rickabaugh, Director of the Institute @ CESA #1, explained that their work began with a white paper written by superintendents in the CESA #1 region. The paper laid out the arguments supporting a system redesign rather than reform work that just tweaked the old system. Their conclusion was that if they wanted change, they had to take it on themselves—no one was coming to help.

Shortly after publication of the white paper, Wisconsin joined the Innovation Lab Network, a group of states organized by the Council of Chief State School Officers, to implement student-centered approaches to learning. Wisconsin named CESA #1 as the site for the state's Innovation Lab, and the Institute @ CESA #1 was created. The Institute chose to focus on personalized learning to redesign public education. It believes that personalizing learning with students holds the greatest promise to transform the current educational design and create the capacity in the system to make the vision of getting learning right the first time for all learners a reality.

A personalized learning system allows all students to learn in the ways they learn best based on their needs, abilities, and preferences. Personalized learning also requires that the learner be a resource to his or her own learning, not simply a receptacle to be filled. Personalization is more than individualized learning or differentiated instruction. The Institute believes in three core components to a personalized learning system:

> "It seems like we were dismantling the systems we were charged to protect and not able to fully support the children we were supposed to develop. We then started on a journey to learn what could be done to make the system work for all learners without adding significant costs. We wrote a white paper that laid out the arguments and gave us hope that the system could be redesigned to have greater capacity instead of incremental reform work that was nothing more than tweaking the old system. Our initial inclination was that the cavalry was not going to save us and that the leadership had to come from the field. We still hold that view."
>
> —Jim Rickabaugh, Director, Institute @ CESA #1

- Comprehensive, data-rich learner profiles
- Customized learning paths
- Proficiency-based progress

The Institute developed a change strategy based on its honeycomb model, shown in Figure 4.1. This strategy guides its member districts as they participate in the Personalized Learning Initiative and is based on change in three areas: learning and teaching, relationships and roles, and structures and policies, to be addressed in three subsequent phases (Rickabaugh, 2012).

Under its model, using the core components as the innovation platform, change begins at the intersection of learning and teaching. This is necessary for any real, lasting transformation to take place; it's evident when examining past reform efforts that those that begin with structure and policy do not lead to dramatically different results. Fundamental changes to learning and teaching practices will then lead to changing roles and relationships for both educators and learners. Schools should not

**Figure 4.1** The Honeycomb Model

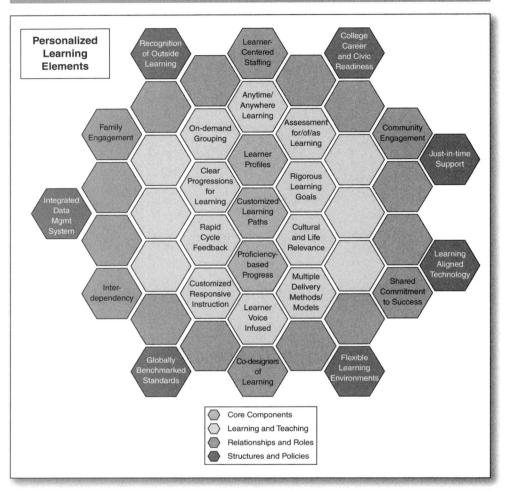

*Source:* http://theinstituteatcesa1.org

make structural changes until these new ways of learning and teaching begin to "bump up" against existing structures. Policy changes should be the very last thing addressed and should only be implemented to stabilize the transformed system.

The Institute uses an action network strategy to align and organize the work of the twenty-nine districts currently involved in the Personalized Learning Initiative. Some have been involved since the beginning, while others just joined the movement this year. Results have been very promising from those districts integrating multiple elements of the honeycomb into a cohesive personalized learning environment (Institute @ CESA #1, 2013).

# RESEARCHING PERSONALIZED LEARNING MODELS

## Characteristics

The personalized learning models in this chapter were chosen from a huge list of schools and districts. It was tough to choose some models over others. So included here is a wide range of models across grade levels with varying types of characteristics. The specific characteristics are listed in the sidebars with each model. Some of the characteristics identified include the following:

| | | |
|---|---|---|
| *Voice and Choice* | *Competency-Based* | *Multi-Age Classrooms* |
| *Play-Based Approach* | *Personal Learning Plans* | *Coaching Program* |
| *UDL for All Learners* | *Project-Based Learning* | *Technology Solutions* |
| *Internships* | *Flexible Learning Spaces* | *Inquiry-Based* |
| *Flexible Time* | *Community Partnerships* | *Self-Directed Learning* |

At the end of this chapter are some examples comparing some of the models with similar characteristics.

## Criteria

Schools and districts considering personalizing learning usually want to see examples and visit models for ideas on why they would want to adopt or adapt a model. Use the following criteria to help you determine if you want to adopt or adapt a model for your personalized learning system:

- Model is clear and defined (e.g., as personalized learning, competency-based or performance-based, or project-based.
- There is a shared vision and belief system about teaching and learning that includes all stakeholders.
- Policies are clearly described and refer to state and local school board policies that support the model.
- Alignment to Common Core State Standards and other standards.
- Partnerships may include community organizations, parents, businesses, and nonprofit and educational organizations with a clear description of what their partnerships involve.

- Resources may include examples, projects, stories, brochures, presentations, lessons, videos, rubrics, forms, and checklists.
- Data include summative and formative assessments, analysis of test results, examples of rubrics, outcomes, and evidence of learning.
- Contact information includes a contact form, contact information for multiple people, and other ways to reach the model.

Choose the characteristics that relate to your focus. Then use the previous criteria for any model that could support your journey in personalizing learning. The following models and examples are just a sampling of personalized learning environments starting to pop up everywhere.

## TRANSFORMATIVE LARGE-SCALE MODELS

### Montessori Education

Maria Montessori (1870–1952), Italian physician and educator, developed an educational approach focusing on the learner in the 1920s. Montessori education serves toddlers to children eighteen years old and is practiced in around 20,000 schools worldwide. Montessori education emphasizes independence, freedom within limits, and respect for a child's natural psychological development. The Montessori approach includes the following:

> **Why adapt or adopt the Montessori model?**
>
> - Multi-age classrooms
> - Constructivist model
> - Learning based on choice
> - Flexible time
> - Self-directed learning

- Classrooms with mixed ages
- Learners having choices of activity
- Large blocks of uninterrupted time
- Learners learning by doing and working with materials rather than by direct instruction
- A Constructivist model where learners discover as they learn

Montessori is an educational approach based on a model of human development with two basic elements:

- Learners of all ages interact with their environments by engaging in construction of their own learning.
- Young children, especially under the age of six, follow an innate path of cognitive development motivated to learn.

Montessori believed that children who have the freedom to choose what they want to learn and are able to move freely within an environment would move toward what is optimum for their development. Children are seen as driving their behavior in every stage of development. Montessori believed education should respond to and facilitate learning around each child's

- Self-preservation
- Orientation to the environment
- Exploration
- Communication
- Work described as "purposeful activity"
- Manipulation of the environment

**Pause/Think/Reflect**

According to Montessori, children naturally engage in self-directed learning and independent study. Teachers should act as observers and facilitators of that learning and not as lecturers or commanders.

Association Montessori Internationale, 2013; Shaw, 2013

### *Montessori's Alumni*

The Montessori educational approach has an interesting group of alumni: Google's founders Larry Page and Sergei Brin, Amazon's Jeff Bezos, videogame pioneer Will Wright, and Wikipedia founder Jimmy Wales, not to mention Julia Child. Barbara Walters interviewed Larry Page and Sergey Brin, who credited their years as Montessori students as a major factor behind their success, on the ABC-TV special *The 10 Most Fascinating People of 2004*. Walters asked them if their college professor parents were a factor behind their success. They said that it was their going to a Montessori school where they learned to be self-directed and self-starters. They said that Montessori education allowed them to learn to think for themselves and gave them freedom to pursue their own interests.

Daniel Pink's bestseller *Drive* discusses our changing understanding of motivation and what leads to high performance and success, especially as we advance into the twenty-first century. Within that context, Pink showcases Montessori as one of a select group of "forward-thinking" educational models that "get it" when it comes to education and motivation.

Pink (2009) writes about Montessori schools:

Many of the key tenets of a Montessori education resonate with the principles of Motivation 3.0—that children naturally engage in self-directed learning and independent study; that teachers should act as observers and facilitators of that learning, and not as lecturers or commanders; and that children are naturally inclined to experience periods of intense focus, concentration, and flow that adults should do their best not to interrupt. Although Montessori schools are rare at the junior high and high school levels, every school, educator, and parent can learn from its enduring and successful approach. (p. 182)

## The Walker Learning Approach

### Play-Based and Personalized Approach for Preschool to Year 8 in Australia

The Walker Learning Approach (WLA) is an Australian-designed teaching and learning approach (pedagogy) that authentically personalizes learning and is developmentally and culturally appropriate. Learning is real, relevant, and meaningful for all children regardless of their age, culture, family context, socioeconomic background, or geographical position. The Walker Learning Approach has been developed over twenty years using an action research model. The pedagogical platform places the child at the center and uses developmental psychology, biology, and neurology alongside cultural and environmental influences as the basis for practical application across the Australian setting. Developmental psychology in recent years has been misinterpreted and misrepresented by some aspects of the educational academic forum with the assumption that the Piagetian model of a lockstep, monocultural stage ("norm") of developmental milestones prevails.

This is not what developmental psychology in the twenty-first century purports, nor does it represent the platform of the Walker Learning Approach. Developmental psychology recognizes key elements of genetic predisposition; assists in areas of temperament and personality; informs greatly in areas of brain development and stimulation; is cross-cultural; and informs in key areas including motivation, engagement, behavior, development, cognitive function, learning, and areas requiring intervention. It works alongside recognition of the influences of culture, environment, health, nutrition, and exposure and opportunity. The need to integrate and work in

**Figure 4.2** The Walker Learning Approach

the **Walker Learning Approach**

DEVELOPMENTALLY & CULTURALLY APPROPRIATE PRACTICE

**Why adapt or adopt the Walker Learning Approach model?**

- Research around pedagogy and personalized learning
- Action research model
- Learning is real, relevant, and meaningful
- Play-based approach
- Learning is culturally and developmentally appropriate
- Self-directed producers and learners

**Pause/Reflect/Discuss**

How do we facilitate the work of youth as self-directed producers and learners?

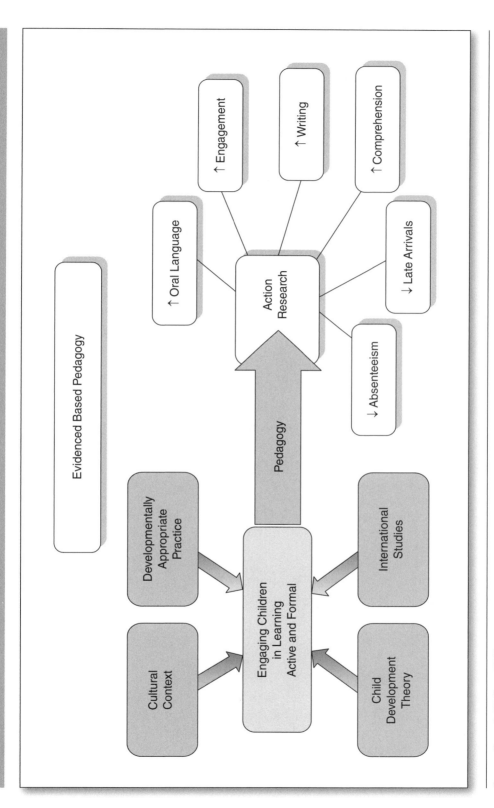

**Figure 4.3** Evidence-Based Pedagogy

*Source:* Bass & Walker, 2013

The Walker Learning Approach is the first pedagogy to be designed for Australian schools, successfully providing teaching and learning that

- personalizes and engages learners in active learning alongside explicit and formalized instruction.
- is culturally and developmentally appropriate across all demographic regions of the country, from remote indigenous communities to elite independent schools.

tandem with the empirical evidence of science, psychology, neuropsychology, and cultural influences on learning is critical, and the WLA does just that (Walker, 2012).

The Walker Learning Approach is an exciting and refreshing philosophy that places the child at the center of the curriculum and teaching strategies; it ensures authentic personalized learning. It is based on decades of research on play-based and personalized learning and social constructivism. It is not a program or an inquiry model sitting discreetly or separately from other curriculum areas. It is a total approach to teaching and learning that combines the need for children to be active participants in their learning through hands-on and creative exploration and investigation that sits alongside formal instruction.

Figure 4.3 (see page 125) illustrates the Walker Learning Approach's belief that pedagogy is based on action research.

Some of the key goals for children's learning are to promote in them the ability to think laterally and creatively: to be able to self-initiate, to explore the properties and elements of things, to problem solve, to take risks, to think deeply, to construct ideas and meaning, to use their own understandings and discover new ones, to become interested in endless possibilities and opportunities, and to become increasingly intrinsically motivated to learn, to find out, to try, to have a go, and to develop resiliency.

## Reggio Emilia Approach

**Why adapt or adopt the Reggio Emilia Approach?**

- Learning is visible
- Learning spaces are the third educator
- Learning is based on self-interests
- Learning through interactions with others
- Learning is documented by adults

Loris Malaguzzi (1920–1994) founded the Reggio Emilia approach in Reggio Emilia, a city in northern Italy, after World War II for municipal child care and education programs serving children younger than six. This approach requires children to be seen as competent, resourceful, curious, imaginative, and inventive and possess a desire to interact and communicate with others.

The Reggio vision of the child as a competent learner has produced a strong child-directed curriculum model that has a purposive progression. There is no scope and sequence and teachers do not provide focused instruction in reading and writing. Children learn through interaction with peers, parents, and staff in a friendly learning environment.

- The environment of the school is seen as the third educator, after the teacher and the parent.
- Children actively participate in their learning by following their own interests.
- The teacher and parent are essential resources as collaborators in the child's process of learning.
- Teachers make learning visible by documenting activities and tracking children's thoughts and ideas as they play together or work with materials.

The Reggio approach does not have defined methods, standards, or an accreditation process. Educators in Reggio Emilia schools see themselves as a reference point for learners. They provide a way of engaging in dialogue that starts with learners and their questions. Educators and parents use documentation to promote an understanding of their child's learning and development.

The learning spaces in a Reggio class invite curiosity, creativity, and collaboration. The Reggio Emilia approach is expanding across K–12, especially the Reggio influence on design of the learning environment (Klein, 2008; Reggio Kids, 2014).

> **Pause/Think/Reflect**
>
> How does the environment foster children's curiosity and creativity?

## Coalition of Essential Schools

In 1984, Ted Sizer founded the Coalition of Essential Schools (CES) to bring together examples of the radical school restructuring that was the focus of *Horace's Compromise,* Sizer's work about the state of American high schools. The book follows Horace, a veteran English teacher in a normal American high school. Horace starts early and works way into the night doing what he can to support each and every learner. With fifty-minute

> **Why adapt or adopt the Coalition of Essential Schools model?**
>
> - School restructured around powerful learning and trust
> - Small, personalized learning communities
> - Coaching model
> - Equitable and intellectually challenging schools
> - Honors diversity
> - Demonstration of mastery in exhibitions

periods, a requirement to grade each learner, and taking on additional commitments, Horace realizes his high standards are higher than is possible within his traditional school setting. Teachers like Horace were still held responsible for learners learning even though the system was broken (Sizer, 2004).

This premise is why Sizer and others developed CES to create and sustain personalized, equitable, and intellectually challenging schools. Visit an Essential School and you will see places of powerful learning where all learners have the chance to reach their fullest potential. Essential Schools include hundreds of schools and more than two dozen CES Affiliate Centers that serve learners from pre-kindergarten through high school in urban, suburban, and rural communities as small schools and schools within large comprehensive schools.

CES practice includes small, personalized learning communities where teachers and learners know each other well in a climate of trust, decency, and high expectations for all. Essential Schools work to create academic success for every learner by sharing decision making and helping all learners use their minds well through standards-aligned interdisciplinary studies, community-based real-world learning, and performance-based assessment.

### The CES Common Principles

The CES Common Principles are a guiding philosophy rather than a replicable model for schools.

Based on years of research and practice, the CES principles reflect the wisdom of thousands of educators who are successfully engaged in creating personalized, equitable, and academically challenging schools for all young people.

1. *Learning to use one's mind well.* The school should focus on helping young people learn to use their minds well. Schools should not be "comprehensive" if such a claim is made at the expense of the school's central intellectual purpose.

2. *Less is more, depth over coverage.* The school's goals should be simple: that each student master a limited number of essential skills and areas of knowledge. While these skills and areas will, to varying degrees, reflect the traditional academic disciplines, the program's design should be shaped by the intellectual and imaginative powers and competencies that the students need, rather than by "subjects"

as conventionally defined. The aphorism "less is more" should dominate: curricular decisions should be guided by the aim of thorough student mastery and achievement rather than by an effort to merely cover content.

3. *Goals apply to all students.* The school's goals should apply to all students, while the means to these goals will vary as those students themselves vary. School practice should be tailor-made to meet the needs of every group or class of students.

4. *Personalization.* Teaching and learning should be personalized to the maximum feasible extent. Efforts should be directed toward a goal that no teacher have direct responsibility for more than 80 students in the high school and middle school and no more than 20 in the elementary school. To capitalize on this personalization, decisions about the details of the course of study, the use of students' and teachers' time and the choice of teaching materials and specific pedagogies must be unreservedly placed in the hands of the principal and staff.

5. *Student-as-worker, teacher-as-coach.* The governing practical metaphor of the school should be student-as-worker, rather than the more familiar metaphor of teacher-as-deliverer-of-instructional-services. Accordingly, a prominent pedagogy will be coaching, to provoke students to learn how to learn and thus to teach themselves.

6. *Demonstration of mastery.* Teaching and learning should be documented and assessed with tools based on student performance of real tasks. Students not yet at appropriate levels of competence should be provided intensive support and resources to assist them quickly to meet those standards. Multiple forms of evidence, ranging from ongoing observation of the learner to completion of specific projects, should be used to better understand the learner's strengths and needs, and to plan for further assistance. Students should have opportunities to exhibit their expertise before family and community. The diploma should be awarded upon a successful final demonstration of mastery for graduation—an "Exhibition." As the diploma is awarded when earned, the school's program proceeds with no strict age grading and with no system of "credits earned" by "time spent" in class. The emphasis is on the students' demonstration that they can do important things.

7. *A tone of decency and trust.* The tone of the school should explicitly and self-consciously stress values of unanxious expectation ("I won't threaten you but I expect much of you"), of trust (until abused) and of decency (the values of fairness, generosity and tolerance). Incentives appropriate to the school's particular students and teachers should be emphasized. Parents should be key collaborators and vital members of the school community.

8. *Commitment to the entire school.* The principal and teachers should perceive themselves as generalists first (teachers and scholars in general education) and specialists second (experts in but one particular discipline). Staff should expect multiple obligations (teacher-counselor-manager) and a sense of commitment to the entire school.

9. *Resources dedicated to teaching and learning.* Ultimate administrative and budget targets should include student loads that promote personalization, substantial time for collective planning by teachers, competitive salaries for staff, and an ultimate per pupil cost not to exceed that at traditional schools by more than 10 percent. To accomplish this, administrative plans may have to show the phased reduction or elimination of some services now provided students in many traditional schools.

10. *Democracy and equity.* The school should demonstrate non-discriminatory and inclusive policies, practices, and pedagogies. It should model democratic practices that involve all who are directly affected by the school. The school should honor diversity and build on the strength of its communities, deliberately and explicitly challenging all forms of inequity.

*Source:* Coalition of Essential Schools, 2014

### Kathleen's Story

My youngest son attended Souhegan High School, a member of the Coalition of Essential Schools, in Amherst, New Hampshire from 1997 to 2001 where he learned how he learns best. In his sophomore year, he led a parent/teacher/peer conference where he used a two-year portfolio to reflect on his learning.

This was a turning point for him as he struggled with speaking to an audience, and now he was articulating what and how he learned to teachers, peers, and his parents. He finally understood who he was as a learner and forged ahead the next two years invested in his learning with the guidance of some outstanding educators who always provided him excellent feedback in his writing and projects. He went on to Clark University where he graduated with honors.

*Big Picture Learning's motto is that "education is everyone's business."*

## Big Picture Learning Schools

Big Picture Learning's (BPL) mission is the education of a nation, one learner at a time. Dennis Littky and Elliot Washor established Big Picture Learning in 1995 with the sole mission of encouraging, inciting, and effecting change in the U. S. educational system.

BPL's vision is to make changes in K–adult education by generating and sustaining innovative, personalized learning environments that work with their community. At the core of Big Picture Learning's mission is a commitment to equity for all learners, especially underserved urban learners, and the expectation that these learners can achieve success. Big Picture Learning designs innovative learning environments, researches and replicates new models for learning, and trains educators to serve as leaders in their schools and communities.

Learners find their career path at a Big Picture Learning School by job shadowing and working on projects they are passionate about. One Wow example is a project where a ninth grader's uncle was shot and killed in a bar. The person who shot him was never caught. This learner worked to get legislation to have cameras placed on the doors of bars. He had to talk to people and check the laws. He was persistent and would not give up. He found some camera companies to donate cameras to use as examples. His work paid off, and cameras were placed on the doors. This is just one example of authentic learning about something someone was really interested in (Big Picture Learning, 2014).

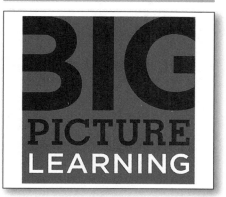

**Figure 4.4** Big Picture Learning

---

**Why adapt or adopt the Big Picture Learning model?**

- Educators as leaders
- Community of learners with equity for all
- Learning through internships
- Learners find and follow career path
- Continuously improving school culture
- Schools have more autonomy

---

**Pause/Think/Reflect**

The Big Picture Learning philosophy started with a question: "If we didn't know there was such a thing as school, what would it be?"

Elliot Washor

Elliot Washor, co-founder of Big Picture Learning, believes the Wow is personalization when the focus is on the learner.

Since our beginnings, personalization has been at the core of our work. We strive for schools to be communities where every learner is known through their interests, academics and how they are doing socially and emotionally in and outside of school. Here the twist is that the learner is known well because it is the learner who tells and the teacher who listens and observes rather than adults who are only telling what they know or suggesting what you need to know.

In this real time environment, there are lots of variables to how, when, what and why a learner learns. These variables change all the time and they are hard to measure and hard to predict. The good news is that this keeps all of us engaged and on our toes. Figuring out things is what we are good at as humans. It makes everyone a part of a community that listens, observes and communicates. (Washor, 2014)

> *"Design is in the doing."*
>
> —Elliot Washor

There are over sixty BPL schools in fourteen states, with schools in Australia, Israel, and the Netherlands. Most of the learners at their first school, the MET, were high-poverty at-risk students who demonstrated increased graduation rates. This got the attention of the Gates Foundation, who funded them to now expand to fifty-two charter schools in the United States with fifty in other countries for a total of 26,000 students. BPL schools have more **autonomy**, younger staff, and a smaller size of fewer than two hundred students.

In Big Picture Learning Schools learners are individuals within a community of learners. The Big Picture Learning design grapples deeply with the culture of schools and how it makes deep learning as well as community possible. When you visit a Big Picture Learning school consider the following questions:

- How can schools be welcoming and transformative places for learners, staff, and families?
- What is the relationship between school culture and the success of our learners?
- How can school staff work intentionally on school culture? (Big Picture Schools, 2014)

The Big Picture Learning Cycle can be broken down into the following six stages after starting with your interests and passions as a foundation for learning:

1. Make it work for you: the learning plan
2. Pursue your passions: internship placement
3. Make it real: learning through internship
4. Organize and do it
5. Exhibit it
6. Reflect and assess it

*"It is the learner who tells and the teacher who listens and observes rather than adults who are only telling what they know or suggesting what you need to know."*

—Elliot Washor

## EdVisions Schools

Keven Kroehler started EdVisions in 1997 with teachers who put together what school should be with learners working on what they are passionate about. EdVision's vision is to change schools and schooling by establishing a network of over forty schools in eleven states with fundamental differences in teaching, learning, and leading that will provide meaningful options for learners, parents, and educators.

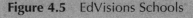

**Figure 4.5** EdVisions Schools

Their mission is to create schools that enhance relationships and build relevant learning environments that empower learners, parents, and teachers to make choices. These learning environments incorporate self-directed, **project-based learning** to build

**Why adapt or adopt
EdVisions Schools model?**

- Small learning communities with mentoring available
- Self-directed learners that have autonomy
- Project-based learning
- Personalized learning plans
- Professional development plans

student autonomy through relevant learning opportunities; create learner belongingness through full-time advisories; and empower teachers via teacher-led and democratically governed schools. To create engaging schools of this nature requires EdVisions to engage in dialogue concerning the nature of learning and assessment that aligns with whole-child development rather than academic achievement alone (EdVisions Schools, 2011).

*"What does school look like?"*

—Keven Kroehler

Keven Kroehler explained that most schools want their graduates to go on to lead successful lives. For example, Minneapolis Public Schools has this mission: "We support [student] growth into knowledgeable, skilled and confident citizens capable of succeeding in their work, personal and family lives into the 21st century" (Kroehler, 2014). He shared EdVisions mission and why hope matters for all learners.

Since the designing of the first EdVisions school in the early 1990's, we have held to a mission of success in the future for our learners. As we consider reforming schools, it seems to me that we should ask, "What is a proven way to get this future success?" We all have our own answers to this question, but EdVisions' schools have built on the research that says learners that can set reasonable goals for themselves, make plans to meet those goals, and persist to actually achieve those goals are well positioned for success in the future. The late Dr. Rick Snyder out of the University of Kansas began this work, EdVisions has done research around this idea, and Dr. Shane Lopez now at the Gallup Student Poll continues with this work. The late Dr. Rick Snyder defined hope as a learner's ability to:

- set reasonable goals,
- make plans for those goals, and
- persist to achieve those goals.

When we focus on hope, we are focusing on a disposition in learners that sets them up for future success. I do want to point out that this idea of hope is more than just a skill that can be taught in a class; it needs to grow inside a learner and become part of who s/he is. The research that EdVisions has worked on regarding hope focuses on what needs to exist in schools to build this hope. In the end we have come up with a recipe that schools can use to increase hope based on Dr. Mark Van Ryzin and Dr. Ron Newell's book *Assessing What Really Matters in Schools* [Newell, Ryzin, & Meier, 2009]. When learners have autonomy, a mastery goal orientation, academic press from adults, and a feeling of belongingness with the teacher and peers, then the school has an environment conducive to engaging and motivating learners. When that happens, learners also build hope. (Kroehler, 2014)

> *"Are we turning out productive learners, or simply academic achievers?"*
>
> —Keven Kroehler

## Expeditionary Learning Schools

Expeditionary Learning (EL) partners with schools, districts, and charter boards to open new schools and transform existing schools. They provide school leaders and teachers with professional development, curriculum planning resources, and new school structures to boost learner engagement, character, and achievement.

### *About EL Learners*

Learners are energized by motivation and engagement through high-level tasks and active roles in the classroom. They use case studies and projects to connect to real-world audiences and compel them to care and contribute. They set clear expectations and follow-through for respect and responsibility, teamwork and contribution, and

**Why adapt or adopt the Expeditionary Learning Schools model?**

- High-level tasks and active roles
- Problem-solving and critical-thinking skills
- Connecting learners to real-world audiences
- Safe school culture where everyone is respected
- Collaborative community of practice

commitment to high-quality work. There is a school culture where learners feel safe, respected, and pushed to be their best selves. Learners are encouraged to participate in deep cognitive challenges and given important responsibilities that prepare them to be leaders. Projects develop the critical-thinking and problem-solving skills learners need to succeed in college and beyond.

### About EL Teachers

Professional development is active and immediately useful in instruction. Teachers are respected as professionals and develop their growth as leaders that catalyze improvement in new and veteran teachers. Teachers use judgment and creativity when addressing standards and assessment practices that occur daily in the classroom. Practice is guided by models of teacher and learners' work. There is a collaborative community of practice to support each other.

There are 165 EL schools in thirty-one states and the District of Columbia, with over 45,000 learners and 4,000 teachers and leaders where each school shares stories of motivated learners. EL develops projects that demonstrate learners' motivation and habits of work and character that produce high-quality products that matter in the real world. The power of these projects is how learners not only get involved in the projects but find a problem and drive the project based on what they believe matters (Expeditionary Learning, 2013a).

It's all about the stories and learners' voices. Here are two examples of learners at EL schools driving their learning.

Monarch Academy in Glen Burnie, Maryland, had eighth-grade students partner with the Maryland Historical Society to document civil rights–era stories. They did over twenty-two interviews with those in their eighties and asked what it was like growing up as an African American in the 1950s. They interviewed Charles Culver, eighty-one, who was very candid about what it was like, and the interviewers learned that there were many important moments to the civil rights movement—even small moments that made a difference (Monarch Academy, 2012).

Seventh-grade learners at Four Rivers Charter Public School in Greenfield, Massachusetts, created the *Life in a Vernal Pool* field guide as part of an expedition on vernal pools. Designed for young children, the field guide includes paintings, descriptions, and original folktales about animals that live in and around vernal pools. Sections for each animal include description, habitat, diet, natural history, taxonomy, and life cycle. The book was donated to the local public library. Thanks to these seventh graders' thorough research and advocacy, they achieved real change in their community (Expeditionary Learning, 2013b).

These are just two examples of learners in EL schools following what they are interested in, using inquiry, and investigating problems using critical-thinking and problem-solving skills.

## Kunskapsskolan Education Design

Kunskapsskolan (KED) was founded in 1999 and currently operates twenty-eight secondary schools for learners ages twelve to sixteen and eight schools for sixteen- to nineteen-year-olds, totaling 10,000 learners in Sweden and other countries. KED's mission is to provide schools where learners, through personalized learning and clear goals, will stretch their boundaries and learn more than they thought possible.

KED is learner-centered. Personalized education means that the school and the teachers start from and adapt themselves to learners' goals, ambitions, and their potentials—not the opposite. KED has expanded to other countries, including the United States (Kunskapskolan Education, 2014).

> **Why adapt or adopt Kunskapsskolan Education Design model?**
>
> - Teaching adapts to learner's goals
> - Each learner has a personal learning coach
> - Learners and teachers are partners in learning
> - Inquiry-based curriculum
> - Leveraging all resources to meet learners' needs

## Vittra Schools in Sweden

Vittra runs thirty schools in Sweden and wants learning to take place everywhere in its schools, so it threw out the "old-school" thinking of straight desks in a line in a four-walled classroom. It eliminated all of its classrooms in favor of an environment that fosters children's "curiosity and creativity." The schools are nontraditional in every sense: there are no

> **Why adapt or adopt the Vittra Schools model?**
>
> - Environments foster curiosity and creativity
> - Free admission for Swedish citizens
> - No letter grades
> - Flexible spaces for K–12
> - Inviting furniture made for flexible learning spaces

letter grades, and learners learn in groups at their level, not necessarily by age. Admission to the school is free, as long as the child has a personal number (like a social security number) and one of the child's parents is a Swedish taxpayer.

Architect Rosan Bosch designed one of the Vittra schools, Telefonplan, so children could work independently in opened spaces while lounging or go to "the village" to work on group projects. All of the furniture in the school is meant to aid learners in engaging in conversations while working on projects. Telefonplan has five learning spaces:

1. *The Cave* is a private space to concentrate on learning.

2. *The Lab* is a flexible space with lab trolleys for experimentation and practical work to discover and explore colors, shapes, and materials.

3. *The Camp Fire* is an important space for large as well as small groups because learning is a social process.

4. *The Watering Hole* is a place where learners can drop in for a while and then move on.

5. *The Showoff* is the place where learners can show off progress and discoveries.

Vittra Schools reach kindergarten through twelfth grade. One thing clear from these examples is that opening the walls, moving or changing the furniture, and allowing flexible places encourages creativity. It works for all ages. More of the examples and models we share in this chapter have new learning spaces. The environment and spaces make a difference in how learners learn (Vittra Schools, 2013).

## High Tech High

**Why adapt or adopt the High Tech High model?**

- Internships, fieldwork, and community service
- Project-based activities based on passions
- Twenty-first-century skills
- Teachers as curriculum designers

The roots of the High Tech High (HTH) program and curriculum lie in earlier work of Larry Rosenstock and colleagues in the New Urban High School Project (NUHS), an initiative of the U.S. Department of Education's Office of Vocational and Adult Education (1996–1999). High Tech High began in 2000 as a single charter high school launched by a coalition of San Diego business leaders and educators.

The aim was to select, study, and assist six inner-city high schools that were using school-to-work strategies, such as internships and other forms of field work, as a lever for whole-school change. It has evolved into an integrated network of schools spanning Grades K–12, housing a comprehensive teacher certification program and a new, innovative Graduate School of Education.

High Tech High operates eleven schools in San Diego County in California: two elementary schools, four middle schools, and five high schools. These schools serve a diverse, lottery-selected learner population; all embody the High Tech High four design principles:

> **Pause/Reflect/Discuss**
>
> How do we ensure authentic personalized learning?

1. *Personalization*

High Tech High teachers know their learners well and are committed to a learner-centered approach that supports and challenges each student. Through projects, learners pursue their passions and continually reflect on their learning and growth. Learners with special needs are supported through a full inclusion model. Each High Tech High learner has a faculty advisor who meets regularly with a small group of learners to build community, support their academic progress, and plan for their future. Advisors also visit each of their advisee's homes and serve as a point of contact for the family.

2. *Adult World Connection*

HTH learners connect their studies to the world beyond school through field studies, community service, internships, and consultation with outside experts. Learners routinely create work for authentic audiences and exhibit that work in professional venues. All high school learners complete substantial internships in the world of work and service, where they develop projects that contribute to the workplace. The HTH facilities have a distinctive "workplace" feel, with windowed seminar rooms, small-group learning and project areas, laboratories equipped with the latest technology, ubiquitous wireless laptop access, and common areas where artwork and prototypes are displayed.

3. *Common Intellectual Mission*

High Tech High schools are diverse and integrated. Enrollment is non-selective via a zip code–based lottery, and there is no tracking of learners by perceived academic ability. All HTH learners pursue a rigorous curriculum that provides the foundation for entry and success at the University of California and elsewhere, as well as success in the world of work. Schools articulate common expectations for learning that value twenty-first-century skills, the integration of hands and minds, and the merging of academic disciplines. Assessment is performance based: all learners develop projects, solve problems, and present findings to community panels. All learners are required to complete an academic internship, a substantial senior project, and a personal digital portfolio. Teachers employ a variety of approaches to accommodate diverse learners and recognize the value of having learners from different backgrounds working together.

4. *Teacher as Designer*

High Tech High teachers are program and curriculum designers. They work in interdisciplinary teams to design the courses they teach. They take the lead in staff meetings and action groups addressing school issues. They participate in critical decisions regarding curriculum, assessment, professional development, hiring, and other significant areas of the school. The schedule supports team teaching, and teachers have ample planning time to devise integrated projects, common rubrics for assessment, and common rituals by which all learners demonstrate their learning and progress toward graduation.

HTH's personalized, hands-on approach to learning, along with its emphasis on connecting to the adult world through internships, has afforded traditionally underserved learners access to college and other postsecondary options. Teachers are positioned for success, too, working in teams that deal with the same cohort of learners. They come to school an hour before learners each day to plan, discuss student work, and engage in professional development activities (High Tech High, 2012).

## Sudbury Valley Schools

Sudbury Valley Schools was founded in 1968 in Framingham, Massachusetts. The model has three basic goals: educational freedom, democratic governance, and personal responsibility.

---

**Why adapt or adopt the Sudbury Valley Schools model?**

- **Self-governance** of school by learners and staff
- Learners learn at their own pace
- Freedom to pursue own interests
- Play is important to learn

---

Since its founding in 1968, Sudbury Valley has been a place where children can enjoy life, liberty and the pursuit of happiness as they grow up in the newly emerging world. From the beginning of their enrollment, no matter what their age, students are given the freedom to use their time as they wish, and the responsibility for designing their path to adulthood.

Students are able to develop traits that are key to achieving success: They are comfortable learning new things; confident enough to rely on their own judgment; and capable of pursuing their passions to a high level of competence. Children at Sudbury Valley are adaptable to rapid change, open to innovation and creative in solving new problems. Beyond that, they grow to be trustworthy and responsible individuals, and function as contributing members of a free society.

At Sudbury Valley, students from pre-school through high school age explore the world freely at their own pace and in their own unique ways. They develop the ability to direct their own lives, be accountable for their actions, set priorities, allocate resources, deal with complex ethical issues, and work with others in a vibrant community. Sudbury Valley Schools offers children opportunities to have a voice in their learning and in a choice how they learn. The focus is on self-governance, freedom to choose, and the importance of play.

### Self-Governance

Everyone has an equal vote in managing the school. That includes every student and every staff member. There are weekly school meetings on issues like staff hiring, behavior, financing and how to use the facilities. Responsibilities are delegated to either students or staff members. Everyone participates in Sudbury Valley's judicial system that is the key to establishing the student's confidence in the school.

### Freedom to Choose

The school's philosophy is based on the fact that children naturally want to learn the skills needed to grow into capable adults. And just like grownups, they want to be free to choose how they will become successful. Given the freedom to pursue their interests for as long as the interest lasts, and the structure to ensure their activities are neither infringed upon nor infringe on the rights of others, children learn what they need. The freedom to choose how one will spend one's time every day, coupled with the obligation to fulfill one's duties as a member of the community, builds personal responsibility and citizenship.

## Importance of Play

When given the time and the space to decide what they want to do, students look deeply within themselves and discover just what it is that they need to be doing at any given moment. They learn to trust themselves and their own needs, so that they are able to make decisions about their actions throughout the school day. Without the constant barrage of adult agendas placed on them, students learn what it is like to be responsible for knowing themselves and finding out what their individual passions are. (Sudbury Valley School, 2013)

> **Pause/Reflect/Discuss**
>
> How do we connect with young people in a democratic learning community?

Sudbury Valley Schools offers a place where learners learn in an organic manner. They play, have a voice in how their school is governed, and do not attend regular classes. If you get a chance, set up a time to visit one of their schools to see self-directed learners of all ages.

## PERSONALIZED LEARNING DISTRICT MODELS

Some districts are jumping into personalized learning feet first. Here are a few districts that provide different approaches to personalize learning.

### Adams County School District 50, Colorado

Adams County School District 50 systemically introduces competency-based pathways starting with elementary school so high school learners are not confronted with not being able to graduate. Their concern was that too many learners were graduating without the mastery of skills and content required to be successful in life. The problem (not unique to their district) was that too many learners were moving through the system and getting a high school diploma by simply showing up for class, making some effort, and staying out of trouble. Too many learners had gaps in their learning that were never filled along the way.

Replacing grades with Levels 1–12 that incorporate standards from

> **Why adapt or adopt the Adams County School District 50 model?**
>
> - Learning at your own pace
> - Support and scaffolding for struggling learners
> - Competency-based pathways
> - No traditional letter grades and grade levels
> - Multi-age classrooms

elementary school through high school graduation, Adams County School District 50 is supporting teachers as they develop consensus on what proficiency looks like. Teachers work together around rubrics to determine when a learner's work should be considered emerging, developing, proficient, or advanced. The Colorado State Board of Education realized this last year and voted to implement Competency-Based High School Graduation Guidelines that are being phased in over the next seven years. Adams County School District 50's leadership testified in support of this proposal and the state is looking to them for leadership on this complicated issue. In their district learning is personalized, the constant, and time is the variable.

### Learning Is Personalized

Learners progress at their own pace with teacher guidance demonstrating proficiency on Learning Targets. Learning is personalized through goal setting and voice and choice with instruction. There are multiple opportunities over time to demonstrate competency of Learning Targets and no retention for struggling learners. They receive support and scaffolding through the Blended Services Model.

### Learning Is the Constant

Learners are placed at their appropriate development instructional level in each of the ten content areas based on demonstrated performance. Curriculum is guaranteed with Learning Targets and supporting materials made available to teachers, learners, and parents. Evidence toward proficiency for all Learning Targets is measured and recorded over time where the learner must score proficient or better before the next performance level. Learning progress is reported on a proficiency scale from 0.0 through 4.0. There are no traditional letter grades.

### Time Is the Variable

Learners advance to the next performance level in a content area once proficiency or better has been achieved and validated. Progression can occur at any point during the course of the year for any content area. At the beginning of the traditional school year, learners resume their learning at the point where they left off the previous year. There is no social promotion. Learners are typically in different performance levels for different content areas. Multi-age classrooms are the norm not the exception (Adams County School District 50, 2011).

## Colorado Springs School District 11

**Figure 4.6** Colorado Springs School District 11

**Why adapt or adopt the Colorado Springs School District 11 model?**

- Personalized learning lead educators
- Exemplar lessons
- On-demand resources
- Technology solutions for professional development

Greg Wilborn, Personalized Learning Coordinator, shared Colorado Springs School District 11's personalized learning vision:

> The desire to provide all learners with a personalized learning experience enabled by universal access to education through technology, wherever and whenever they choose. The provision of a personalized experience for each individual will drive learners' motivation to learn. They will have the opportunity to work individually, in groups, or as a whole class, locally, nationally and internationally. (Wilborn, 2012)

The Personalized Learning Lead Educator Group is instrumental in the development of exemplar lessons, demonstration classrooms, and ultimately demonstration schools that will be specific to leveled tiers ensuring appropriate differentiation.

### The Personalized Learning Lead Educator Group

- Shares research
- Develops learning resources around their area of expertise
- Delivers exemplar lessons that can be viewed by other teachers (live and/or recorded)
- Explores new and existing technologies
- Produces and/or finds guidance notes (e.g., podcasts, video) in their area of expertise
- Develops resources that promote an on-demand approach to professional development
- Uses technology to increase the flexibility of professional development (e.g., webinars)

According to the Colorado Springs School District 11 website (2011) the staff and school community are committed to the graduate who achieves the following:

Academic Preparedness: the foundation required for either higher education or workforce readiness.

Cultural Competence: the ability to understand and interpret political and cultural events from multiple perspectives in a global society.

High-Functioning Team Member: the ability to collaborate, facilitate, or contribute to the work of a group, and the ability to distinguish when each role is required.

Innovative Thinking and Problem-Solving Skills: the ability to identify pertinent from extraneous information in decision making.

Effective Use of Information Technology: the ability to identify and utilize appropriate media and technological tools.

Vital Participation in Civic Responsibility: the ability to share knowledge and participate productively as a member of a democratic society.

Effective Communication Skills: the ability to interact and correspond at various levels through a variety of mediums.

## Kennebec Intra-District Schools (KIDS) Regional School Unit, Maine (RSU 2)

RSU 2 is a K–12 performance-based system with a transparent curriculum. They have competencies aligned to measurement topics for every grade level. Learners move toward their learning targets by receiving a score of 3 on each these topics to demonstrate proficiency at their own pace. They have an internal data system to track every learner on every topic.

RSU 2 set out to create a standards-based, learner-centered education environment in March 2010 where they formed a committee that consisted of parents, teachers, administrators, and high school learners from each community in RSU 2. Their primary accomplishment of this committee was to develop a shared vision for RSU 2. They did exactly that. In January of 2011 the RSU 2 School Board

**Why adapt or adopt the RSU 2 model?**

- Shared vision and belief system
- K–12 performance-based system
- Standards-based, learner-centered framework
- Assessment and data system that supports and tracks learning
- 1:1 supports learner-centered environment

approved the committee's recommended shared vision: *The vision of RSU 2 is to be a system of student-centered learning.*

They took the next step by creating the RSU 2's Standards-Based, Learner-Centered Framework. What stands out in this framework is that they first developed a set of guiding principles with ten beliefs for each one of these topics:

- Children and learning
- Teachers and teaching
- Learning communities

To support these beliefs, they devised a set of commitments to fulfill their vision and beliefs:

- Standards-based curriculum design
- Assessment practices that support learning
- Learner-centered instructional strategies
- Use and develop effective, learner-centered teaching strategies
- Monitoring learning and providing feedback
- Continuous improvement

They also developed a process for standards-based learner-centered structures along with a set of action steps that includes curriculum and instruction, leadership, articulation agreements with higher education, and community learning partnerships. One example of an action step that encourages learner-centered environments is to focus on developing learner-centered instructional strategies including regrouping and strategic intervention. RSU 2 is well on their way to creating learning environments where every learner is motivated to learn (Kennebec Intra-District Schools, 2013).

## Taylor County Schools, Kentucky

Taylor County Schools uses **performance-based education** as a system of teaching and learning that places learners in grade-level content areas based on mental capacity rather than chronological age. Taylor County School's mission statement:

> **Why adapt or adopt the Taylor County Schools model?**
>
> - Performance-based education
> - Zero percent dropout policy
> - Career and college readiness
> - Community partnerships

Roger Cook, Superintendent, transformed Taylor County Schools into a performance-based educational system, challenged teachers and learners to meet twenty-first-century expectations with rigor and relevance, and spearheaded the effort to fund new, much-needed facilities. Part of the Performance-Based Education model is a zero percent dropout policy. Potential dropouts are required to meet with their guidance counselor, as well as Cook, to create a new plan tailored to their needs. Some of the students, for example, choose to complete classes online in the Virtual Program and find this environment better suited to their needs.

Roger Cook

Teachers in the district are highly trained professionals challenged to make learning fun, identify problems, and intervene when needed. Weekly, certified teachers participate in professional development during Early Release Fridays. The zero percent policy is aimed at learners in all grade levels. Each school runs a weekly watch list for struggling learners and those with poor attendance. The school counselor is contacted first and a number of interventions can be put in place based on the learner's needs. Those might include a home visit or support from the family resource center for basic needs.

> *"Providing an Equal Opportunity for ALL Learners to Reach their Maximum Potential"*
>
> —Roger Cook, Superintendent, Taylor County Schools, Kentucky

Roger shared the story of a learner who wanted to drop out to work on automobiles in his father's garage.

I agreed to let him work on automobiles all day but it had to be done at the area Vocational Technical Center. This is also a part of our school district. I talked with the Vo-Tech principal and, at first, he did not agree to allow the sixteen-year-old sophomore to stay down in his building all day working on automobiles. I then told the principal that the other sixty-eight learners going to his school would not be going either unless he agreed and changed his mind. He had to be given his math as it related to an internal combustion engine, same with science and all of his subjects as they related to automobiles. Reading technical manuals gave him his reading grade. This learner went on to graduate with his class and he did it his way. (Cook, 2013)

**Pause/Think/Reflect**

How can performance-based systems keep learners in school? How can other districts adapt Taylor County Schools' performance-based system?

Cook shared that more than one-third of all Taylor's learners are taking or have taken classes one or more grades above their chronological age. There are well over three hundred elementary learners taking middle  school content and five hundred high school credits earned by middle school learners. There are some fifth graders taking high school algebra for high school credit, and some seniors are graduating from high school with enough college hours to be midterm sophomores in college (Cook, 2013).

## Bartholomew Consolidated School Corporation (BCSC), Indiana

**Why adapt or adopt the BCSC model?**

- BYOD (Bring Your Own Device)
- Universal Design for Learning
- Implementation plan and resources
- UDL coordinators and facilitators
- Supportive system for UDL across K–12

BCSC is a school district serving 12,000 learners in the town of Columbus, Indiana. BCSC began a district-wide framework for implementation of Universal Design for Learning in 2006. Initially, BCSC began this process by conducting an internal inquiry and examination of how they deliver special education. This evolved into a district-level approach to removing barriers in the learning environment for all learners by addressing learner variability. BCSC has three district UDL coordinators and nine UDL facilitators serving sixteen buildings. The implementation of Universal Design for Learning as a framework for designing and evaluating curriculum, instruction, and learning environments in the BCSC is a dynamic process, challenging in its scope, but crucial to the academic success of all learners.

The BCSC addressed teacher requests for assistance with implementing the UDL process by designing a referral tool. This resource is an opportunity for collaborative conversations and problem solving when needed around the implementation of the UDL framework with learning environments, the curriculum, and lessons. BCSC is in the process of creating a tool to support learners as expert learners and a rubric to serve as a professional growth tool around expert learning.

> *BCSC demonstrates a community commitment to deeper learning for one . . . and all.*

The stages of UDL implementation are flexible and fluid, allowing BCSC to revisit the process when considering new district initiatives or examining current ones. BCSC believes that UDL implementation is an ongoing process with expert learners as the goals. (National Center for Universal Design for Learning, 2013)

## Verona Area School District, Wisconsin

Verona Area School District (VASD) is building a personalized learning system based on a coaching platform.

Betty Wottreng, Director of Technology Services, leads the Personalized Learning Initiative as educators across VASD have built a common language around personalizing learning. The excitement about personalized learning grew, and VASD realized they needed a way to build a self-sustainable model with people on the ground who could support teachers on a daily basis.

Coaching is about building a human infrastructure based on a train-the-trainer model where lead coaches support site coaches who support your teachers. Teachers become partners in learning with their learners as learners take ownership of their learning. Teachers are working collaboratively with the support of personalized learning coaches and each other.

**Why adapt or adopt the Verona Area Schools model?**

- Personalized learning coaches
- Self-sustainable personalized learning system
- Personalized learning plans
- Building a common language
- Resources and models

**Figure 4.7** Verona Area School District

The next step was to take their core beliefs and align them to personalized learning. VASD's core beliefs are shared here.

Betty Wottreng

### *Why we believe what we believe!*

- Our world, including Verona, Fitchburg, Madison and all the surrounding areas is changing dramatically and rapidly.
- The needs of all of the learners and families we serve contribute to that change and compel us as an organization to change to meet those needs.

- Unfortunately, some of the learners in our school district are not succeeding.
- We believe this has an enormous negative impact on learners, educators, parents, policy makers, employers, employees, residents, homeowners, and citizens. As a community, we must take responsibility for EVERY learner.

### How will we know every learner is successful?

- Every learner in VASD has a personalized learning plan that provides a path to discovery and achievement and that plan is reviewed and changed at least annually based on the learner's needs.
- Every learner's parent, guardian or advocate participates directly in the design, implementation, and outcomes of that learner's personalized learning plans.
- Every learner meets or exceeds the goals of his or her personalized learning plan every school year.
- Every VAHS learner graduates.

VASD is committed to make these beliefs and goals happen. Ten school teams connected the dots of their initiatives and programs under the personalized learning umbrella. Each school team took one initiative and demonstrated what the concept would look like in a personalized  learning environment. What every team found is that personalized learning can be the umbrella, and most initiatives do fit under this umbrella. Teaching and learning are different and better in Verona Area Schools. (Verona Area School District, 2014)

> *"I have always considered myself a process-driven person, and constantly work that angle with learners—"how did we arrive at this" and "why is this important" serve as cornerstones in this approach. Personalized learning seems to be a shift of paradigms from the teacher modeling and defining the learning process, to the learner understanding the learning process in such great extent that they define their own path."*
>
> —Noah Weibel, sixth-grade history/ social science teacher, Savannah Oaks Middle School, VASD

## Henry County Schools, Georgia

Aaryn Schmuhl is Assistant Superintendent for Learning and Leadership at Henry County Schools. He manages professional learning communities for improving academic achievement, designs and implements job-embedded professional development, and leads the district in its implementation of personalized learning.

**Why adapt or adopt the Henry County Schools model?**

- Coaching
- Implementation plan
- Building models
- Mastery of rigorous standards
- Personalized learning plans

Henry County Schools is a large suburban district located approximately thirty miles south of Atlanta. HCS is a diverse district with an approximately 53 percent free and reduced lunch rate and 60 percent nonwhite learner population that includes a wide variety of demographics within each of the fifty-one schools. Over the past decade, learner enrollment has doubled to nearly 41,000, as has the percentage of learners who are economically disadvantaged, yet learner performance has generally held steady or improved over time.

**Figure 4.8**   Henry County Schools

HENRY COUNTY SCHOOLS

District leadership has a strong commitment to create personalized learning opportunities for students in schools and across the district. HCS has been working on progressive school reform, including a focus on creating pockets of innovative learning options, over the past five years. While Henry County Schools has taken several bold and concrete steps toward establishing personalized learning as the norm of the district, there is much work yet ahead to make PL sustained and systemic change with regard to better preparing learners to be college and career ready.

Aaryn Schmuhl

HCS's vision for personalized learning comprises the following five tenets:

1. *Competency Based/Flexible Pacing:* A system of competency-based learning with common standards for all learners and schools, wherein time is flexible, but learning is constant.

**The HCS Vision**

Henry County Schools ensures educational success for each student by inspiring a culture of creators and achievers. We believe all learners will excel in an environment where

- Achievement reflects mastery of rigorous standards
- Learning experiences are relevant and engaging
- Relationships are supportive and nurturing

HCS works to create learning environments that exemplify these principles organized around three areas, all of which stand to benefit from the adoption of personalized learning: student achievement, culture/climate/community, and quality assurance (i.e., effective leading and teaching).

2. *Twenty-First-Century Skills for College and Career Readiness:* District-wide approach to developing and measuring communication, collaboration, creativity, and critical thinking.

3. *Technology-Enabled Learning:* HCS will develop infrastructure to support tech-enabled learning including wireless, LMS, and data systems. Over the course of their Henry County career, all learners will receive a blend of face-to-face and digitally-enabled instruction in order to ensure facility in both.

4. *Project-Based Learning/Authentic Assessment:* Real and relevant learning experiences (e.g., service learning and internships) that promote greater learner engagement, voice, and agency in order to make learning more relevant to students.

5. *Learner Profiles/Personalized Learning Plans:* A learner-centered culture built around individual learning plans co-created by students, parents, and teachers.

### *HCS has a high level implementation plan with three layers*

1. *Launch* a cohort of 6 schools each year that are ready to personalize learning and serve as models across the district. Selected redesign schools engage in 1.5 full years of visioning, strategic planning, and training prior to launch.

2. *Develop* capacity to enable remaining schools to implement in future cohorts. The implementation plan calls for a small number of schools to redesign each year until all 51 schools are models of personalized learning.

3. *Build* awareness and support of PL among community at large through stakeholder engagement with families, businesses, higher ed, and various state-level entities. (Henry County Schools, 2014)

# PERSONALIZED LEARNING SCHOOL MODELS

## Mt. Abraham Union Middle/High School, Vermont

John H. Clarke worked for twenty years at Mt. Abraham Union Middle/High School in Bristol, Vermont, on personalization in several roles. Clarke (2013) helped develop the Pathways Program and wrote *Personalized Learning: Student-Designed Pathways to High School Graduation.* John wrote about **personal pathways** to graduation to show how a relatively large high school could develop reliable processes for personalizing the experience of all its learners. The transformation is feasible but surely not quick and easy.

> **Why adapt or adopt the Mt. Abraham Union Middle/High School Pathways model?**
>
> • Personal pathways
> • Apprenticeships
> • Mentors and advisory program
> • Goal setting
> • Independent learning

Personal pathways at Mt. Abraham Union Middle/High School engage learners in looking at their talents, skills, interests, and aspirations with a skillful personalized learning advisor to discover the things that drive them forward. Learners in Mt. Abraham Union Middle/High School self-select to take courses in Personalized Learning (PL). Those who want to learn intensively through PL, take 4 or more of their 8 courses in PL and are considered full-time, or "Pathways" learners. Other learners may choose to self-select just 1–3 Personalized Learning options such as DUO's (Do Unto Others), Independent Studies, Independent Learning Opportunities (self-directed core credit courses), Virtual High School courses and Dual Enrollment college courses.

> **Pause/Think/Reflect**
>
> The pathways are another way to graduate at Mt. Abraham:
>
> • Decide (think about your interests, talents, and aspirations)
> • Design it! (apply those here)
> • Do it!
> • Show it! (exhibition presentation)
> • Graduate

Learners and their advisor begin to ask questions and set goals that open a desirable pathway to the future. Then learners test possible pathways, making site visits to professionals in their interest area; finding a mentor for in-depth experiences; taking college courses, virtual courses, or conventional courses; and searching for ideas from the widest possible array of choices, including community experience, reading, and other media. Invariably, learners change direction as the semesters unfold, but they are gathering evidence from all their explorations to show they are meeting the school's graduation standards. Each learner has an "e-portfolio" website where work is developed and stored, assembled in collaboration with the advisor. Learners refine the collection of evidence to show evidence of competency in five areas:

- Communication
- Critical thinking
- Collaboration
- Global citizenship
- Independent learning

Independent work at Pathways usually takes the form of a personal project—clearly defined processes and products. Learners have designed an enormous array of pathways: filmmaking, music production, medieval weapons, firefighting, computer programming, blacksmithing, game design, emergency rescue, nursing, film, theater, architecture, forestry, taxidermy . . . the list goes on. It is about looking for ways to engage learners. When engagement is not there, they don't care about their work and don't do it. The personal projects start with personal questions. In grouping learners by subjects, teachers are making assumptions about why they put effort into learning. Quizzes or grades are extrinsic motivators and may work for some of the population. But personal goals and questions about those goals intrinsically motivate learners.

**Pause/Think/Reflect**

How can learners test and design their own learning pathways?

Advising, mentoring, and team leadership are new roles for teachers at Mt. Abraham Union Middle/High School. The Personalized Learning department depends on four teachers with much of their time devoted to advising and program development. Teaching roles develop as the need expands. Rather than changing teacher contracts to define these fluid roles, all are identified as "teaching" (Mt. Abraham Union Middle/High School, 2013).

## KM Explore, Wisconsin

Lisa Welch and Wanda Richardson are K–1 co-teachers with forty-four learners in one large classroom at KM Explore, a K–5 elementary charter school in Wales, Wisconsin, in the Kettle Moraine School District. The school embraces the notion of a "generative curriculum" grown from the collective voices and choices of the community of learners, families, and educators of the school itself. Learning at KM

Explore is on a continuum where each learner is on a self-propelled journey embedded in a community of learners.

Lisa Welch and Wanda Richardson

### *The Five Pillars at KM Explore*

In the 2013–2014 year, teachers in the Kettle Moraine School District in Wisconsin began an exciting adventure by starting KM Explore with a foundation built on the following five pillars:

- Optimal learning spaces
- Generative curriculum
- Multi-age learning
- Habits of mind
- Collaborative teaching and learning

KM Explore involves learners in the design of a different kind of school. By being multi-age in structure, community-based in function, and integrated in its curriculum design, KM Explore learners provide evidence of learning in a manner that is meaningful to them. A fluid and adaptable schedule removes traditional boundaries of learning. Integrated curriculum design, the creative process, and high-level questioning are woven throughout the learning experience. The fundamentals of reading, writing, and math are foundational to this generative curriculum as they are embedded and integrated into the day-to-day work.

Inside KM Explore, you will find furniture similar to a home setting where learners are encouraged to move and find comfort while learning. The furniture is movable and can be arranged for collaborative work as well as quiet space.

Anytime, anywhere learning is encouraged. It is not uncommon for learners to access their learning plans at home and come to school with artifacts of their learning. Here are three of the five pillars in more detail.

**Why adapt or adopt the KM Explore model?**

- Multi-age classrooms
- Generative curriculum
- Co-teaching
- Habits of mind
- Flexible learning spaces

**Figure 4.9** KM Explore

**Pause/Think/Reflect**

How can a multi-age and community-based program personalize learning?

### Generative Curriculum

Learning is generated through these connections and the discovery of our community at large. An example can be a walk to simply notice the street names around us, a walk around the playground. They learn by discovering, questioning, and then suggesting strategies. They saw the band practicing and asked if they could collaborate with the high school band. They ended up marching in the homecoming parade.

### Habits of Mind

The whole child is important and there are certain skills and mindsets that are simply not traditionally acknowledged through academia. These habits of mind play a vital role in life-long learning and the ability to meet goals as well as create new ones. The habits that focused on are persisting, managing impulsivity, thinking flexibly and listening with empathy and understanding. Each week, the learners also listen to "Mission Monday" video to think about the message that is given and to apply it to their daily interactions with peers, family and the community around them. The goal is to also employ these habits to their daily goals in learning.

> Though the learners are in groups due to logistics, they like to embrace the notion that they are "ageless and gradeless."

### Collaborative Teaching and Learning

Learners are encouraged to collaborate with peers to meet their learning goals. There is much talking and collaborating throughout the school. The noise level sometimes becomes higher than in a traditional classroom but is also embraced as evidence of learning through collaboration.

Teachers also model and work in a collaborative team as learners. No learner is thought of as an individual teacher's "responsibility," but rather everyone works as a team to create the best learning environment for each child. There is the daily modeling of collaboration that comes through in our learners' actions within the classroom.

KM Explore's goal is to help a learner be an architect of how their learning will look. Just as each building in a community looks different, each plan the learner builds will look different as well. If we start this "blueprint" right away in kindergarten, there is no telling what their "building" of learning will look like into high school and beyond! Though the learners are in groups due to logistics, they like to embrace the notion that they are *ageless and gradeless* (Welch & Richardson, 2013).

*"Our goal at KM Explore is to help a learner become an architect of how their learning will look."*

—Lisa Welch and Wanda Richardson,
K–1 co-teachers, KM Explore

## The Inquiry Hub, British Columbia

The Inquiry Hub (Vancouver, Canada) was inspired by conversations around SD43 Coquitlam District's vision of "Learning Without Boundaries." David Truss, Vice Principal, shared that the Inquiry Hub provides ninth-through twelfth-grade learners an innovative, technology driven, full-time program that allows learners to pursue their own learning by shaping their educational experience around their interests and questions instead of structured classes.

Instead of traditional style classes, learners participate in workshops on specific topics, and a significant part of the day is designed by learners in collaboration with teachers and other learners. In the morning, teachers and learners start off with a topical workshop. Then learners work on online courses guided by their teachers. In the afternoon they work on their inquiry project individually and/or collaboratively. Learners are encouraged to think about thinking and take two requisite courses:

**Why adapt or adopt the Inquiry Hub model?**

- Inquiry-based
- Digital learning
- Learner-driven around interests
- Project-based

**Figure 4.10**   The Inquiry Hub

David Truss

1. *Principles of Inquiry* looks at domains of inquiry, questions development, and researches design.

2. *Applications of Digital Learning* explores social networking and creates a positive digital

**Pause/Think/Reflect**

"We are working on the simple premise that if we help learners develop meaningful and engaging questions around their own interests, passions and ideas that matter to them, then the learning will be rich and meaningful to.our entire learning community."

—David Truss, Vice Principal, The Inquiry Hub

footprint, search and research, and principles of digital presentation.

There are two larger learning commons areas and also smaller conference rooms that groups of learners can work in. Learners are empowered to work with peers, meet with their teachers, or use their time working independently. Transforming learning at the Inquiry Hub follows the Seven Principles that any school can use as they personalize learning (Inquiry Hub, 2013).

1. *Inquiry (give learners a voice):* Learners seek and explore their own questions.

2. *Voice (give learners a voice):* Provide learners with meaningful opportunities to share.

3. *Audience (give learners an audience):* Student work is shared with more than teachers and peers.

4. *Community (give learners a community to collaborate with):* Collaboration with teachers and peers with global and local communities.

5. *Leadership (give learners opportunities to lead):* Learners as lead learners in our school and in our world.

6. *Play (give learners opportunities to play):* School as a learning sandbox.

7. *Networks (give learners digitally connected space to learn):* Connected learning in both physical and digital spaces.

### Creating Your Own Project at the Inquiry Hub

The Green Inquiry Project was the brainchild of learners Shauna, Sophia, and Hannah who wrote a proposal and received a wildlife grant as part of their environmental sustainability group. David Truss shared about a topic that took on a life of its own.

Their project focuses on the development of a garden to produce organic fruits, vegetables, and herbs. The aim of the project is to connect youth with the land by providing an opportunity to plant, grow, and harvest their own food.

Learners learn about the environment and agriculture by cultivating their own produce, a hands-on experience, rather than simply reading about it. In addition, the garden offers a place for learners to interact and learn with each other and partner groups. Partner groups may include the resident daycare, alternative education programs, and community residents, for example senior citizens. In April 2013, the community came together, and everyone helped build and maintain the garden. (Truss, 2013)

**Pause/Think/Reflect**

The girls along with three other learners shared during a December 2013 webinar two quotes about what they are learning at the Inquiry Hub that all of us can use.

"Learning how to learn to fail"

"Learning differences not disabilities"

Now the girls have taken the garden a step further and are doing hydroponic gardening. Learners may have one interest that is a large project but then another one that is something they want to explore. Two learners wanted to rebuild a lawn mower. Another learner wanted to create a wristband computer.

## Science Leadership Academy (SLA), Pennsylvania

The Science Leadership Academy (SLA) is a partnership high school between the School District of Philadelphia and The Franklin Institute. SLA is an inquiry-driven, project-based high school focused on twenty-first-century learning that opened its doors on September 7, 2006.

Chris Lehman, SLA Principal, shared that SLA provides a rigorous college-preparatory curriculum with a focus on

**Why adapt or adopt the SLA model?**

- Inquiry-driven
- Project-based
- Entrepreneurships
- 1:1 Laptop Program
- Leadership training

science, technology, mathematics, and entrepreneurship. Learners at SLA learn in a project-based environment where the core values of inquiry, research, collaboration, presentation, and reflection are emphasized in all classes. SLA is built on the notion that inquiry is the very first step in the process of learning by asking these three questions:

"How do we *learn?*"

"What can we *create?*"

"What does it mean to *lead?*"

SLA is a project-based twenty-first-century school with a 1:1 laptop program. At SLA, they believe learning should not stop with the school walls or at the end of the school day. They believe learning should—and does—happen 24/7/365 (Science Leadership Academy, 2014). Learning is theme-based:

Ninth grade: Identity

Tenth grade: Systems

Eleventh grade: Change

Twelfth grade: Creation

*"For my classroom, I still strongly believe in the concept of student as worker, teacher as coach and I continue to structure learning so that students—and not the teacher—are the focus. And yet, the more I've become aware of my own learning process, the more I've come to value the importance of strategic modeling for students."*

—Joshua Block, high school humanities teacher, SLA (Block, 2013)

### Second Campus of SLA

Science Leadership Academy opened a second campus in Philadelphia called the Beeber School. Using a project-based inquiry approach to learning math is not easier, but kids are learning the material in ways that are relevant to them. Teaching a topic like math without the traditional sequencing can be hard for everyone in the community to understand and requires tolerance for failure. The payoff is when, for example, a learner becomes a senior and chooses mechanical engineering as an elective because he loves solving problems and has been learning to do it all through high school (Schwartz, 2014).

## COMMON CHARACTERISTICS OF MODELS

When you research personalized learning models, consider what characteristics you want to adopt or adapt. Consider the criteria from the beginning of this chapter when you do your research. The following is a list of characteristics and the models that share these characteristics.

*Competency-based, proficiency-based, or performance-based:*

Coalition of Essential Schools (CES), Big Picture Learning (BPL), Kennebec Intra-District (RSU 2), Adams County District 50, Henry County Schools, and Taylor County Schools.

*Multi-age classrooms:*

Walker Learning Approach, Reggio Emilia, Sudbury Valley Schools, Adams County District 50, Henry County Schools, and KM Explore.

*Flexible learning spaces:*

High Tech High, Reggio Emilia, KM Explore, and Vittra Schools.

*Personal learning paths:*

Montessori, Coalition of Essential Schools (CES), KED, Sudbury, Adams County District 50, Verona Area Schools, Henry County Schools, and Mt. Abraham Union Middle/High School.

*Community partnerships:*

Mt. Abraham Union Middle/High School, Science Leadership Academy, Big Picture Learning (BPL), Inquiry Hub, and Taylor County Schools.

*Play-based learning:*

Walker Learning Approach, Sudbury Valley, and Inquiry Hub.

*PL coaches:*

BPL, Colorado Springs, Kunskapsskolan (KED), Bartholomew Schools (UDL coaches), Verona Area Schools, and Henry County Schools.

*Technology Solutions:*

Colorado Springs (on-demand resources), Kennebec Intra-District (1:1), Inquiry Hub, and Bartholomew (BYOD).

There are so many more connections and characteristics that could be included here, but consider this a place to start your journey.

## CHAPTER 4 REVIEW

- Review how learners test and design their own learning pathways.
- Research information about a generative curriculum.
- Learn why a multi-age and community-based program can personalize learning.
- Investigate how the learner is important and how habits of mind play a vital role in lifelong learning.
- Learn how an inquiry-based approach can give learners voice.

## RESOURCES

- Reggio Children Loris Malaguzzi Foundation Homepage: www.reggiochildrenfoundation.org
- The Walker Learning Approach: http://walkerlearning.com.au/info/home
- Why Are Finland's Schools Successful? (*The Smithsonian*): www.smithsonianmag.com/people-places/Why-Are-Finlands-Schools-Successful.html
- Ingredients for the World's Best Education System: http://asiasociety.org/video/education/ingredients-worlds-best-education-system
- Adams County School District 50 Wiki: http://wiki.adams50.org/mediawiki/index.php/SBS:Instructional_Resources
- Colorado State School Graduation Guidelines: www.cde.state.co.us/sites/default/files/documents/secondaryinitiatives/downloads/adoptedgraduationguidelines2013.pdf

# 5 Why Personalize Learning?

*"The beautiful thing about learning is that nobody can take it away from you."*

—B. B. King

The rationale to personalize learning is for learners to own and drive their learning. This means changing how we teach and design learning environments. When you begin personalizing learning by transforming teaching and learning, there may be resistance from teachers, parents, and even learners. Teachers may want to continue teaching the same way they have always taught, especially if test scores are high, support and funding is limited, or other reasons to continue with the status quo. Learners may be concerned about grades. Parents may not understand why children need to take responsibility for their learning. If someone asks you why you would personalize learning, what would you say? This chapter pulls the key points from the book together so you can build that rationale.

## UNIVERSAL DESIGN FOR LEARNING FOR ALL LEARNERS

All of us as learners are affected by different factors: our families, technology, peers, the speed of information, how we interact with others, social-emotional issues, and our birth order. Every learner in your class is unique and different from every other learner. Even though we know this, schools still continue to teach the same curriculum at the same pace by grade levels based on their ages to all the children in their class—"one size fits all."

Universal Design for Learning (UDL) is the lens that guides the design of personalized learning environments and is the framework

**Pause/Think/Reflect**

How do you determine how each learner learns best?

that applies to *all* learners who have **variability** in their learning. Remember the research in Chapter 2 from Dr. Todd Rose on why everyone is unique and no one is average. You can determine all learners' needs by using the principles of UDL to understand their strengths, challenges, aptitudes, interests, talents, and aspirations with their Personal Learner Profile.

UDL provides a blueprint for creating instructional goals, methods, materials, and assessments that work for everyone—not a single, one-size-fits-all solution but rather flexible approaches that can be customized and adjusted for individual needs. Teachers can design a Class Learning Snapshot based on four diverse learners to design instructional and learning strategies that will meet most of the learners in their class. UDL reduces the barriers to the curriculum by maximizing the learning for all learners. It is about how learners access information, engage with content, and express what they know and understand.

## EXPERT LEARNERS

The goal in education is to help turn learners into expert learners—individuals who want to learn, who know how to learn, and who, in their own individual and flexible ways, are well prepared for a lifetime of learning. This means every learner, no matter what age, needs to develop characteristics of expert learners adapted from the UDL principles.

*Expert learners focus on and work strategically toward their goals by*

- knowing how they learn best.
- developing their own personal learning plans.
- designing learning strategies that scaffold meeting goals.
- monitoring their progress as they learn.
- adjusting their learning when they realize learning is not effective.

*Expert learners are resourceful and knowledgeable by*

- activating prior knowledge to identify, organize, and assimilate new information.
- using multiple strategies to access information.

- choosing the appropriate tools and resources that support the task at hand.
- turning information into useable knowledge that is easy to understand and express.

*Expert learners are motivated and engaged to learn by*

- having a purpose in their learning.
- being able to demonstrate mastery of what they learned.
- setting challenging goals that push their learning.
- sustaining the effort to meet the goals and not giving up.

(Center for Applied Special Technology, 2011)

Expert learners are learners who are self-directed, self-regulated, motivated, and engaged to learn who are able to monitor their progress and make connections with prior learning. They have a purpose to learn something they are interested

**Pause/Think/Reflect**

How do we prepare all learners to become expert learners?

in. This sounds great; however, this doesn't just happen overnight or even all the time. Plus, learners may not be an expert on every concept, strategy, or skill. The continuum to develop expert learners shown in Figure 5.1 provides the journey learners of all ages can go on to build expertise.

**Figure 5.1** Continuum of an Expert Learner

When learners include their voice and have opportunities for choice, this changes how they interact with the content, the teacher, and each other. The teacher can still be directing the learning but can invite learners to share their ideas and voice their opinions. The teacher can also provide multiple methods, tools, and strategies for learners to access information, engage with the content, and express what they know and understand.

## Motivation, Engagement, and Voice

Students at the Center explores the roles that learner-centered approaches can play to deepen learning and prepare young people to meet the demands and engage the opportunities of the twenty-first century. It authored nine research reports on learner-centered approaches. In the research report *Motivation, Engagement, and Student Voice,* Dr. Eric Toshalis and Dr. Michael Nakkula concluded that motivation, engagement, and voice (see Figure 5.2) are the trifecta of learner-centered learning.

**Figure 5.2** Motivation, Engagement, and Voice

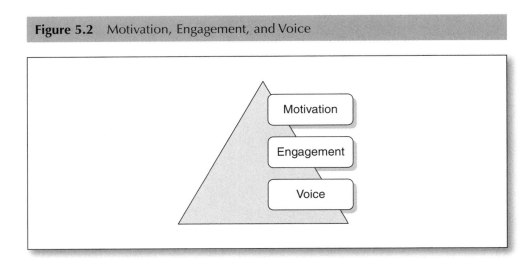

"*Without motivation, there is no push to learn.*

*Without engagement there is no way to learn.*

*Without voice, there is no authenticity in the learning.*"

—Dr. Eric Toshalis and Dr. Michael Nakkula

## Learner Voice

Toshalis and Nakkula explained in the research paper that the spectrum on learner voice–oriented activities is where learners can start articulating their perspectives as stakeholders in their learning to directing collective activities. They can move from data sources to leaders of change. Most learner voice activity in schools resides in expression, consultation, and participation. The goal is for learners to have a voice that moves to partnership, activism, and leadership roles. Most activity for learners in schools resides at the left side of the spectrum in Figure 5.3. As one moves from left to right across the spectrum, roles, responsibilities, and decision-making authority grow.

**Figure 5.3**  Spectrum of Learner Voice–Oriented Activity

Starting on the left side of the spectrum, learners are provided opportunities to express themselves that may involve sharing opinions, creating art, performing theater, and giving their perspectives. The middle areas are where activities blend these orientations in ways that recognize learners as stakeholders while providing opportunities for them to collaborate with, but not yet lead, adults to achieve specific goals. When learners have regular opportunities to advocate for changes, they can share responsibilities with adults as partners in learning. Moving toward the right side of the spectrum, learners can affect systemic change by organizing and applying pressure about issues that concern them. When learners move to the right side of the spectrum, they are prepared to lead as problem solvers and decision makers to affect change.

When learners act in a way to produce meaningful change, agency is the key to learner voice. The more educators give learners choice, control, challenge, and opportunities to collaborate, the more the learner is motivated and engaged in the learning and eventually taking on the leadership role (Toshalis & Nakkula, 2013).

## Learners Have Choices

When learners have a choice in what they are learning, especially if it is something they are passionate about or interested in, they jump in and sometimes get lost in the task or project. This is called "flow," and you can see and hear the engagement. The room changes. Learners want to share and talk about what they are learning in one corner. In another silent area, there might be learners fixated on a book or something they are reading. They are also in flow and lost in the text. When the teacher encourages voice and choice, it opens the door to noise and what Chris Edwards calls "messy learning." It is not predictable. This is where learning is becoming personal to the learner. Bell schedules or grade levels don't work as well in this type of environment. Learners are not only in the flow and engaged in learning now, they are totally immersed.

Learner-centered environments offer active and collaborative learning where learners are able to generate questions, organize inquiry projects, and monitor their own products and progress. Teachers have been taught to manage and control the learning environment. To encourage learners to own and drive their learning, teachers' roles need to change.

A few teachers try new ideas behind closed doors, and many are recognized in their districts for being innovative and taking risks. But, in some cases, their colleagues voiced their disapproval of what was happening in their classrooms. Early adopters created project-based learning activities that encouraged collaborative problem-solving and independent learning. Technology was included that grabbed these kids, but it wasn't just the technology. It was how teachers who co-designed projects that included voice and choice gave control of the learning to the learners and how the learners took responsibility for their learning. The kids loved it. So did the teachers who realized how much their learners were motivated and engaged in the learning process. Yet something is happening in schools where kids are less engaged and dropping out of school.

## DECLINING ENGAGEMENT

The Gallup Student Poll shown in Figure 5.4 surveyed nearly 500,000 learners in Grades 5 through 12 from more than 1,700 public schools in thirty-seven states in 2012. It found that nearly eight in ten elementary learners who participated in the poll are engaged with school. By middle school that falls to about six in ten learners. And by high school, only four in ten learners qualify as engaged. Our educational system sends learners and our country's future over the school cliff every year.

Engagement with school and learning is a gold standard that every parent, teacher, and school strives to achieve. If we were doing right by our learners and our future, these numbers would be the absolute opposite. For each year learners progress in school, they should be more engaged, not less.

The drop in engagement for each year learners are in school is a national failure. Gallup lists why this might be happening—ranging from our overzealous focus on standardized testing and curricula to the lack of experiential and project-based learning activities for learners—not to mention the lack of pathways for learners who will not or do not want to go on to college.

**Figure 5.4** The School Cliff

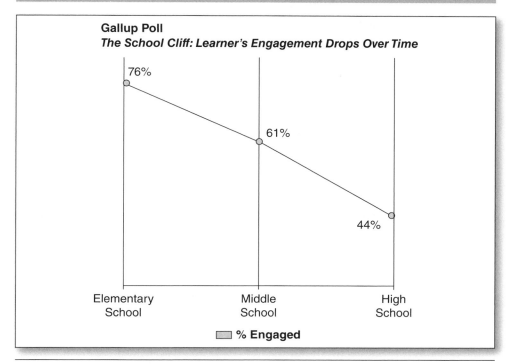

**Gallup Poll**
*The School Cliff: Learner's Engagement Drops Over Time*

*Source:* Gallup, Inc., *The School Cliff.* January 7, 2013.

Another question in the poll asked if learners plan to start their own business. Forty-five percent of the learners in Grades 5 through 12 say they plan to start their own business someday. That is a ton of entrepreneurial energy in our schools. Yet a mere 5 percent have spent more than one hour in the last week working, interning, or exposed to a real business. We not only fail to embrace entrepreneurial learners in our schools, we actually neutralize them. Schools were designed to create compliant workers not independent out-of-the-box thinkers. This is going to have to change if we want our nation to survive (Busteed, 2013).

> **Pause/Think/Reflect**
>
> How do you measure engagement?

### Graduation Rates

A 2013 report from the Department of Education shows that high school graduation rates are at their highest level since 1974. According to the report, during the 2009–10 school year, 78.2 percent of high school learners nationwide graduated on time, about a 5 percent increase from the 73.4 percent recorded in 2005–2006. Vermont had the nation's highest graduation rate at 85 percent with the District of Columbia finishing last at 57 percent. From 2000 to 2010, graduation rates were up in forty-six states, although the size of those gains varies widely—from a tenth of a percentage point in Virginia to 31.5 percentage points in Tennessee (see Figure 5.5).

**Figure 5.5** Graduation Rates

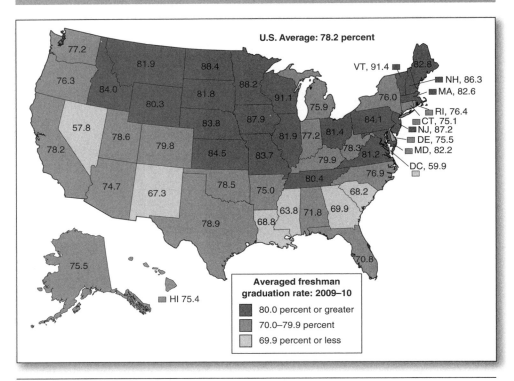

*Source:* U.S. Department of Education, National Center for Education Statistics, Common Core of Data (CCD), "State Dropout and Completion Data File," 2009–10.

Yet many learners—around 1 million a year—leave high school without a diploma. The prospect for these learners of landing a good-paying job or earning a postsecondary credential is likely to be dim. While much attention has gone to identifying teenagers who are at risk of dropping out and finding ways to keep them in school, comparatively fewer efforts have been expended on bringing back the learners who have already left. Here's what that group of 27 million teenagers looks like nationally:

- More than 20 million are in school, either K–12 or higher ed.
- 5.1 million graduated but are not enrolled in a postsecondary institution.
- 1.8 million young adults (which includes a disproportionate percentage of minorities) have left school without a diploma. Of those, 1.2 million of them—66 percent—are not working (Diplomas Count, 2013).

## Dropout Rates

In the United States one child drops out of high school every twenty-six seconds, equaling 1.2 million learners a year.

The National Center for Educational Statistics report *Status Dropout Rates* lists the status dropout rate as the percentage of sixteen- through twenty-four-year-olds who are not enrolled in school and have not earned a high school credential (either a diploma or an equivalency credential such as a General Educational Development [GED] certificate).

**Pause/Think/Reflect**

One child dropping out of school every twenty-six seconds is appalling. One child dropping out of school is too many. We need to find out why children are losing hope before they give up. Every child is worth it.

The status dropout rate declined from 12 percent in 1990 to 7 percent in 2011. Reflecting the overall decline in the status dropout rate from 1990 and 2011, the rates also declined for Whites (from 9 percent to 5 percent), Blacks (from 13 percent to 7 percent), and Hispanics (from 32 percent to 14 percent). Over this period, the status dropout rate was lowest for Whites, followed by Blacks and Hispanics. The gap between Whites and Hispanics narrowed from 23 percentage points in 1990 to 9 percentage points in 2011; the gap between Whites and Blacks during this same time was not measurably different (National Center for Education Statistics, 2014).

The following are 2009 median earnings for full-time workers age twenty-five and by educational attainment.

- $24,520—Not a High School Graduate
- $30,915—GED or Alternative Credential
- $33,213—Regular High School Diploma
- $39,867—Some College or Associate's Degree
- $56,472—Bachelor's Degree
- $73,248—Advanced Degree

*Source:* U.S. Census Bureau, 2009

Comparing those who drop out of high school with those who complete high school, the average high school dropout costs the economy approximately $240,000 over his or her lifetime in terms of lower tax contributions, higher reliance on Medicaid and Medicare, higher rates of criminal activity, and higher reliance on welfare (Levin & Belfield, 2007).

## U. S. College Completion Rates

According to the National Center for Education Statistics (2013), the 2011 graduation rate for full-time, first-time undergraduate learners who began their pursuit of a bachelor's degree at a four-year degree-granting institution in fall 2005 was 59 percent. That is, 59 percent of full-time, first-time learners who began seeking a bachelor's degree at a four-year institution in fall 2005 completed the degree at that institution within six years.

**Pause/Think/Reflect**

We need to ask graduates what they need to prepare them for college. Have you asked your graduates how they are doing? What about surveying them on what skills they wish they had learned in high school?

Although high school graduates are attending college in record numbers, four in ten are not adequately prepared for the course load that awaits them and are thus forced into remedial classes when they start college. This fact contributes to a staggering number of learners pursuing a bachelor's degree—42 percent to drop out. This number is about 30 percent higher at the two-year or community college level.

The U. S. Census Bureau in 2009 reported that, nationally, 9 percent of eighteen- to twenty-four-year-olds and only 27.5% of those twenty-five years and older had a bachelor's degree or more. Massachusetts has the highest completion rate with 37.8 percent of citizens twenty-five years and older having a bachelor degree. In West Virginia, the completion rate is the lowest with only 17.1 percent of the population having bachelor's degrees (National Center for Education Statistics, 2013).

## Failure to Educate

According to the Council on Foreign Relations (2012) report *U.S. Education Reform and National Security,* declines in U.S. education performance are jeopardizing U. S. national security, including the country's ability to compete in a high-skills global marketplace.

**Pause/Think/Reflect**

Not preparing our children for the global marketplace is a concern for all of us. Our learners can learn and compete if we provide learning opportunities where they learn how to be self-directed learners.

Task Force chair Joel Klein, former head of New York City public schools, warns us that the educational failure puts the United States' future economic prosperity, global position, and physical safety at risk. The report goes on to state that the country will not be able to keep pace—much less lead—globally unless it moves to fix the problems it has allowed to fester for too long. According to the Council's report, the lack of educational preparedness poses threats on five national security fronts:

1. Economic growth and competitiveness
2. Physical safety

3. Intellectual property

4. U. S. global awareness

5. U. S. unity and cohesion

Too many young people are not employable in an increasingly high-skilled and global economy, and too many are not qualified to join the military because they are physically unfit, have criminal records, or have inadequate education (Council on Foreign Relations, 2012).

## PREPARING FOR THE FUTURE

Schools are educating our learners for jobs that are not there anymore. If you look at the world now, everything is changing: business, government, banking, and education. We are in a transitional period with many of us kicking and screaming afraid to go where we have to go. The world is going to change whether we like it or not. Employers are looking for candidates with the following skills and values:

- Communications skills (listening, verbal, written)
- Analytical/research skills
- Digital literacy
- Flexibility/adaptability
- Managing multiple priorities
- Interpersonal abilities
- Leadership/management skills
- Multicultural sensitivity/awareness
- Planning/organizing
- Problem-Solving/reasoning/creativity
- Teamwork/collaboration (Hansen & Hansen, n.d.)

Teaching and learning need to address these skills and encourage learners to find their passions and how they learn best. Standardized tests put so much pressure on teachers since they are evaluated based on the final scores and are accountable for their learners' learning. Since No Child Left Behind (NCLB), teachers have been teaching to the test instead of teaching to the real world. Teachers and schools are punished.

> **Pause/Think/Reflect**
>
> Standardized tests put the focus on instruction not on learning.

Schools are closed. Teachers and principals are reassigned. Teachers are leaving the profession because of the pressures.

Employers are looking for people who are creative and have ambition and a passion for what they do. When you look at Generation Y and Z, they are building these skills outside of school. They are collaborating by using social media, playing games, developing leadership skills, participating in global collaborations, and increasing their interpersonal skills. The problem is education's focus does not teach these skills. Since teaching has become teaching to the test and memorizing facts, it seems obvious that our learners are not prepared in school for the jobs available today and definitely not prepared for jobs in the future.

## DIGITAL, CONNECTED, AND GLOBAL

The world is different today. All of us are more connected to each other, with more innovative learning experiences available now than we ever thought possible. It doesn't matter how old you are, where you live, and what you want to learn, you can connect to people, resources, and courses so you, the learner, can learn what you want when you want to. This means what is called "school" is different. Teachers and learners are different. Roles change.

Learners are more networked now at a younger age than ever before. Common Sense Media (2013) found that 29 percent of five- to eight-year-olds use a computer several times a week and 10 percent several times a day. Most interesting was the percentage of children who have ever used a smartphone, tablet, or similar device to play games, watch videos, or use other apps:

- 10 percent for newborn to one-year-olds
- 39 percent for two- to four-year-olds
- 52 percent for five- to eight-year-olds (Common Sense Media, 2013)

Even though the number of younger children using technology is growing, most of the use is around games and play. There's nothing wrong with that because we do learn from play. The idea is not to just be a connected learner but an engaged learner. Younger children may be engaged in play using these tools, but the tools don't necessarily support understanding or meaning making. When kids are playing, they are in the discovery mode and there is little or no self-regulation happening. Children need to develop a set of cognitive skills so they can think deeper about their learning.

Mimi Ito, Cultural Anthropologist at the University of California, Irvine, who specializes in youth and technology and is one of the principal investigators in the new Connected Learning Research Network, reported a growing gap between in-school and out-of-school learning as more and more young people's learning, attention, and access to information is happening outside of the classroom and through online networks. She believes that this can be disturbing, but there is good news. New technology also hands us opportunities for bringing young people, educators, and parents together in cross-generational learning driven by shared interests and goals (Ito, 2010).

Connie Yowell, Director of Education for U.S. programs for the MacArthur Foundation, shared that connected learning represents a path forward and that it is the learning that is socially rich and interest fueled. In other words, it is based on the kind of learning that decades of research shows is the most powerful and most effective. And connected learning is oriented toward cultivating educational and economic opportunity for all young people.

*At the core of Connected Learning are three values:*

- Equity
- Full participation
- Social connection

*These values are based on the three learning principles:*

- Interest powered
- Peer supported
- Academically oriented

*Connected Learning builds on the three design principles:*

- Shared purpose
- Production centered
- Openly networked (Yowell, 2013)

The world faces global challenges that require global solutions. These challenges call for changes in how we think and learn. The Global Education First Initiative is a key part of the UN Secretary General's Initiative on Education and aims to raise the political profile of education and strengthen the global movement to achieve quality education.

**Pause/Think/Reflect**

The world is smaller and becoming more connected each day. It is also more competitive than ever. Learning needs to change to prepare learners of all ages to be global citizens and have the skills and values they will need to meet their learning goals for college and career.

The Initiative on Education (2012) states very clearly that it is not enough anymore for education to put the emphasis on producing individuals who can read, write, and count. Education must be transformative and bring shared values to life. It must cultivate an active care for the world and for those with whom we share it. Education must also be relevant in answering the big questions of the day. Technological solutions, political regulation, or financial instruments alone cannot achieve sustainable development. It requires transforming the way people think and act. Education must fully assume its central role in helping people to forge more just, peaceful, tolerant, and inclusive societies. It must give people the understanding, skills, and values they need to cooperate in resolving the interconnected challenges of the twenty-first century (Global Education First Initiative, 2012).

So let's go back to K–12 schools and figure out how to transform learning so we engage our learners and prepare them for their future.

## FIXED TRADITIONAL SYSTEMS VS. FLEXIBLE LEARNING SYSTEMS

Think about your current system along with the programs and initiatives you are mandated to do or used to doing. Before you can really change anything, you need to know where you are. Compare the following initiatives and practices in a fixed traditional system with those in a flexible personalized learning system.

- Carnegie Unit vs. **Competency-Based**
- Fixed Grade Levels vs. Multi-Age/Co-Teaching
- **RTI** in a Traditional Classroom vs. RTL in a Personalized Learning System
- Structured Classrooms vs. Flexible Learning Spaces
- Computer Labs vs. 1:1/BYOD
- Print vs. Digital
- Assessment OF, FOR, and AS Learning

### Carnegie Unit vs. Competency-Based

Table 5.1 compares the Carnegie Unit, where learning is based on seat time, with competency-based learning, where learners advance based on evidence that demonstrates mastery of learning.

**Table 5.1** Carnegie Unit vs. Competency-Based

| Carnegie Unit | Competency-Based |
|---|---|
| Learners progress based on seat time. | Learners advance upon mastery. |
| Learners count credits. | Learners provide evidence of learning. |
| Bell schedules and structured time for classes. | Learners receive just-in-time support based on their individual learning needs. |
| Equal opportunity for all learners. | Learning outcomes emphasize competencies that include application and creation of knowledge along with the development of important skills and dispositions. |
| Everyone takes the same curriculum. | Learners select courses based on career or college plans. |
| Learning takes place in school. | Learning takes place anytime, anywhere. |

*Source:* Personalize Learning, LLC

### Carnegie Unit

Under the leadership of Harvard president Charles Eliot in 1893, the Committee of Ten undertook a broad and comprehensive exploration of the role of the high school in American life, concluding, significantly, that all public high school learners should follow a college preparatory curriculum, regardless of their backgrounds, their intention to stay in school through graduation, or their plans to pursue higher education.

> **Pause/Think/Reflect**
>
> Does "seat time" equal learning?

Eliot, author of the final report, wrote that "every subject which is taught at all in a secondary school should be taught in the same way and to the same extent to every pupil so long as he pursues it, no matter what the probable destination of the pupil may be, or at what point his education is to cease". (National Education Association of the United States, 1894).

The Carnegie Unit lives with us today—truly, nothing structural has changed in U. S. education since 1910. We still measure academics via seat time. We count our credits—both at the secondary and postsecondary level—by hours spent "in instruction" on specified subjects (Mirel, 2006).

### Competency-Based

Competency-based pathways are a reengineering of our education system around learning—a reengineering designed for success in which failure is no longer an option. Competency-based may be called performance-based or proficiency-based. Competency-based approaches build on standard reforms, offering a new value proposition, according to Sturgis (2013):

> **Pause/Think/Reflect**
>
> Design for success where failure is no longer an option.

"By aligning all of our resources (in schools, the community, and online) around learning to enable learners to progress upon mastery, our country can increase productivity in the education system, while simultaneously raising achievement levels overall and reducing the achievement gap."

A growing number of education leaders understand that the traditional time-based ways of organizing learning (courses, grades, Carnegie Unit, and the assumption that learning takes place in the classroom) contribute to the reconstruction of inequity in our public school system. Use of the Carnegie Unit is changing (see Chapter 4), and more than twenty-nine states are offering alternative methods for credit recovery.

## Fred Bramante's Journey

Fred Bramante is a former eighth-grade science teacher from Stamford, Connecticut, an entrepreneur, a former candidate for governor, the past Chairman of the New Hampshire State Board of Education, and co-author of the book *Off the Clock: Moving from Time to Competency* with Rose Colby. Fred shared about competency-based systems:

> A good competency-based system will make a difference for all learners, because kids will be learning what they love instead of trying to jump through traditional school hoops. They will be the primary drivers of their learning. Imagine a student saying I would like Mrs. Jones for English, but I want to use my karate lessons for my physical education. I want to play in a rock band for my music and do world history online. I want to learn automotive at the car dealership and want to learn space science at the planetarium. All of these become possibilities in a competency-based world where learning can take place anytime, anyplace, anyhow, and at any pace. I've always said that if kids can own how they learn, where they learn, when they learn, then why would anyone drop out of school? (Bramante, 2013)

## Fixed Grade Levels vs. Multi-Age Co-Teaching

Table 5.2 provides an overview of how fixed grade levels isolate teachers and learners in classrooms by grade level compared to multi-age co-teaching where teachers as part of a team may collaborate in one large classroom with multiple grade levels.

**Pause/Think/Reflect**

How can your school be restructured to be more competency-based?

**Table 5.2**   Fixed Grade Levels vs. Multi-Age Co-Teaching

| Fixed Grade Levels | Multi-Age Co-Teaching |
|---|---|
| Teachers are isolated in one classroom. | Teachers plan and collaborate as part of a team. |
| Learners advance to the next grade based on scores and seat time. | Learners progress based on evidence of learning and demonstrating mastery. |
| Classrooms have doors that close. | Classrooms have doors that open and learning can happen anywhere. |
| The teacher needs to manage the classroom and is the disciplinarian. | Teachers work as a team to identify learners who need additional support and coaching. |
| There are learning targets based on the grade level. | Teachers work with learners to identify learning goals based on evidence of learning. |

*Source:* Personalize Learning, LLC

### Fixed Grade Levels

Our schools and classrooms continue to reflect an industrial model. Our children move along an assembly line, from kindergarten to Grade 12, where we install math, reading, science, and social studies—in compliance with government standards—blueprints that define and sequence what our learners should be taught during their years of formal education.

> *"We are getting better and better at things that don't work."*

The United States and other countries use ordinal numbers like *first* for identifying grades. Typical ages and grade groupings in public and private schools may be found through the U.S. Department of Education. Generally, school follows a progression from elementary school (K–5), to

**Pause/Think/Reflect**

How is your school moving toward multi-age and/or multidiscipline collaborative teaching teams?

middle school (6–8), to high school (9–12). However, there are a rising number of variations, the most popular being elementary (K–4), to intermediate (5–6), to middle (7–8), to high school (9–12). Many different variations exist across the country and in other countries. Some countries, such as Finland, have children start school at age seven (What Is the History of the K–12 Education System?, 2013).

### Multi-Age Co-Teaching

Teams are typically composed of two to four teachers working collaboratively to plan thematic units and lesson plans in order to provide a more supportive environment for learners. When teachers like Lisa Welch and Wanda Richardson at KM Explore co-teach, learners stay or loop with their teachers. Both the multi-age and looping mean that a cohort of learners stays together with the same teacher for at least two years. This allows teachers to get to know the personalities, needs, and interests of each learner and develop a strong relationship with learners and their parents. In Finland, learners stay with the same teacher for at least five years.

Children experience increased opportunities to lead and follow, collaborate, and make stable peer relationships. And only about half the learners are new each year for a class that runs two years. When learners have the same teacher for several years, they are used to consistent routines and require fewer year-to-year adjustments. Teachers work together to identify learners who need additional support and support them to meet their learning goals based on evidence of learning.

**Picture This!**

The K–1 classroom at KM Explore encourages learners to teach each other class "seminars." A learner older or younger than other learners spends fifteen minutes during the morning teaching others in the class skills the learner has acquired. Learners are able to sign up for a seminar if the topic interests them. Everyone is either teaching or learning from each other.

*"The most fruitful experience in a child's education is her collaboration with more experienced or skilled partners."*

—Lev Vygotsky

## RTI in a Traditional Classroom vs. RTL in a Personalized Learning System

Table 5.3 demonstrates that Response to Intervention (RTI) looks different in a personalized learning system. In a traditional classroom, there tends to be a focus on disabilities and working with struggling learners after they might have failed. Response to Learning (RTL) focuses as learners learn so they can monitor their progress and provide support as they learn.

**Table 5.3** RTI vs. RTL

| RTI in a Traditional Classroom | RTL in a Personalized Learning System |
|---|---|
| Multilevel instruction aimed at all learners. | Targets all learners' specific learning needs when needed, as needed. |
| Part of reauthorization of the Individuals with Disabilities Education Act (IDEA). | Provides intervention for all learners that need additional support. |
| Teachers spend more time being compliant filling out forms than working with at-risk learners. | Uses intervention based on learning goals as part of the PLE right from the beginning. |
| Focuses on what is wrong with learners and their weaknesses instead of strengths. | Designs learning strategies that focus on the learner's strengths. |
| Learning outcomes cover all required standards. | Focuses on standards and skills learners need to succeed in the future. |

*Source:* Personalize Learning, LLC

### *Response to Intervention (RTI) in a Traditional Classroom*

RTI is multilevel instruction aimed at all learners and is required by the Individuals with Disabilities Education Act (IDEA). Learning outcomes cover all required standards, yet the focus is on what is wrong with learners and their weaknesses instead of their strengths. Teachers tend to spend more time trying to be compliant and filling out forms than working with at-risk students. RTI is classified in three tiers. In all tiers, the teacher provides interventions and is responsible for the learning.

*Tier 1*—Core Instruction
Intervention for all learners by differentiating instruction

*Tier 2*—Group Interventions
Strategic intervention using formative data to increase intensity and time on tasks

*Tier 3*—Intensive Interventions
Identify at-risk learners for individualized support

### Response to Learning (RTL) in a Personalized Learning System

Response to Learning (RTL) is actually RTI for all learners. Instead of waiting until a learner fails, you can target all learners' specific learning needs when they are needed, as needed. In fact, in a personalized learning environment (PLE), learners own and drive their learning by designing their learning goals with their teacher. The teacher uses interventions based on the learning goals right from the beginning of the learning process. The teacher designs learning strategies identified through the Universal Design for Learning (UDL) lens so needed interventions can be identified earlier.

**Pause/Think/Reflect**

How do you see RTL addressing the needs of all learners in your classroom or school?

When teachers and learners work together to understand how learners learn best using their UDL lens, then learners can take responsibility for their learning so they can acquire the skills and knowledge they need to succeed in their future. Teachers and learners work together so learners receive additional support before they fail. Failure is no longer an option under a personalized learning environment.

**Figure 5.6** Response to Learning (RTL)

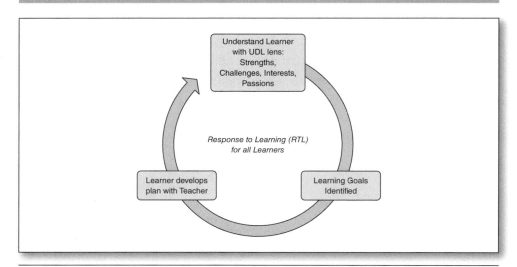

*Source:* Personalize Learning, LLC

Figure 5.6 reinforces the importance of responding to learning for all learners, not just those who are struggling or at risk. All learners can identify their strengths, challenges, interests, and passions using the UDL lens and create and monitor their learning goals and plan as they learn.

## Structured Classrooms vs. Flexible Learning Spaces

Traditional classrooms were structured for learners to be compliant and the teacher directing the learning. Table 5.4 compares these structured classrooms with desks in rows to flexible learning spaces designed for the variability of the learners in the classroom.

**Table 5.4**    Structured Classrooms vs. Flexible Learning Spaces

| Structured Classrooms | Flexible Learning Spaces |
|---|---|
| Designed in the industrial age. | Designed for different learning needs. |
| Teachers as manager and disciplinarian. | Teacher as facilitator and partner in learning. |
| No learner voice and choice. | Learners own how and where they learn. |
| Seating arrangements to maintain order and control. | Different seating patterns and configurations. |
| Uniformity where all learners are the same and want to fit in. | Foster creativity, not just productivity. |

*Source:* Personalize Learning, LLC

### *Structured Classrooms*

Traditional teacher-centered classrooms have been a mainstay of American education since the first public schools were opened in the nineteenth century. However, when considering traditional methods of instruction, many teachers could mistakenly equate longevity with effectiveness. Socratic questioning can be powerful in the hands of an able teacher, but as the demographic pursuing a comprehensive, college-preparatory education changes, teachers must respond by changing their instructional practices.

Education today is designed to meet the needs of nineteenth-century Industrial Revolution employers that needed millions of assembly line workers, all similarly skilled and able to work for a simple wage.

The image in Figure 5.7 is from the 1940s, but it brings back memories for

> **Consider This!**
>
> Just integrating technology doesn't make a difference if the structure is still built on an industrial model.

**Figure 5.7**  Industrial Age Classroom

*Source:* http://commons.wikimedia.org/wiki/File:StateLibQld_1_100348.jpg

many Baby Boomers who were learners in the 1950s and 60s. Learners put their heads down when told to do so by the teacher. Learners never questioned authority. Does this look familiar? Seating arrangements in a classroom are a way to maintain order and control and are an important part of classroom management._

### Flexible Learning Spaces

The twenty-first century is challenging old notions of learning spaces. The idea that learners must be seated at desks working in rows is quickly becoming archaic. Technology and collaborative work environments are changing the design of learning spaces. Experts hope that the emerging paradigm will translate into improved learning spaces and influence future architectural design.

In a personalized learning environment, flexible learning zones are designed to give learners options to learn, collaborate, create, and design. Chris Edwards, a Year 2 teacher in the United Kingdom who discussed messy learning in Chapter 4, shared how his young learners (around seven years old) find that they can self-direct the learning by

**Pause/Think/Reflect**

What is the climate and culture of your classroom, and how could you make it more effective?

going to the appropriate learning space for each task. They stand at the creation zone and sit in beanbag chairs in the reading zone. The learners are busy using the space in the room effectively to work individually or with others. Chris redesigned his classroom (see Figure 5.8) using existing furniture, something teachers can do right now.

**Figure 5.8** Chris Edwards's Classroom Redesign

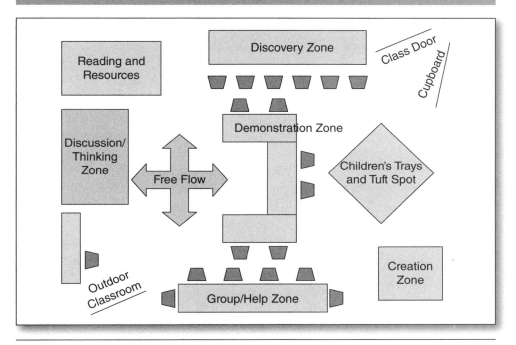

*Source:* Personalize Learning, LLC

## Computer Labs vs. 1:1/BYOD

Computer labs were designed to manage the limited computers in a school all in one place. Table 5.5 contrasts computer labs with a one user–one device approach.

**Table 5.5** Computer Labs vs. 1:1/BYOD

| Computer Labs | 1:1/BYOD |
| --- | --- |
| About the computers and software available. | About the learner and task. |
| Teacher or technology directed. | Learner-centered. |

*(Continued)*

| Table 5.5 (Continued) | |
| --- | --- |
| **Computer Labs** | **1:1/BYOD** |
| No or limited learner voice and choice. | Learners have voice and choice. |
| Schedule limits learning and work on activities. | Learners learn anytime, anywhere. |
| Availability controlled by tech department. | Learner drives learning using mobile device. |
| Limited access as a shared resource. | Learners can collaborate in classroom. |

### *Computer Labs*

For a long time, computers in labs were the only way for learners to access and use technology. After more computers became available in classrooms, labs were used to learn how to program, create music, or edit videos. Professional developers used labs for workshops that were mostly teacher led. Since the computer lab was a separate room that learners went to weekly based on scheduling issues, the lab was also set up as an elective or prep time. This meant that classroom teachers used that time for prep while a computer teacher, librarian, or paraprofessional taught or managed the computer lab. In most cases, when learners go to a computer lab, technology is not integrated into the curriculum.

**Pause/Think/Reflect**

Just putting technology in learners' hands or providing access to computers doesn't always mean learners are learning.

Computer labs still exist in the majority of traditional schools in the United States and around the world. The room layout can be one of the most frustrating things about teaching in a lab. Since many of the computers are desktops on tables that are fixed because of electrical outlets, the computers do not lend themselves to project-based and collaborative activities. Labs do not look exactly the same and often come in three configurations:

1. Lined up in rows like in a typing or sewing class

2. Configured in a U-shape around the edge of the room to accommodate electrical access for the teacher who can quickly see what is on the screens

3. Grouped in small pods or clusters on round or hexagonal tables spaced about the room

Computer labs today are maintained for several reasons:

- Security
- Promoting digital literacy skills that requires a dedicated room and teacher
- Climate control to protect desktop computers
- Standardized testing and adaptive learning systems
- Access for learners for afterschool or community events (Trucano, 2011)

### 1:1/BYOD

In a personalized learning environment, you provide flexibility in the ways learners access and engage with the content and express what they know. Optimally, all learners can have their own device to do that or possibly a choice of devices. Many schools have introduced 1:1 computing with iPads, Chromebooks, or other tablets whereas other schools have introduced BYOD (Bring your Own Device). Anytime, anywhere learning requires the use of a device for each learner.

Brett Clark, a Technology Director from Jeffersonville, Indiana, was recently asked to set up a 1:1 initiative in his school district. To gain support for a 1:1 movement, he came up with the following Six Pillars of a 1:1 Initiative.

> **Consider This!**
>
> If you are planning to purchase technology, consider the goal for integrating technology for learners first and how it supports their learning.

1. *Learning initiative.* A 1:1 movement cannot be about the device. It must be about the learning.

2. *Professional development.* There can never be enough professional development. Professional development should focus on how to actually use and maintain the device and how to successfully implement the device, which includes knowing when to put the device away.

3. *Infrastructure.* Like any great technological advancement, it does not matter what it does if it does not work.

4. *Digital citizenship.* How we conduct ourselves online and offline matters.

5. *Choice.* Bring-your-own-device means learners choose the device they want to use. Yet there is not one device that does it all. So in some cases, learners have multiple devices.

6. *Time and patience.* Moving from a traditional classroom to a 1:1 classroom takes time and patience. All major stakeholders need time to adjust to having technology and information at their fingertips. Very few things bring instant and sustainable success (Clark, 2013).

## Print vs. Digital

Table 5.6 compares print with digital text and shows why one might be better than the other for specific learners. Some research states that print is easier for learners to read whereas digital makes content more accessible.

**Table 5.6**   Print vs. Digital

| Print | Digital |
|---|---|
| Print is read 20 percent faster than digital text. | Learn material faster. |
| Easier to translate text into conceptual knowledge. | Enriches curriculum and instructional materials. |
| Do not need Internet connection or bandwidth. | Holds more than 100 times the content of print. |
| Not all learners can afford mobile devices. | Interactive features not available in print. |
| Technology is more distracting than print. | Content updated as needed. |

### Print

The print world is alive and well in almost every school on the planet. We are probably producing more hard-copy materials and print textbooks than at any time in history.

The brain interprets printed and digital text in different ways, and people generally read digital text 20 to 30 percent slower than print. According to Pulitzer Prize–winning technology writer Nicholas Carr, peer-reviewed studies show that reading hyperlinked text may increase the brain's "cognitive load," lowering the ability to process, store, and retain information, or "translate the new material into conceptual knowledge" (Noyes & Garland, 2008).

Many learners do not have sufficient home Internet bandwidth to use tablets. Learners "need home broadband to access digital content and to complete Internet based homework" (Digital Textbook Collaborative, 2012). According to FCC Chairman Julius Genachowski and Secretary of Education Arne Duncan, about a third of Americans—100 million people—do not have broadband Internet at home. A 2010 FCC survey found that nearly 80 percent of K–12 schools reported broadband connections that were "inadequate to meet their current needs" (Digital Textbook Collaborative, 2012).

The Joan Ganz Cooney Center released a QuickStudy that analyzed how three- to six-year-old children use and retain information from printed books, e-books, and enhanced e-books. They had the children read each book type and then tested their retention, interactivity, and co-reading experience.

- The Cooney Center recommends that parents and preschool teachers choose print or basic e-books (rather than enhanced e-books) if they want to deliver the best literacy-building experiences.
- They found that the interactive features of the more visually engaging enhanced e-book actually distracted both adults and children alike, making it tough for both to recall key points of what they just read. There is a silver lining to enhanced e-books though: they may prompt less motivated readers to pick up this type of book rather than none at all.
- Children who read enhanced e-books recalled fewer details than children who read the other types of books.
- As expected, enhanced e-books were more engaging and interactive, but print and basic e-books did a better job at literacy building (Lepi, 2012).

### *Digital*

Digital books and materials will be a reality in many schools, if they are not already, as educational publishers project that all textbooks will be produced in a digital format by 2017. Digital versions of books and materials provide greater flexibility to understand content and concepts. Digital content offers multiple means of representation of information for any learning environment, anywhere, anytime. Above all, it provides access to content and information that so many learners have been denied due to learning or reading disabilities or for those who may speak another language.

Self-directed learning, a much-sought goal of twenty-first-century education, can really blossom with digital content. As learners become more adept at using digital content and building their digital literacy, they are able to choose their own sources for learning rather than simply being fed lessons through the filter of a textbook or a single teacher. In the optimal scenario, the learner is inspired to expand learning beyond school, and that means shifting effortlessly from school-sanctioned lessons to other resources, a feat made easier with digital content.

Digital content is more flexible and cost-effective than print materials such as textbooks. Digital resources can be updated easily without the cost of reprinting. They are available anytime, anywhere for learners and teachers to access in the classroom or at home. They can be personalized to meet the individual needs of learners. And they allow for richer content, including high-definition graphics, videos, simulations, interactive lessons, virtual labs, and online assessments.

> **Pause/Think/Reflect**
>
> How does the brain perceive text in digital or print forms?

Young children have been seen as early as eight to ten months sweeping their fingers across an iPad's touchscreen, pinching, swiping, and clicking on icons. Children who have only known technology may not know what to do with paper. One father who took a video of his one-year-old using an iPad stated that "a magazine is an iPad that does not work." For these young children who have been interacting with digital technologies from a very early age, books and magazines seem useless to them. There are concerns, however, about reading on a screen that is pixelated, has glare, and flickers (Jabr, 2013).

## Assessment OF, FOR, and AS Learning

Table 5.7 explains how assessment differs in individualization and differentiation situations compared to personalization. All three environments can involve Assessment OF, FOR, and AS; however, in personalization, learners are more involved in monitoring their progress as they learn. In the other environments, the teacher may be responsible for assessments that refer to summative and formative assessments. In those cases, learners may not have a voice in how their learning is assessed.

**Table 5.7**  Assessment OF, FOR, and AS Learning

| Fixed Traditional System | | Flexible Learning System |
|---|---|---|
| *Individualization* | *Differentiation* | *Personalization* |
| Assessment **OF** Learning | Assessment **OF** and **FOR** Learning | Assessment **AS** and **FOR** Learning with minimum **OF** Learning |
| Summative assessment is grade-based and involves time-based testing that confirms what learners know. | Assessment involves time-based testing, and teachers provide feedback to advance learning. | Teachers develop capacity so learners become independent learners who set goals, monitor progress, and reflect on learning and assessments based on mastery. |

### Assessment OF Learning

Assessment OF Learning is where the teacher measures learner performance using summative assessments to confirm what learners know and can do. It refers to strategies designed to confirm what learners know, demonstrate whether or not they have met curriculum outcomes or the goals of their individualized programs, or certify proficiency and make decisions about learners' future programs or placements in relation to others. Teachers concentrate on ensuring that they have used assessment to provide accurate and sound statements of learners' proficiency. Effective Assessment OF Learning requires that teachers provide the following:

- A rationale for undertaking a particular assessment of learning at a particular time
- Clear descriptions of the intended learning
- Processes that make it possible for learners to demonstrate their competence and skill
- A range of alternative mechanisms for assessing the same outcomes
- Public and defensible reference points for making judgments
- Transparent approaches to interpretation
- Descriptions of the assessment process
- Strategies for recourse in the event of disagreement about the decisions

### Assessment FOR Learning

Assessment FOR Learning is where the teacher and peers provide feedback to the learner throughout the learning process. Assessment FOR Learning provides information about what learners already know and can do, so that teachers can design the most appropriate next steps in instruction. Assessment FOR Learning is designed to give teachers information to modify and differentiate teaching and learning activities. It acknowledges that individual learners learn in idiosyncratic ways, but it also recognizes that there are predictable patterns and pathways that many learners follow. It requires careful design on the part of teachers so that they use the resulting information to determine not only what learners know but also to gain insights into how, when, and whether learners apply what they know. Teachers can also use this information to streamline and target instruction and resources and to provide feedback to learners to help them advance their learning. Assessment FOR Learning occurs throughout the learning process. It is interactive, with teachers doing the following:

- Aligning instruction with the targeted outcomes
- Identifying particular learning needs of learners or groups

- Selecting and adapting materials and resources
- Creating differentiated teaching strategies and learning opportunities for helping individual learners move forward in their learning
- Providing immediate feedback and direction to learners

### Assessment AS Learning

Assessment AS Learning is where learners monitor their progress and reflect on their own learning. It is based on research about how learning happens and is characterized by learners reflecting on their own learning, monitoring their progress, and making adjustments to their learning so that they achieve deeper understanding. Reporting in Assessment AS Learning is the responsibility of learners who can learn to articulate and defend the nature and quality of their learning. When learners reflect on their own learning and communicate it to others, they are intensifying their understanding about a topic, their own learning strengths, and the areas in which they need to develop further and advance their learning.

The teacher's role in promoting the development of independent learners through assessment as learning is the following:

- Model and teach the skills of self-assessment
- Guide learners in setting goals and monitor their progress toward them
- Provide exemplars and models of good practice and quality work that reflect curriculum outcomes
- Work with learners to develop clear criteria of good practice
- Guide learners in developing internal feedback or self-monitoring mechanisms to validate and question their own thinking and to become comfortable with the ambiguity and uncertainty that is inevitable in learning anything new
- Provide regular and challenging opportunities to practice, so that learners can become confident, competent self-assessors
- Monitor learners' metacognitive processes as well as their learning and provide descriptive feedback
- Create an environment where it is safe for learners to take chances and where support is readily available (Earl & Katz, 2006)

**Pause/Think/Reflect**

What are your assessment strategies? How do you use assessment of, for, and as learning in your classroom? How can you move to an environment that includes more assessment as learning?

You might see assessment of, for, and as learning happening in your classroom. In the world of standardized tests, teachers and schools are accountable for the learning, not the learners. When you move to assessment as learning, the types of assessments change. Learners are not only more responsible for their learning, they are also more accountable and can monitor their progress. This is what personalizing learning is all about.

## CONTINUUM OF AN EXPERT LEARNER

Now that you have reviewed fixed versus flexible systems, refer back to Figure 5.1, Continuum of an Expert Learner, as it relates to motivation, ownership, purpose, and self-regulation. Learners will want to learn if they are intrinsically motivated. Right now in traditional classrooms around the country, learners are motivated by extrinsic factors: grades, praise, and moving to the next grade level.

Motivation changes as learners respond to and prepare for their learning. Instead of grouping unmotivated learners together and moving them away from motivated learners, it would be better first to determine what motivates learners. Researchers now largely agree "that even though there may be individual differences in biological aptitudes for learning certain things like music or sports, most functional intelligence is learnable and hence also teachable (Bransford, Derry, Berliner, Hammerness, & Beckett, 2005).

### Motivation to Learn

Kathleen Cushman is an expert on adolescent learning and motivation who began her work with the Coalition of Essential Schools. She started as a co-founder of the Francis J. Parker Charter School in Devens, Massachusetts. She is co-founder of What Kids Can Do with Barbara Cervone, and author of *Fires in the Mind, Fires in the Bathroom* and *The Motivation Equation*, among other titles. Kathleen authored the "8 Universal Factors that Motivate Kids."

1. *We feel OK.* Creating well-being in a learning environment is the crucial first step, according to both kids and scientists. Threats to our physical or emotional safety—from hunger to humiliation—shut down learning as we respond to more primal signals.

2. *It matters.* A personal connection or a real-world issue can make all the difference to whether we care about an academic task. Offering a choice on some aspect of the work also sends its value up, and so does the chance to work on things with friends.

3. *It's active.* From constructing a model to collaborating on a puzzle, we start to "own" new information when our hands and minds engage our thinking processes more fully.

4. *It stretches us.* Extreme frustration can shut down learning, but a stretch that's both challenging and achievable gives the learner a buzz of excitement. (Don't forget to notice small successes along the way!)

5. *We have a coach.* We do much better with someone around who will help us make sure we're getting it right—watching us practice and giving us tips, with plenty of time to learn from our mistakes.

6. *We have to use it.* Doing something with information not only shows that we know it but also makes it stick in our minds. The most fun is to perform what we've learned or teach it to others—but even a pop quiz will do the trick.

7. *We think back on it.* What did I learn? What would I do differently next time? How have I grown and changed? Making time for us to reflect on questions like these has a huge effect on deepening our learning—yet it's the easiest thing to skip.

8. *We plan our next steps.* Planning any venture—an argument, a project, even what we're going to say next—is a creative adventure. It forces us to remember information in order to develop an idea or solve a problem. Hand us the keys to our learning and watch us take those intellectual risks! (Cushman, 2013)

Kathleen shared that these eight factors taken together give us a critical lens through which we can analyze what's going wrong—and what's going right—as we teach and as we learn.

## Growth Mindset

 A growth mindset is an important outcome to consider when you begin to design a personalized learning environment. This is actually a social and emotional part of the bigger puzzle. If you don't believe in yourself or think you cannot do something, it is difficult to get motivated to do something. You can almost determine the first day in your classroom who has a fixed mindset and who has a growth mindset. The two mindsets are contrasted in Table 5.8.

**Table 5.8** Fixed Mindset vs. Growth Mindset

| Fixed Mindset | Growth Mindset |
|---|---|
| Intelligence or talent is a fixed trait. | Most abilities can be developed with brains and talent as a starting point. |
| Teachers spend time documenting intelligence or talent instead of developing them. | Learners have a love of learning and resilience that is essential for great accomplishments. |

The focus in traditional school is to avoid failure. The focus in a personalized learning environment is to learn how to fail and learn from failure. One reason we give up or believe that we cannot do something is because of the focus on failing. Teachers can change that by believing in themselves as learners. Growth-minded teachers love to learn and love teaching as a way to learn about themselves. Everything is a learning opportunity and teachable moment for these teachers. Carol Dweck (2006) writes in her book *Mindset* that "the growth mindset is based on the belief that your basic qualities are things you can cultivate through your efforts. Although people may differ in every which way—in their initial talents and aptitudes, interest, or temperament— everyone can change and grow through application and experience" (p. 7).

> **Pause/Think/Reflect**
>
> We all fail at some things, but does that mean we are failures? How can learners persevere so they don't give up?

Mindsets frame what is taking place in our heads. Fixed mindsets interpret things differently from growth mindsets. Those with a fixed mindset create an internal dialogue judging themselves and others. They put a very strong evaluation on each and every piece of information. People with a growth mindset are constantly monitoring what's going on, but their internal dialogue focuses more on what they can learn from something and how can they improve. Probably the best thing you as a teacher can do is to model how to develop a growth mindset so your learners realize they too can change and believe in themselves. It is about persevering when times are tough and getting back up if you fall (Dweck, 2006).

## Ownership of Learning

Ownership of learning is about learners driving their own learning. When learners own their learning, they are more motivated and take responsibility for their learning. When learners have a stake in their learning, they often discover purpose in their learning.

### *Learners can drive their learning to . . .*

- meet their personal learning goals and align them to Common Core and other standards;
- determine how they will demonstrate mastery of learning; and
- discover their interests, aspirations, talents, and strengths to help them meet their college, career, and life goals.

> **Pause/Think/Reflect**
>
> Do you think you can change one activity in one lesson so your learners can drive their learning?

Chris Watkins, researcher at the University of London, Institute of Education, developed a driving metaphor, mentioned in Chapter 1, to better understand the concept of driving your learning.

Imagine what driving your own learning means for you. You have your hands on the wheel, steering; you are watching where you are going and making decisions as you go on your journey. As you are driving, you are noticing what is happening as you drive and how that relates to where you want to be. These are the same core processes that are key to being an effective learner. Watkins discussed that learning, just like driving, involves planning, monitoring, and reflecting. His research demonstrates that when learners drive the learning it leads to . . .

- Greater engagement and intrinsic motivation
- Learners setting higher challenges
- Learners evaluating their work
- Better problem solving

### *Responsibility vs. Accountability*

 The word *responsibility* has been used interchangeably with the word *accountability* when it comes to teachers, teaching, and learning. The national dialogue on public education over the last decade has been characterized by the need to improve our schools, elevate achievement, and hold accountable those educators and institutions that fail to meet those expectations.

The current reliance on high-stakes standardized tests as the sole assessment of learner achievement, teacher efficacy, and primary motivator of individual and institutional performance has come under fire. Being obsessed with measuring adequate yearly progress (AYP), we sometimes forget the importance of cultivating a love of learning, a passion for inquiry, and a zeal for creative expression. Even the movement to raise standards may fail if teachers are not supported to understand the connections among motivation, engagement, and voice (Toshalis & Nakkula, 2013).

Where does intrinsic motivation factor in the equation? Evaluations of teachers are often based on learner performance and data, so teachers feel not only accountable but responsible for what their learners learn. Doesn't this seem backward?

When learners take responsibility to write something they are interested in for an audience of their peers, they are motivated to write, read each other's work, and want to learn and do more.

*Responsibility* means a moral obligation and something taken upon one's self. Most of the teachers we know feel wholly and morally responsible for their learners. That's why most of us went into the profession: to make a difference.

*Accountability* is more of a social contract or social obligation. Accountability can be measurable. If teachers are accountable for their learners' learning, then why would learners feel responsible for their own learning?

If these are the correct definitions then *accountability* refers to making, keeping, and managing agreements and expectations where *responsibility* is the feeling of ownership. So that's it! Being responsible for our own learning. This also means that all learners need to be held accountable for what they learn by taking responsibility for their own learning. Teachers usually feel a responsibility to create an environment that engages and motivates learners to want to learn, but that does not mean they have to be accountable for what learners learn.

Motivation is related to whether or not learners have opportunities to be autonomous and to make important academic choices. Having choices

> **Counterproductive Effects in the Classroom**
>
> Encouraging learner-driven learning requires several actions; one is naming the problem. Some of the current climate may be having counterproductive effects in the classroom. Teachers may not even realize they may be enabling behaviors where learners will only do what they are told to do. Mary Ellen Weimer (2002) states:
>
> - The more structured we make the environment, the more structure learners need.
> - The more we decide for learners, the more they expect us to decide.
> - The more motivation we provide, the less they find within themselves.
> - The more responsibility for learning we try to assume, the less they accept on their own.
> - The more control we exert, the more restive their response.

> **Pause/Think/Reflect**
>
> If teachers are accountable for what their learners are learning, are learners only learning for their teachers or a grade, not for themselves?

allows learners to feel that they have control or ownership over their own learning. This, in turn, helps them develop a sense of responsibility and self-motivation (McCombs, 2014).

When learners feel a sense of ownership, they want to engage in academic tasks and persist in learning. If teachers and learners are learners first, then responsibility comes with being a learner. Learners of all ages become responsible for their learning when they own and drive their learning.

### Finding Purpose

When learners pursue their passion or interest, they are intrinsically motivated to learn. It is something they want to do. Just imagine if you could learn about something you are interested in and passionate about and find it is your purpose. When you pursue your purpose, you tend to self-direct your learning by setting goals and planning how you will meet those goals. You do this because you believe in your purpose. When you work toward a goal you really believe in, you self-regulate your learning and monitor your progress.

Purpose is about making a difference in the world. We need to give learners opportunities where they can experience something that can make a difference in their lives and others.' When you find a purpose for learning, you can bring purpose into your adult life that is powerful in so many ways because it impacts you emotionally and socially. You persevere to learn more. You actually learn by trying, failing, and trying again. Failure is not an option. It is about developing agency and owning your journey. Your purpose is your reason to learn and grow.

### Self-Regulation

Self-regulation provides a learner-centered perspective on the various dimensions of engagement. The self-regulation theory is concerned with what learners do to generate and sustain their engagement. It begins with the recognition that learners are active participants in their own learning. This echoes constructivists' observations about building rather than just absorbing knowledge. To be self-regulated is to be goal directed, to demonstrate control over and be responsible for your own focus and effort when engaged in a learning activity.

Cognitively, "self-regulated learners plan, set goals, organize, self-monitor, and self-evaluate at various points during the process of building new knowledge or skills. These processes enable learners to be self-aware, knowledgeable, and decisive in their approach to learning" (Zimmerman, 1990).

Self-regulated learners tend to be self-starters who show effort and persistence during learning, who seek out advice, information, and places where they are most likely to learn. An example of a self-regulated learner is a learner who might read a paragraph and then ask herself what the paragraph was all about and may realize she cannot remember. She then self-regulates her own learning by going back and rereading the paragraph for understanding—all on her own.

## SO WHY WOULD YOU PERSONALIZE LEARNING?

When teachers transform their teaching, learning changes. Figure 5.1, Continuum of an Expert Learner, guided the design of this chapter and can be used to help you define learners in your school or district. Use the continuum and the rationale in this chapter to help you guide how you will personalize learning.

Personalizing learning takes time, patience, and commitment. If someone asked you why you would want to personalize learning and you only had sixty seconds in an elevator, you would have to quickly come up with something profound about personalized learning. Teachers are so creative and created speeches in multiple forms, such as videos, cartoons, and text. Here are two teachers from the Verona Area School District in Wisconsin who wanted to share their speeches with you.

### Response to Learners

*We CHOOSE teaching*

*We do not teach math, reading, or science*

*We support, encourage, engage, and empower learners*

*ALL learners*

*We do not assess, report, grade*

*We team with learners to set meaningful goals and provide evidence of learning*

*We believe ALL learners can and will achieve at high levels*

*We do not close our doors*

*We work as a TEAM to design, support, and respond to learners*

*ALL learners*

*Anytime, anywhere*

*We do not track, retain, or marginalize*

*We build relationships, recognize talents, encourage passions*

*We foster hope*

*We CHOOSE Personalized Learning*

---

*Source:* Jennie Clement, Learning Resource Coordinator, Glacier Edge Elementary, Wisconsin

## Visualize an Environment Where . . .

*ALL LEARNERS . . .*

- *Experience equity/respect/success*
- *Enjoy the experience of belonging*
- *Are invited to use their interests/strengths/passions/desires/goals to create their own learning journey*
- *Are . . .*

  - Challenged
  - Motivated
  - Engaged
  - Independent
  - Collaborative
  - Powerful

- *Are passionate and connect with other passionate learners near and far*
- *Are in control of their learning because they have been equipped to be self-aware/reflective/expert learners*
- *Are learning partners with family/school/community/world*
- *Use technology flexibly to obtain information/to interact with information/ to create and share new learning*
- *Have supportive relationships with teachers who believe in them and guide them*

---

*Source:* Amy Buss, Learning Resource Coordinator, Sugar Creek Elementary, Wisconsin

When you look at the rationale in this chapter, the characteristics of expert learners, and the sixty-second speeches, do you have a better idea of what personalized meaning means for your learners? What about your role as a teacher or administrator?

## CHAPTER 5 REVIEW

- To have a better idea of learner voice, refer to the Spectrum of Learner Voice–Oriented Activity in Figure 5.3 and what that means for your learners.
- Review the UDL principles and characteristics of expert learners so learners can have choices in how they access information, engage with content, and express what they know and understand.
- Read through the "8 Universal Factors that Motivate Learners" and ask your own learners what motivates them to learn.
- Read through the skills and values learners need for their future. Then consider how learners will acquire these skills and values.
- Review the fixed vs. flexible systems. Choose an initiative to research in more detail and describe what it will look like in a flexible system.
- Choose and summarize one concept as a rationale to personalize learning.
- Create a sixty-second elevator speech about personalizing learning.

## RESOURCES

- Turning Students Into Good Digital Citizens: http://thejournal .com/articles/2012/04/09/rethinking-digital-citizenship.aspx
- The Current State of Mobile Learning in Education: http://edu demic.com/2012/08/state-of-mobile-learning-education
- Connected Learning Research Network: http://clrn.dmlhub.net
- Dropout Rates Infographic: http://visual.ly/dropout-epidemic
- CompetencyWorks: www.competencyworks.org
- Center on Response to Intervention: www.rti4success.org
- Finding Coherence With RTI and Personalized Learning: http:// cesa1transformation.wordpress.com/2012/05/23/finding-coher ence-with-rti-and-personalized-learning
- Six Pillars of a 1:1 Initiative: http://smartblogs.com/educa tion/2013/01/16/the-6-pillars-11-initiative-brett-clark/
- UDL and Expert Learners (National Center on Universal Design for Learning) www.udlcenter.org/aboutudl/expertlearners

# 6

# Your Turn to Personalize Learning

*"If culture changes, everything changes."*

—Michael Fullan

## CULTURE SHIFT

When you turn the learning over to your learners, that's a culture shift. When learners take control of their learning and have a voice in how they learn, that's a culture shift. Veteran teachers have teaching strategies and lessons all prepared. When teachers first hear what it means to change teaching practice and transform their lessons, some are concerned with what it will mean for them or their learners, assuming they are interested at all. Just getting teachers to recognize and call students "learners" has been a struggle. Even if something is not working, it is easier for people to stay with the status quo. Now is the time to change school culture and shake up the system. We have to for our learners because it is all about them and their future.

### Traditional Classrooms to Learner-Centered Environments

To review, in a learner-centered environment, engagement becomes more active. Noise level increases from group work. Learners are moving around the class self-directing their learning. They may be working independently or with one or more other learners. This changes how you teach. Table 6.1 shows how learner-centered environments are different from traditional classrooms.

**Table 6.1** Traditional Classrooms vs. Learner-Centered Environments

| Traditional Classrooms | Learner-Centered Environments |
|---|---|
| Learners learning same material at same time. | Learning driven by learners' goals. |
| Low level of engagement (passive). | High level of engagement (active). |
| Students placed in grade level based on age and earn letter grades "to pass." | Learners progress through levels based on performance and demonstrating mastery. |
| Progression to the next grade level only occurs at end of the school year. Learning is "fragmented" from year to year and perpetuates social promotion and retention. | Progression to the next performance level can occur on any day during the course of the year. Learning has a "continuous flow" throughout the years and ends social promotion and retention. |
| Multi-age classrooms are the exception. | Multi-age classrooms are the norm. |
| The pace of learning is directed by the teacher, technology, or curriculum. | Learners accelerate the pace of learning through goal setting, voice, and choice. |
| Predominantly whole-group approach to teaching. | Predominantly small-group or one-on-one approach to learning. |
| Fixed learning spaces that encourage direct instruction. | Flexible learning spaces that encourage independent and collaborative group work. |
| Teachers teach in isolation, usually one classroom in one grade level per year. | Teachers co-teach with one or more teachers and are part of a community of practice. |
| Commercially created artifacts are displayed in the classroom and hallway. | Artifacts as evidence of learning from the learners are everywhere in the learning environment. |
| Teachers use student data to drive instruction and to know their learners. | Learners create a Personal Learner Profile based on how they learn best. Teachers create a Class Learning Snapshot based on four diverse learners. |

*Source:* Personalize Learning, LLC 2013

## Systemic Change Causes Culture Shift

To ensure deeper learning, to encourage problem-solving and thinking skills, and to develop and nurture highly motivated and engaged learners requires mobilizing the energy and capacities of all teachers. In turn, to mobilize teachers, we must improve teachers' working conditions and morale. To do this, we need leaders who can create a fundamental transformation in the learning cultures of schools and of the teaching profession itself. When we personalize learning in one classroom, learners' attitudes change about their roles in the learning process. They are more involved and engaged in their learning, and that energy spills out into the hall and goes home.

You might have heard kids say that they want the teacher who makes learning fun or challenges them. Not every teacher can be that teacher. This is more than something the principal as the instructional leader can change alone. This involves what Michael Fullan calls the right drivers.

> *"Everyone, ultimately, has a stake in the caliber of schools, and education is everyone's business."*
>
> —Michael Fullan, The Moral Imperative of School Leadership

## Wrong vs. Right Drivers

Michael Fullan (2011) outlines the wrong and right drivers for systemic change in Table 6.2. He lays out four criteria that must be met by the drivers for change and reform at a district and system level.

- Foster intrinsic motivation of teachers and learners
- Engage educators and learners in continuous improvement of instruction and learning
- Inspire collective or team work
- Affect teachers and learners—100 percent

**Table 6.2**   Wrong vs. Right Drivers

| Wrong Drivers | Right Drivers |
|---|---|
| Accountability | Capacity building |
| Individual teacher and leadership quality | Collaborative work |
| Technology | Pedagogy |
| Fragment strategies | System-ness |

*Source:* Fullan, 2011

Fullan mentions "system-ness" as a right driver. Building a system around personalized learning means everyone is involved. We know teachers like Kevin McLaughlin who took risks and other teachers resisted. This made it difficult for the teacher who personalized learning. In some cases, teachers believed and fought and worked so hard, but they just couldn't fight the system and gave up. Our system is broken, and it's time to really look at personalizing learning as a way to transform education.

> *"Culture has been defined as the way we do things around here."*
>
> —Rick DuFour

Schools have been doing things the same way for hundreds of years. Changing teaching and learning takes time, and some educators and parents aren't ready to change to a personalized learning system.

> *"To transform an entire system to a learner-centered culture, all stakeholders in the school community need to agree on the shared vision and goals."*
>
> —Rick DuFour

Culture shift is defined as lasting changes to the shared ways of thinking, beliefs, values, procedures, and relationships of the stakeholders. A school needs trust in changing beliefs, values, and relationships. Change is a difficult process. There are so many types of relationships in schools that impact how people think about school (DuFour, 2004).

## Transforming Schools Is the Culture Shift

Robert Evans (1996) explains in his book *The Human Side of School Change* that "transformation begins with trust." School change requires a belief in the potential of improving people, but it also requires an acceptance of people as they are. Change means something different to different people. Evans argues that the key factor in change is what it means to those who must implement it, in that its primary meaning encourages resistance. It provokes loss, challenges competence, creates confusion, and causes conflict.

> *"Real change is always personal: organizational change is always incremental."*
>
> —Robert Evans

Probably the biggest factor needed to improve schools is hope. Evans explains that we cannot hope to transform schools with just a commitment from all stakeholders. In the best of schools, with the best resources, and the most skillful leadership, the timeframe for transforming culture, structure, belief, and practice is years (Evans, 1996).

Personalizing learning is more than putting a device in learners' hands. It is more than creating one lesson with voice and choice. The Stages of Personalized Learning Environments were created to provide a process for teachers who are tentative to start. Like Evans states, the timeframe for implementation is years. Initiatives fail because the expectations were to change in one or two years. Realistically, changing the culture of the school involves many factors that keep change from happening. Change is scary for some, and the status quo is comfortable. Today our learners are demanding that schools change. The world is changing, and learners hope for learning environments that engage and motivate them. They want the focus to be on learning.

## READINESS FOR CULTURE SHIFT

**Readiness** is defined as a developmental point at which a person, organization, or system has the capacity and willingness to engage in a particular activity. Creating readiness for change is a critical component of both initiating and scaling up the use of evidence-based practices and other innovations in education. Readiness is an under-emphasized part of the implementation process.

> *Where are you in the process of personalizing learning?*

### Concerns-Based Adoption Model (CBAM) for Personalized Learning

In facilitating change, you need to know what concerns you or other educators may have about personalizing learning, especially your most intense concerns. These concerns will have a powerful influence on the implementation of change and how you will sustain the transformation to personalize learning. CBAM offers several ways to identify these concerns. As an educator or change agent, you can use this model to identify concerns, interpret them, and then act on them. Table 6.3 describes each stage of concern and strategies to guide change.

What stage are you in when it comes to personalizing learning? If you are at the informational stage, you want to find out more about what that means for you and your learners. As a coach or administrator, you can identify the stage of concern most of the teachers on your staff are working in.

**Table 6.3** CBAM: Stages of Concern About Personalized Learning

| Stages | Description | Strategies to Guide Change |
|---|---|---|
| *Awareness* | • May or may not know about personalizing learning.<br>• May or may not be ready to change roles and let go so learners own their learning. | • Involve teachers in discussions and decisions.<br>• Share enough information to stir interest but not to overwhelm.<br>• Provide open environment where all questions are allowed.<br>• Minimize gossip and inaccurate sharing of information. |
| *Informational* | • Wants to learn more about personalized learning.<br>• Curious about what will happen to their role as teachers and how to start with learners. | • Share information through all forms of media.<br>• Find those that are taking risks in and out of the school and have them share what they are doing.<br>• Help teachers see how moving to a personalized learning approach relates to their teaching practice.<br>• Be enthusiastic about those that try something new and share their successes. |
| *Personal* | • Have concerns about how changing their role will affect their effectiveness.<br>• Does not want to look foolish in front of learners.<br>• Might say "What's in it for me?" (WIIFM) | • Realize that these concerns are common and legitimize their existence.<br>• Connect teachers with similar concerns with those who will be supportive.<br>• Share small steps that are attainable. |
| *Management* | • Wants practical suggestions before jumping in.<br>• Needs help with specific problems often. | • Explain details of specific strategies of personalized learning.<br>• Offer the How in small steps.<br>• Help teachers create their own learning plan with realistic goals based on how learners learn best. |

*(Continued)*

**Table 6.3** (CBAM Continued)

| Stages | Description | Strategies to Guide Change |
|---|---|---|
| *Consequence* | • Wants to know how personalizing learning will impact learners and their academic achievement.<br>• Concerned about how it will impact their teaching and relationships with their learners. | • Share lessons or projects that encourage learner voice and choice.<br>• Share research that provides evidence of learning and change in teaching practice. |
| *Collaborative* | • Interested in sharing lessons and projects with other teachers.<br>• Encourages learners to co-design lessons with them.<br>• Willing to offer support to other teachers.<br>• Participates in and may even lead a professional learning community or community of practice around personalized learning. | • Provide teachers opportunities to attend conferences or visit other teachers or schools that have personalized learning.<br>• Provide common planning time to discuss what's working and learn from each other.<br>• Encourage teachers to team teach. |
| *Refocusing* | • Looks for ways to transform to learner-driven environment.<br>• Serves on committee involving the change.<br>• Writes and speaks about personalizing learning to other educators. | • Encourage these teachers to research and test new ideas and strategies with their learners.<br>• Provide access to all resources so they can refine their ideas and put them into practice.<br>• Allow these teachers to take risks and share results. |

*Source:* Bray & McClaskey, 2012. Creative Commons License. [Adapted from Hord, Rutherford, Huling-Austin, Hall, & Knoll, 1987.]

If 50 percent of your staff are at the awareness stage of concern, then you review the strategies for change in the right column. During lunch in the faculty room, you can involve teachers in discussions and decisions. Then share enough information to stir interest but not overwhelm them.

You may find that there are more teachers at the personal and management stages of concern than you thought. The strategies to guide change can support teachers, but for some it will take one-on-one coaching and maybe even modeling in the classroom.

## Fixen's Stages of Implementation

Dean L. Fixen and colleagues (Fixen, Blase, Horner, & Sugal, 2009) write in their report *Scaling Up Evidence-Based Practices in Education* about moving ahead on implementation when people are not ready. Teachers may be "resistant to change" because they are not "ready for change." Fixen designed the Stages of Implementation for the readiness to change. Fixen's stages were adapted to relate to adopting a personalized learning environment (see Table 6.4). Fixen states that in education "readiness for change" is something that needs to be developed, nurtured, and sustained (Fixen et al., 2009).

**Table 6.4**    Fixen's Stages of Implementation Adapted to Relate to Personalized Learning

| | |
|---|---|
| ***Exploration*** | • Identify the need to personalize learning<br>• Learning about possible strategies for solutions<br>• What it takes to implement personalizing learning effectively<br>• Developing stakeholders and champions<br>• Deciding to proceed |
| ***Installation*** | Teachers establish the resources required to implement personalized learning with fidelity and good outcomes for teachers and learners. |
| ***Initial Implementation*** | Stage One Personalized Learning Environment (PLE) is when teachers are infusing voice and choice in their lessons. We call this dipping your toes into personalizing learning. Fixen calls it the "awkward stage." |
| ***Full Implementation*** | When all teachers have dipped their toes into personalizing learning, some teachers have moved to Stage Two PLE where they are co-designers of curriculum and the learning environment with their learners. |
| ***Innovation*** | When all teachers are personalizing learning and the system has measured the success, the system itself has changed the way teaching and learning are delivered across the school or district. Teachers may have adopted competency-based learning, changed assessment strategies, and moved to Stage Three PLE, learner-driven environments. |
| ***Sustainability*** | A coaching program provides ongoing job-embedded support for teachers, and learners are teaching each other. The system is generative because it is continually comparing outcomes against current practice and modifying practice to achieve valued outcomes. |

*Source:* Adapted from Fixen et al., 2009

## Your Readiness to Personalize Learning

How do you know if your school or district is ready to personalize learning? There are multiple strategies to assess your readiness. First you need to know who is on board, who is ready to take some risks, and who is ready for creative, collaborative, and innovative experiences for their learners and themselves. A school may think it is ready, but there might be some teachers still in the awareness stage and others in the refocusing stage (refer to CBAM in Table 6.3).

A school can use Fixen's Stages of Implementation to determine the stage of the entire staff. However, administrators may not have enough information about each teacher's concerns and may need more criteria to determine readiness. To that end, administrators can adopt the following strategies:

- Interview teachers and ask them to share some lessons that include learner voice and choice, how they feel about giving more control of the learning to the learner, and their hopes for teaching and learning.
- Observe teaching and learning in the classroom, learner participation, the look and feel of the learning environment, and examples of assessments and reflection on learning.
- Conduct pre-assessment surveys for teachers that ask about the following:
    o Instructional design
    o Comfort level of learning environment
    o How learners learn best
    o Teaching and assessment strategies
    o Level of technology integration
    o Tools, apps, and website to support learning
    o Stage of concern based on CBAM
    o Culture and climate in classroom
    o Example of lesson or project
    o Snapshot of culture in classroom

- Conduct pre-assessment surveys for schools that determine, in addition to the information in the previous survey, more specifics about the following:
    o Competency-based education
    o Aligning to Common Core State Standards
    o Technology, including bandwidth, support, and levels of integration
    o Current initiatives and programs
    o Professional development
    o Culture of school

# CHANGING THE CULTURE (FOR EDUCATIONAL LEADERS)

Personalizing learning means changing the culture. It also means changing the current system to a personalized learning system that can be self-sustaining. Let's first define what a Personalized Learning System is and what it can look like from the perspective of the district, the school, the teacher, and the learner. That means beginning with the end in mind.

## What Is a Personalized Learning System (PLS)?

A **Personalized Learning System** is a culture shift and a change in process that impacts the entire school community. Moving to learner-centered personalized learning environments is more than just handing over the keys to learners so they drive their own learning right away. It means creating a self-sustaining system that will need human and technological infrastructures to support it. The human infrastructure will include a multilayer coaching model to support the teachers in creating personalized learning environments where lessons are transformed and universally designed. The technological infrastructure entails supporting teaching and learning where every learner has access to learning 365/24/7. Before you begin to consider your first steps, let's take a look at the bigger picture.

### Begin With the End in Mind

What can a Personalized Learning System look like from the perspective of the district, the school, the teacher, and the learner? As shown in Figure 6.1, each position takes on a different role and perspective.

Notice that each element of a PLS has different roles to play in the process. Elements are woven into a framework where each piece fits together to create a culture where every learner becomes self-directed and independent. All the pieces work together so that learners are prepared to make choices for college and career. The first steps needed to begin your journey to change the culture and create a self-sustaining personalized learning system involve the following:

- Connecting the dots under the personalized learning umbrella
- Creating a shared vision, belief system, and commitment to personalize learning
- Developing a strategic plan for the self-sustaining personalized learning system

**Figure 6.1** Building a Self-Sustainable Personalized Learning System (PLS)

| | | | |
|---|---|---|---|
| Each District | Creates Vision, Beliefs and Commitments with Stakeholders | Establishes a Community of Practice (CoP) | Develops and Implements a Strategic Plan to support a PLS |
| Each School | Establishes Trust and Respect as Part of the Culture | Allows for Flexibility in Curriculium and Classroom Redesign | Supports Teachers in Developing Learner-Centered PLEs |
| Each Teacher | Understands each Learner's Strengths, Challenges, and Interests | Includes Learner Voice and Choice in Lessons | Develops Personal Professional Goals to Support PLE |
| Each Learner | Understands How They Learn and has Voice and Choice in Their Learning | Selects and Uses Appropriate Tools to Support Learning | Becomes a Self-Directed Learner Prepared for College and Career |

Source: Personalize Learning, LLC, 2013

## Connect the Dots Under the Personalized Learning Umbrella

Now that you have an understanding of personalized learning, how do you make it work in your current system? You know that when you personalize learning, teacher and learner roles change. But something else happens: how you teach changes, and existing initiatives and programs are impacted. The issue here is that personalizing learning is not a new initiative that you add to your repertoire. You probably have heard teachers and others say, "Personalized Learning is one more fad—it will go away" and "This is just like something else in our district, and that didn't work." Instead of putting up barriers to moving ahead, consider personalized learning as the umbrella that connects the dots of all your initiatives and programs, as shown in Figure 6.2. These initiatives and programs will look different if teaching and learning roles change.

Some people confuse the terms *personalized* and *personalization* as something that is done *to* the learner. If you change the concept so

 everything starts *with* the learner and you connect your programs, initiatives, and teaching strategies under the umbrella, it doesn't matter what you call it. It's the big picture of transforming teaching and learning so the focus

**Figure 6.2**   Personalized Learning Umbrella

Source: Personalize Learning, LLC, 2013

is on the learner instead of the instruction, the curriculum, or the technology. Learning is always personal to the learner.

## Shared Vision and Belief System

Creating a shared vision, a belief system, and a commitment to personalizing learning are essential elements in establishing a foundation to build a personalized learning system that is self-sustainable. Just like the phrase "it takes a village," it takes the whole school community and key stakeholders to develop a shared vision and belief system around system change. Personalizing learning that changes how teachers teach and learners learn affects everyone in the community. School looks different. Learning changes.

## Now It's Your Turn

Congratulations! You are on your way to the Wow in your school and district. Now it's your turn to create an action plan for your next steps.

Think about how you might get all stakeholders on board and build a set of beliefs that drive the change.

1. Invite teams of teachers to research personalized learning, including sections of this book, and then share their findings.

2. Share results of pre-assessments, the Connect the Dots session, and an overview of the readiness of the district and schools.

3. Ask learners to imagine what a school would look like if they had never seen one before.

4. Interview teachers and learners about what they like about school and what they would change.

5. Create a speech or presentation about personalizing learning to share at parent night, for staff, and when meeting members of the community. Consider creating a sixty-second speech just in case you only have that amount of time to get your message across about personalized learning.

6. Facilitate a shared vision session with key members from each school, including learners to give them voice about their learning.

7. Collect a team of dedicated educators and key stakeholders to develop a strategic plan for personalizing learning.

8. Write a principal or superintendent's message about personalized learning and what that will mean for your school(s).

> *"Personalized learning, by whatever name, is a central design principle for a transformed education system."*
>
> —John Bordeaux

## CHANGING THE CLASSROOM CULTURE (FOR TEACHERS)

### From a Teacher's Perspective

Kevin McLaughlin, a kindergarten teacher from the United Kingdom, shared what it means to have a culture shift in education and in his classroom. Kevin explained that personalizing learning is not something you can pick up and start in your own class tomorrow. But then he went on to say that teachers can take some steps to start. In his blog, he suggested that teachers might want to take into account most if not all of the following:

- It takes a lot of thought and effort.
- It takes time to build up a clear picture of learners in your class and where they are in their own learning.
- It takes courage to stand back as a teacher and let the learning happen on its own accord.
- It requires a vision and belief that it will work.
- It needs careful planning, but still allow for change at a moment's notice.
- It needs the voice of the learner to be listened to, to steer the direction of the learning.
- It needs you to rethink your classroom layout.
- It needs you to rethink your approach to teaching and learning

McLaughlin, 2012a.

Kevin shared that after he started standing back, there were so many Wow moments. But he did share there are not that many other teachers in his school taking this leap and giving learners voice and choice. He really appreciated that he was able to share his story and his learners' journeys.

> **Pause/Think/Reflect**
>
> How do we create a school culture where being a learner is more valuable than being a student?

## Focus on Learning

School is supposed to be about how learners are learning, but the conversations do not seem to be focused on learning. The focus tends to be on instruction and performance. Chris Watkins participates in the Campaign for Learning's Learning to Learn project and wrote *Learning: A Sense-Maker's Guide*, a publication commissioned by ATL, the union for education professionals across the United Kingdom. This guide makes so much sense. It brings everything in this book together. The idea of starting with the learner is all about learning about learning and noticing how we learn.

When you go back and review Chapter 2 on how learners learn, you get that how we make sense of learning is similar to how we make sense of other things. We do it gradually through experiences and build knowledge as we go. Remember the idea of talking, thinking, and reflecting about learning. These are key factors to understanding. *Learning: A Sense-Maker's Guide* notes four teaching practices that can help your learners make sense of their learning.

1. *Notice learning.* Getting in the flow is when learners are engaged in the process. You can see them motivated and immersed in the learning. This is a great time to stop the flow. Really! Ask your learners to step back and notice what happened, what we did to make it happen, what the effects were, how it felt, what helped, how learners were persistent in making it happen, and what might they do with the learning. You might even pick up some new language by noticing the learning that just happened.

2. *Have conversations about learning.* Listen to the conversations. You can ask learners to pair up or work in groups of three or four to discuss what they noticed in their learning. You can prompt them to reflect on why they were doing something, maybe something they might not even realize or take for granted. Some questions you can ask:

   Why did we _____ yesterday?

   Did we find out anything new?

   How can we find out more?

3. *Reflect on your learning.* Reflection is personal and can be recorded in a personal journal or shared in a blog. Reflection helps you notice your learning because you think about it when you write. When you are writing your reflections, new ideas may come to you or you may notice things about your learning you never knew before.

4. *Make learning an object of learning.* You can learn about learning while you are learning about something else. When you have your learners read and experiment to learn something, you can have them notice and reflect on what they learned and how they learned. You could have them reflect on how they handled their feelings during the learning or how they engaged with others as they learned. This is called the cycle of learning (Watkins, 2011).

When you see learners noticing and reflecting on their learning during their learning, that is the Wow of learning. These are the higher-order thinking skills we want our children to adopt: learning about learning and thinking about learning. This makes learning visible. This is what shakes up the classroom dynamics, because when the teacher is lecturing, learners are supposed to be listening. Are they? When you shake up the learning so learning is visible and learners are talking about their learning, the classroom environment is different. This change is that culture shift, the change that learners want now.

> *Changing culture is big. Now is the time.*

After reading this book and other resources about starting with the learner, you now know more about personalizing learning. You also know that turning the learning over so learners own their learning just doesn't happen overnight. If your district and school are moving in this direction, then you can start by doing your research on how personalizing learning will look in your classroom.

## Now It's Your Turn

Congratulations! You are on your way to the Wow in your classroom. Now it's your turn to create an action plan for your next steps. Think about how you might start personalizing learning.

1. Create a speech or presentation about personalizing learning to share with your learners and parents during Back-to-School or Open House night.

2. Determine how you learn best based on access, engage, and express.

3. Summarize your findings and review them with your class.

4. Ask your learners to then determine how they learn best and have them summarize and share their findings with another learner.

5. Take four diverse learners in your class and create a Class Learning Snapshot.

6. Start with one lesson and add some voice and choice.

7. Add more time to a specific activity that engages your learners so you do not have to stop the flow of learning.

8. Use the information from *Learning: A Sense-Maker's Guide* to notice and reflect on learning.

9. Reflect on your own teaching and learning and share with your learners.

10. Use some of the ideas shared in this book and write an action plan for your next steps.

## LOOKING FORWARD

Pulling all the pieces together around the missing piece, the learner, means teaching and learning change. Personalized learning is happening now, and you will see it happening more around the world. Put the *person* back in *personalization.* We end this book by providing the top trends for what personalized learning environments will look like in the near future.

### Top Trends for Personalizing Learning

• *The language will change to* learner *NOT* student. People are going to start using the word *learner* more often. When you use the word *learner* instead of *student,* it changes the context of how learning is happening. Learning now can happen anywhere, anytime, and any way. The learner takes charge and the teacher guides the process.

• *Schools will build a common language around personalized learning.* We will see teachers, learners, parents, and communities pulling together. It is all about focusing on the learner—starting with the learner. You will see more teachers sharing stories of learners taking control of their learning. You will also see teachers at more conferences sharing what teaching and learning looks like when learners take ownership of their learning. You will be seeing the Wow and the sharing of a-ha moments that will amaze you when you see what learners can do.

• *Learners will have more voice and agency.* Voice gives learners a chance to share their opinions about something they believe in. There are so many aspects of school where learners have not been given the opportunity to be active participants. Giving learners voice encourages them to participate in their own learning. When teachers let go, learners take on more leadership roles, especially around issues that matter to them.

• *Districts and schools will connect the dots.* Personalizing learning is neither another initiative nor a fad. It is the umbrella that connects all of the initiatives and programs in the district. Personalized learning means that teaching and learning change. It means looking at the current system with an open mind. Districts will consider what certain programs look like if the teacher is more of a facilitator and learners self-regulate their learning.

• *Districts will develop a shared vision and a set of beliefs around personalized learning.* To transform a system that has been in existence for over a hundred years, expect change to take time. Let all stakeholders have a chance to voice their concerns and ask questions. Build teams who investigate how personalized learning will look in their schools, visit schools where they are personalizing learning, and then develop a vision and plan that starts with the learner.

- *There will be more opportunities for choice where learners own and drive their learning.* Learning *is* personal. When you believe you have a stake in your learning and own your learning, you are more motivated to want to learn. The best thing we can do for our learners is to teach them to learn how to learn and how to think about their thinking. Now with anytime and anywhere learning, learners will need to acquire the skills to choose the most appropriate resources and tools for any task.

- *Purchasing decisions will be around what learners need first.* Technology does make it easier to personalize learning, but learners can take control of their learning with or without it. It is all about changing teacher and learner roles. You can give all learners an iPad or tablet or allow them to bring their own device, but teachers can still teach in a teacher-directed environment. There are teachers using an interactive whiteboard just like they did with their chalkboard. Technology does not change teaching practice unless the teacher understands that learning starts with the learner. It is so easy to get caught up in the lure of technology and believe the marketing from companies who state that their product is the only way to personalize learning or improve achievement.

Schools and districts need to involve teachers and learners in purchasing decisions. Watch for new tools like 3-D printers, Google Glass, and augmented reality programs that will Wow you and your learners. Learners will acquire the skills on their own to learn these tools if they are available to them. Teachers will have more opportunities to play with these tools at conferences and opportunities to drive their own learning with unconferences and Edcamps. You will see more Makerspaces happening where people of all ages can make and build things their way. Learners will be learning by tinkering, playing, investigating, exploring, and building in multiple venues in and outside of school. So think about technology tools supporting anytime, anywhere, and any way learning. This will push learning to be more personal and learners to think deeper on their own.

- *You will see more competency-based systems.* Fred Bramante (2013) defined competency-based systems as "a two-tiered strategy, both top-down and bottom-up. The top-down part is that you change the state regulations. You take out time requirements: 180 days, etc. and put in competency-based regulations that make learning flexible." Fred always tells people that mandating flexibility is an oxymoron. You make it so that the regulations pass much of the control over who owns the system from the system to the parents and the learners. The bottom-up part is where you have to make sure learners and parents actually know what's inside the regulations and know that they don't have to do it the way they've always done it. When learners know they have fun and exciting options, they will take advantage of this flexibility and more and more learners will start taking responsibility for their learning.

- *Learners will have hope and be more engaged because of intrinsic motivation.* All of us as learners need to feel motivated to learn. It cannot just be about getting a grade on an assignment, especially if that assignment is not relevant to the learner. A personal connection or a real-world issue that means something to learners can make all the difference to whether they care about an academic task. Offering a choice on some aspect of the work also sends its value up, and so does the chance to work on things with friends. From constructing a model to collaborating on a puzzle, we start to "own" new information when our hands and minds engage our thinking processes more fully.

- *Teachers will start small and have the time they need to make it work.* All of us as teachers only know what we know or what we were taught. We don't always know what we don't know. The Stages of Personalized Learning Environments were created for a reason. Teachers jumped in and turned over the learning to their learners before they were ready. Some things worked. Some didn't. If you feel comfortable teaching direct instruction and being in control, then letting go will be tough for you. But if you start slow, you can test the waters one lesson at a time.

 Thank you for taking the time to read this book! Use this book as a reference for understanding what personalized learning is and is not; understanding how your learners learn best; sharing models and examples with your colleagues, learners, and parents; and helping guide you in your next steps as you build your own rationale and action plan for personalizing learning.

This is not the end of the story; this is just the beginning of your journey, and what an amazing journey it will be!

> *"The only person who is educated is the one who has learned how to learn . . . and change."*

> —Carl Rogers

# Appendix

## UDL GUIDELINES, VERSION 2

The UDL Guidelines are organized according to the three main principles of Universal Design for Learning: representation, action and expression, and engagement. To include more detail, the principles are broken down into guidelines, where each has a set of supporting checkpoints. In short, they are arranged from *principle (least detail) to guideline to checkpoint (most detail)*.

| Principle | Guidelines | Checkpoints |
|---|---|---|
| **Principle I. Provide Multiple Means of Representation** (the What of learning) Qualities of an expert learner in the What of learning: **RESOURCEFUL AND KNOWLEDGEABLE LEARNER** | *Guideline 1: Provide options for perception* | **Checkpoint 1.1:** Offer ways of customizing the display of information **Checkpoint 1.2:** Offer alternatives for auditory information **Checkpoint 1.3:** Offer alternatives for visual information |
| | *Guideline 2: Provide options for language, mathematical expressions, and symbols* | **Checkpoint 2.1:** Clarify vocabulary and symbols **Checkpoint 2.2:** Clarify syntax and structure **Checkpoint 2.3:** Support decoding of text, mathematical notation, and symbols **Checkpoint 2.4:** Promote understanding across languages **Checkpoint 2.5:** Illustrate through multiple media |

*(Continued)*

(Continued)

| Principle | Guidelines | Checkpoints |
|---|---|---|
| | **Guideline 3:** *Provide options for comprehension* | **Checkpoint 3.1:** Activate or supply background knowledge<br><br>**Checkpoint 3.2:** Highlight patterns, critical features, big ideas, and relationships<br><br>**Checkpoint 3.3:** Guide information processing, visualization, and manipulation<br><br>**Checkpoint 3.4:** Maximize transfer and generalization |
| **Principle II. Provide Multiple Means of Action and Expression**<br><br>(the How of learning)<br><br>Qualities of an expert learner in the How of learning:<br><br>**STRATEGIC AND GOAL-ORIENTATED LEARNER** | **Guideline 4:** *Provide options for physical action* | **Checkpoint 4.1:** Vary the methods for response and navigation<br><br>**Checkpoint 4.2:** Optimize access to tools and assistive technologies |
| | **Guideline 5:** *Provide options for expression and communication* | **Checkpoint 5.1:** Use multiple media for communication<br><br>**Checkpoint 5.2:** Use multiple tools for construction and composition<br><br>**Checkpoint 5.3:** Build fluencies with graduated levels of support for practice and performance |
| | **Guideline 6:** *Provide options for executive functions* | **Checkpoint 6.1:** Guide appropriate goal setting<br><br>**Checkpoint 6.2:** Support planning and strategy development<br><br>**Checkpoint 6.3:** Facilitate managing information and resources<br><br>**Checkpoint 6.4:** Enhance capacity for monitoring progress |

| Principle | Guidelines | Checkpoints |
|---|---|---|
| **Principle III. Provide Multiple Means of Engagement**<br><br>(the Why of learning)<br><br>Qualities of an expert learner in the Why of learning:<br><br>**PURPOSEFUL AND MOTIVATED LEARNER** | *Guideline 7:*<br>*Provide options for recruiting interest* | **Checkpoint 7.1:** Optimize individual choice and autonomy<br><br>**Checkpoint 7.2:** Optimize relevance, value, and authenticity<br><br>**Checkpoint 7.3:** Minimize threats and distractions |
| | *Guideline 8:*<br>*Provide options for sustaining effort and persistence* | **Checkpoint 8.1:** Heighten salience of goals and objectives<br><br>**Checkpoint 8.2:** Vary demands and resources to optimize challenge<br><br>**Checkpoint 8.3:** Foster collaboration and communication<br><br>**Checkpoint 8.4:** Increase mastery-oriented feedback |
| | *Guideline 9:*<br>*Provide options for self-regulation* | **Checkpoint 9.1:** Promote expectations and beliefs that optimize motivation<br><br>**Checkpoint 9.2:** Facilitate personal coping skills and strategies<br><br>**Checkpoint 9.3:** Develop self-assessment and reflection |

# Glossary

1:1 programs:

Anywhere, anytime learning or laptops for learners programs with one device for each learner.

Access:

How a learner first processes information by accessing content through digital media, visual media, printed text, audio, or touch.

Adaptive learning:

Education method that uses computers as interactive teaching devices.

Anticipatory set:

As it relates to the Class Learning Snapshot, the strengths, interests, and challenges that four diverse learners have in accessing information, engaging with content, and expressing what they know.

Assessment AS Learning:

Characterized by learners reflecting on their own learning and making adjustments so they achieve deeper understanding.

Assessment FOR Learning:

Designed to make each learner's understanding visible so that teachers can decide what they can do to help learners progress (formative).

Assessment OF Learning:

Assessment that typically comes at the end of a course or unit of instruction to determine the extent to which

| | |
|---|---|
| | instructional goals have been achieved (summative). |
| Autonomy: | Personal independence and the capacity to make moral decisions and act on them. |
| Blended learning: | Hybrid learning that combines online and on-site opportunities. |
| Carnegie unit: | A system developed in the late nineteenth and early twentieth centuries that based the awarding of academic credit on how much time students spent in direct contact with a classroom teacher. |
| Class Learning Snapshot (CLS): | Helps teachers universally design lessons based on looking at the extremes of four diverse learners in their class instead of the average learner. |
| Class Learning Toolkit (CLT): | Helps teachers plan for the materials and methods that all learners in their class can use during their lessons and units by referring to the CLS. |
| Competency-Based: | Refers to any system of academic instruction, assessment, grading, and reporting based on learners demonstrating mastery of the knowledge and skills they are expected to learn before they progress to the next lesson, get promoted to the next grade level, or receive a diploma. |
| Constructivist theory: | Learning includes the concepts, categories, and problem-solving procedures invented previously by the culture and the ability for learners to "invent" these things for themselves. |

Engage: How learners engage with content and concepts using multiple strategies and tools that will keep their interest and motivation to learn.

Express: How learners express what they know and understand through actions (e.g., writing, acting, presenting, building, drawing, sharing).

Flipped classroom: Encompasses use of technology to leverage the learning in a classroom so a teacher can spend more time interacting with learners instead of lecturing.

Flow: When learners are fully immersed in what they are doing and there is a balance between the challenge of the task and the skill of the learner.

"g": General intelligence is highly predictive of both academic and work success and is necessary to learn complex activities like dance choreography.

Generation Y: The Millennials or First Digitals (1981–1996) prefer technology since they grew up in a digital environment and are adaptable, crave independence, and tend to be optimistic.

Generation Z: The Net Generation (1997–present) is realistic because of the events that have happened in their lives. They are globally aware and connected.

Generative curriculum: Learning is generated through connections and the discovery of the community by discovering, questioning, and then suggesting strategies.

Habits of mind: Play a vital role in lifelong learning and the ability to meet goals as well as create new ones. The habits focus on persisting, managing impulsivity, thinking flexibly, and listening with empathy and understanding.

Individual education plan: Defines the individualized objectives of a learner who has been diagnosed with a disability and is intended to help the learner reach individual education goals identified by the teacher.

Intrinsic motivation: A highly desired form of incentive that stems from a person's internal desire for self-satisfaction or pleasure in performing the task itself.

Learner agency: The capacity of individuals to act independently and to make their own free choices.

Lexile score: Refers to a measurement and tracking of reading abilities and helps choose appropriate reading material for learners' abilities.

Long-term memory: Occurs when information is processed deeply, questions are asked repeatedly to retrieve information and followed by feedback, material is practiced often, and the study of material is spaced over days and weeks.

Mindset: Belief guides a large part of your life. Much of what you think of as your personality actually grows out of this mindset and could prevent you from fulfilling your potential. You have either a fixed mindset or a growth mindset.

More Knowledgeable Other (MKO): Refers to anyone who has a better understanding than the learner with respect to a particular task, process, or concept. The MKO could be a teacher, coach, or adult and could also be peers or technology.

Neuroplasticity: Means the brain can change, be improved, and continues to adapt and learn through life.

Neuroscience: Links observations about cognitive behavior with the actual physical processes that support such behavior.

Performance-based education: A system of teaching and learning that places learners in grade-level content areas based on mental capacity rather than chronological age (e.g., Taylor County Schools).

Personal Learner Profile (PLP): Identifies how learners learn best based on their strengths, challenges, interests, aspirations, talents, and passions.

Personal Learning Backpack (PLB): The PLB is personal to learners based on how they understand how they learn best and includes learning and instructional strategies and resources and tools.

Personal pathways: Engages learners in looking at their talents, skills, interests, and aspirations guided by an advisor so they discover the things that drive them forward.

Personalized Learning Environment: A place is where learning starts with the learner and learner and teacher roles change. Learners understand how they learn best so they can become active participants in

|  | designing their learning goals along with the teacher. Learners take responsibility for their learning. When they own and drive their learning, they are motivated and challenged as they learn so they work harder than their teacher. |
|---|---|
| Personalized Learning System: | A culture shift and a change in process that impacts the entire school community. It means creating a self-sustaining system that will need human and technological infrastructures to support it. |
| Project-Based Learning (PBL): | Dynamic approach to teaching in which learners explore real-world problems and challenges. PBL is not the same as learners doing the same project designed by the teacher. |
| Readiness: | A developmental point at which a person, organization, or system has the capacity and willingness to engage in a particular activity. |
| Response to Intervention (RTI): | A multitier approach to the early identification and support of students with learning and behavior needs (see www.rtinetwork.org). |
| Self-governance: | Every learner and staff member has an equal vote in managing the school. |
| Self-regulation: | Learners are concerned with what they do to generate and sustain their engagement. |
| Sensory memory: | Associated with the senses (e.g., seeing, hearing, touching) where information is stored briefly for processing. |
| Short-term memory: | The stage where further consciousness processing occurs, actively thinking about what has occurred. |

| | |
|---|---|
| Social Interaction: | Where community plays a central role in the process of "making meaning" and plays a fundamental role in the process of cognitive development. |
| Spiral curriculum: | The idea of revisiting basic ideas over and over, building on them and elaborating to the level of full understanding and mastery. |
| Stage One PLE: | Teacher universally designs instruction that encourages learner voice and choice. |
| Stage Two PLE: | Learner and teacher are co-designers of lessons, projects, and assessments. |
| Stage Three PLE: | Learners drive their learning with teacher as partner in learning. |
| UDL Guidelines: | Provide a lens for teachers to understand how learners learn best and assist teachers in planning universally designed lessons that can reduce barriers to learning as well as maximize learning for all learners (see appendix). |
| UDL Principles: | The UDL Principles are multiple means of representation, multiple means of action and expression, and multiple means of engagement. They provide the framework for personalizing learning and assist teachers in planning universally designed lessons that can reduce barriers to learning as well as optimizing levels of challenge and support to meet the needs of all learners. |
| Universal Design for Learning (UDL): | Set of principles for curriculum development that gives equal opportunities for all learners to learn. |

Universally designed:     Implies concerns about accessibility so possible barriers identified for diverse learners are removed and solutions are developed to support those learners.

Variability:     The degree of difference where learners differ from other learners and no one is average.

Working Memory:     Holds limited information for a limited amount of time by using cognitive learning strategies to transfer information from working memory t long-term memory.

Zone of proximal development:     The distance between a learner's ability to perform a task under adult guidance and/or with peer collaboration and the learner's ability to solve the problem independently. Learning occurs in this zone (see McLeod, 2012).

# References

Adams County School District 50. (2011). *Our competency-based system (CBS)*. Retrieved December 29, 2013, from http://www.cbsadams50.org.

Anytime Anywhere Learning Foundation. (2008). *Transforming learning through universal access to technology*. Retrieved November 23, 2013, from http://www.aalf.org/cms/?page=AALF.

Association for Psychological Sciences. (2009, December). *Learning styles debunked*. Retrieved October 15, 2015, from http://www.psychologicalscience.org/index.php/news/releases/learning-styles-debunked-there-is-no-evidence-supporting-auditory-and-visual-learning-psychologists-say.html.

Association Montessori Internationale. (2013). *Montessori research*. Retrieved May 1, 2014, from http://www.montessori-ami.org.

Barron, B., & Darling-Hammond, L. (2008). *Teaching for meaningful learning: A review of research on inquiry-based and cooperative learning*. Retrieved November 24, 2013, from http://www.edutopia.org/pdfs/edutopia-teaching-for-meaningful-learning.pdf.

Bass, S., & Walker, K. (2013, July 8). *The Walker Learning approach: A pedagogical model for a "both way learning" paradigm*. Victoria, Australia.

Bergmann, J., Overmyer, J., & Wilie, B. (2013). *The flipped class: What it is and what it is not*. Retrieved August 10, 2013, from http://www.thedailyriff.com/articles/the-flipped-class-conversation-689.php.

Bergmann, J., & Sams, A. (2012). *Flip your classroom: Reaching every student in every class every day*. Eugene, OR: ISTE.

Big Picture Learning. (2014). *Schools*. Retrieved December 12, 2013, from http://www.bigpicture.org/schools.

Block, J. (2013, October 28). *Strategic modeling: Balancing structure with choice*. Retrieved December 30, 2013, from http://www.edutopia.org/blog/strategic-modeling-balancing-structure-choice-joshua-block.

Boyd, R. (2008, February 7). *Do people only use 10 percent of their brains?* Retrieved November 5, 2013, from http://www.scientificamerican.com/article.cfm?id=people-only-use-10-percent-of-brain.

Bramante, F. (2013, August). *Competency-based: It's all about learning not time*. Retrieved July 22, 2014, from http://www.personalizelearning.com/2013/08/competency-based-its-all-about-learning.html.

Bransford, J., Derry, S., Berliner, D. C., Hammerness, K., & Beckett, K. L. (2005). Theories of learning and their roles in teaching. In L. Darling-Hammond & J. Bransford (Eds.), *Preparing teachers for a changing world*. San Francisco: Wiley & Sons.

Bray, B., & McClaskey, K. (2013, May). A step-by-step guide to personalize learning. *Learning & Leading with Technology*. Retrieved July 22, 2014, from http://www.learningandleading-digital.com/learning_leading/201305#pg14.

British Columbia Ministry of Education. (2011). *Personalized learning in BC: Interactive discussion guide*. Retrieved February 10, 2013, from http://personalizedlearningbc.ca/#/1.

Bruner, J. (2013). *Constructivism and discovery learning*. Retrieved September 10, 2013, from www.lifecircles-inc.com/Learningtheories/constructivism/bruner.html.

Busteed, B. (2013, January 7). *The school cliff: Student engagement drops with each school year*. Retrieved August 10, 2013, from http://thegallupblog.gallup.com/2013/01/the-school-cliff-student-engagement.html.

Carnegie Foundation. (2013, July). *50 state scan of course credit policies*. Retrieved September 12, 2013, from http://commons.carnegiefoundation.org/wp-content/uploads/2013/08/CUP_Policy_PDF1.pdf.

Center for Applied Special Technology. (2013). *Changes in UDL guidelines 2.0*. Retrieved May 1, 2013, from http://www.udlcenter.org/aboutudl/udlguidelines/changes.

Center for Dewey Studies. (2010). *About Dewey—Influence*. Retrieved September 10, 2013, from http://deweycenter.siu.edu/about_influence.html.

Clark, B. (2013, January 16). *6 pillars of a 1:1 initiative*. Retrieved November 10, 2013, from http://smartblogs.com/education/2013/01/16/the-6-pillars-11-initiative-brett-clark.

Clarke, J. (2013). *Personalized learning: Student-designed pathways to high school graduation*. Thousand Oaks, CA. Corwin.

Clarke, J., & Frazer, E. (2003). Making learning personal: Educational practices that work. In J. DiMartino, J. Clarke, & D. Wolk (Eds.), *Personalized learning: Preparing high school students to create their futures* (pp. 174–193). Lanham, MD: Scarecrow Press.

Coalition of Essential Schools. (2014). *The CES common principles*. Retrieved January 5, 2014, from http://www.essentialschools.org/items/4.

Colorado Springs School District 11. (2011). *Home*. Retrieved May 1, 2012, from http://www.d11.org/d11way/Pages/default.aspx.

Common Sense Media. (2013, October). Zero to Eight: Children's Media Use in America 2013. Retrieved January 10, 2014, from Common Sense Media Web site: http://www.commonsensemedia.org/research/zero-to-eight-childrens-media-use-in-america-2013

Concordia University. (2013). *Do standardized tests show an accurate view of students' abilities?* Retrieved October 11, 2013, from http://education.cu-portland.edu/blog/news/do-standardized-test-show-an-accurate-view-of-students-abilities.

Cook, R. (2013, May). Performance-based with zero dropouts. Retrieved July 22, 2014, from http://www.personalizelearning.com/2013/05/performance-based-with-zero-dropouts.html.

Council of Chief State School Officers. (2014). *Innovation Lab Network*. Retrieved December 29, 2013, from http://www.ccsso.org/What_We_Do/Innovation_Lab_Network.html.

Council on Foreign Relations. (2012). *U.S. education reform and national security*. Retrieved September 10, 2013, from http://www.cfr.org/united-states/us-education-reform-national-security/p27618.

Csíkszentmihályi, M. (1990). *Flow: The psychology of optimal experience.* New York: Harper & Row.

Culatta, R. (2013). *Social development theory (Lev Vygotsky).* Retrieved July 22, 2014, from http://www.instructionaldesign.org/theories/social-development.html.

Cushman, K. (2013, November 14). *8 universal secrets of motivated learners.* Retrieved November 14, 2013, from http://www.personalizelearning.com/2013/11/8-universal-secrets-of-motivated.html.

Dekker, S., Lee, N., Howard-Jones, P., & Jolles, J. (2012). Neuromyths in education: Prevalence and predictors of misconceptions among teachers. *Frontiers in Educational Psychology.* Retrieved October 14, 2013, from http://www.frontiersin.org/Educational_Psychology/10.3389/fpsyg.2012.00429/full.

Dewey, J. (1899). *The school and society.* Chicago: University of Chicago Press.

Digital Textbook Collaborative. (2012, February 1). *Digital textbook playbook.* Retrieved November 10, 2013, from http://tablets-textbooks.procon.org/files/Digital_Textbook_Playbook.pdf.

*Diplomas count 2013.* (2013, June 6). Retrieved January 5, 2014, from http://www.edweek.org/media/diplomascount2013_release.pdf.

Doidge, N. (2007). *The brain that changes itself.* New York: Viking.

DuFour, R. (2004). Culture shift doesn't occur overnight—or without conflict. *Leading Edge, 25,* 63–64. Retrieved November 20, 2013, from http://learningforward.org/docs/jsd-fall-2004/dufour254.pdf?sfvrsn=2.

Dweck, C. (2006). *Mindset.* New York: Random House.

Dweck, C. (2010). *What is mindset?* Retrieved June 12, 2013, from http://mindsetonline.com/whatisit/about/index.html.

Earl, L., & Katz, S. (2006). *Rethinking classroom assessment with purpose in mind.* Retrieved April 11, 2013, from http://www.edu.gov.mb.ca/k12/assess/wncp/full_doc.pdf.

EdVisions Schools. (2009). *EdVisions schools design essentials.* Retrieved December 5, 2013, from http://www.edvisions.com/custom/SplashPage.asp.

Edwards, C. (2012, November 17). *Using technology to engage learners.* Retrieved April 19, 2013, from http://messylearningdotcom.wordpress.com/2012/11/17/using-technology-to-engage-learners.

Evans, R. (1996). *The human side of school change.* San Francisco: Jossey-Bass.

Expeditionary Learning. (2013a). *Our approach.* Retrieved December 29, 2013, from http://elschools.org/our-approach.

Expeditionary Learning. (2013b). *Life in a vernal pool field guide.* Retrieved December 29, 2013, from http://elschools.org/student-work/life-vernal-pool-field-guide.

Ferguson, C. (2009, June 14). Not every child is secretly a genius. *The Chronicle Review.* Retrieved January 29, 2014, from http://chronicle.com/article/Not-Every-Child-Is-Secretly/48001.

Fixen, D., Blase, K., Horner, R., & Sugal, G. (2009, February). *Scaling up evidence-based practices in education.* Retrieved January 7, 2014, from http://www.fpg.unc.edu/sites/fpg.unc.edu/files/resources/reports-and-policy-briefs/SISEP-Brief1-ScalingUpEBPInEducation-02-2009.pdf.

Fullan, M. (2011, May). *Choosing the wrong drivers for whole system reform.* Retrieved January 7, 2014, from http://www.michaelfullan.ca/media/13501740430.html.

Gardner, H. (1983). *Frames of mind.* New York: Basic Books.

Gerstein, J. (2011, June). *The flipped classroom model: A full picture.* Retrieved September 30, 2013, from http://usergeneratededucation.wordpress.com/2011/06.

Global Education First Initiative. (2012). *An initiative of the secretary-general.* Retrieved January 25, 2014, from http://www.globaleducationfirst.org.

Groff, J. (2013). Expanding our 'frames' of mind for education and the arts. *Harvard Educational Review, 83,* 15–39. Retrieved May 19, 2013, from http://hepg.org/her/abstract/1217.

Hamdan, N., McKnight, P., McKnight, K., & Arfstrom, K. (2013). *The flipped learning model: A white paper based on the literature review titled a review of flipped learning.* Retrieved November 23, 2013, from http://researchnetwork.pearson.com/wpcontent/uploads/WhitePaper_FlippedLearning.pdf.

Hansen, R., & Hansen, K. (n.d.). *What do employers really want? Top skills and values employers seek from job-seekers.* Retrieved August 20, 2013, from http://www.quintcareers.com/job_skills_values.html.

Hargreaves, D. (2006). *A new shape for schooling.* Retrieved April 12, 2012, from http://webfronter.com/camden/learning/mnu4/images/new_shape_for_schooling_DHH_06.pdf.

Henry County Schools. (2014). *Personalized learning.* Retrieved April 2, 2014, from http://schoolwires.henry.k12.ga.us/Page/60175.

High Tech High. (2012, December 18). *HTH design principles.* Retrieved December 28, 2013, from http://www.hightechhigh.org/about/design-principles.php.

Hinton, C., & Jobs for the Future. (2013). *Brainy approaches to learning.* Retrieved from http://www.studentsatthecenter.org/brainy-approaches-learning.

Hord, S., Rutherford, W., Huling-Austin, L., Hall, G., & Knoll, M. (1987, May). *Taking charge of change.* Alexandria, VA: ASCD.

Inquiry Hub. (2013). *Inquiry Hub.* Retrieved October 25, 2013, from http://www.inquiryhub.org.

Institute @ CESA #1. (2013, August 12). *Personalized learning model.* Retrieved November 3, 2013, from http://www.cesa1.k12.wi.us/institute/designdevelop/personalized-learning-model.cfm.

Ito, M. (2010, November 24). *When youth own the public education agenda.* Retrieved August 10, 2013, from http://www.huffingtonpost.com/mimi-ito/when-youth-own-the-public_b_787866.html.

Jabr, F. (2013, April 11). The reading brain in the digital age: The science of paper versus screens. *Scientific American.* Retrieved November 10, 2013, from http://www.scientificamerican.com/article/reading-paper-screens.

Johansen-Berg, H. (2011, November ). How does our brain learn new information? *Scientific American.* Retrieved October 12, 2013, from http://www.scientificamerican.com/article.cfm?id=how-does-our-brain-learn.

Khan Academy. (2013). *A free world-class education for anyone anywhere.* Retrieved September 15, 2013, from https://www.khanacademy.org/about.

Kennebec Intra-District Schools. (2013). *RSU 2's standards-based, learner-centered framework.* Retrieved July 22, 2014, from http://www.kidsrsu.org/wp-content/uploads/2013/12/Standards-Based-Reform-Action-Plan-V1.pdf.

Kennedy, C. (2013, December 2). *Does student voice lead to student agency?* Retrieved May 1, 2014, from http://cultureofyes.ca/2013/12/02/does-student-voice-lead-to-student-agency.

Klein, A. (2008). *Different approaches to teaching: Comparing three preschool programs.* Retrieved May 1, 2014, from http://www.earlychildhoodnews.com/early-childhood/article_view.aspx?ArticleID=367.

Kroehler, K. (2014, January 28). *Why hope matters.* Retrieved July 22, 2014, from http://www.personalizelearning.com/2014/01/why-hope-matters.html.

Kunskapsskolan Education. (2014) *Welcome to Kunskapsskolan.* Retrieved May 1, 2014, from http://www.kunskapsskolan.se/foretaget/kunskapsskolaninenglish.

Lepi, K. (2012, May 30). *Print vs digital books: New study helps teachers decide.* Retrieved November 10, 2013, from http://www.edudemic.com/print-ebooks.

Levin, H. M., & Belfield, C. R. (2007). *The price we pay: Economic and socialconsequences of inadequate education.* Washington, DC: Brookings Institution Press.

Luskin, B. (2013). The media psychology effect. *Psychology Today.* Retrieved July 22, 2014, from http://www.psychologytoday.com/blog/the-media-psychology-effect/201308/if-i-had-better-brain.

Maine Learning Technology Initiative. (2009). *About MLTI.* Retrieved November 23, 2013, from http://maine.gov/mlti/about/index.shtml.

Marquis, J. (2012, December 23). *6 possible roles for teachers in a personalized learning environment.* Retrieved November 5, 2013, from http://www.teachthought.com/learning/6-possible-roles-for-teachers-in-a-personalized-learning-environment.

Maryland State Department of Education. (2011). *A route for every learner.* Retrieved January 20, 2014, from http://marylandpublicschools.org/NR/rdonlyres/517D465A-F0B5-40DD-BB4B-E98EA716EC46/28188/A_Route_for_Every_Learner_Report_NSG_032511_w.pdf.

McCombs, B. (2014). *Developing autonomous and responsible learners: A key to motivating students.* Retrieved February 1, 2014, from http://www.apa.org/education/k12/learners.aspx.

McGreal, S. (2013, November). The illusory theory of multiple intelligences. *Psychology Today.* Retrieved October 14, 2013, from http://www.psychologytoday.com/blog/unique-everybody-else/201311/the-illusory-theory-multiple-intelligences.

McLaughlin, K. (2012a, April 2). *Personalising learning does more than get results.* Retrieved October 13, 2013, from http://www.ictsteps.com/2012/04/personalising-learning-does-more-than.html.

McLaughlin, K. (2012b, January 15). *Innovating learning requires innovating the classroom too.* Retrieved October 5, 2012, from http://www.ictsteps.com/2012/01/innovating-learning-requires-innovating.html.

McLeod, S. (2012). *Zone of proximal development.* Retrieved September 5, 2013, from http://www.simplypsychology.org/Zone-of-Proximal-Development.html.

MetaMetrics. (2013). *What is a Lexile measure?* Retrieved October 10, 2013, from http://www.lexile.com/about-lexile/lexile-overview.

Mirel, J. (2006). The traditional high school. *EducationNext, 6.* Retrieved September 8, 2013, from http://educationnext.org/the-traditional-high-school.

Monarch Academy. (2012). *Monarch charter schools.* Retrieved May 1, 2014, from http://www.monarch-academy.org/glen-burnie.

Mt. Abraham Union Middle/High School. (2013). *Mt. Abraham Union Middle/High School.* Retrieved December 30, 2013, from http://www.mtabe.k12.vt.us.

NASSP. (2004). *Breaking ranks II: Strategies for leading high school reform.* Retrieved February 6, 2013, from http://www.nassp.org/Content/158/BRII_exec_sum mary.pdf.

National Center for Education Statistics. (2013, May). *Institutional retention and graduation rates for undergraduate students.* Retrieved January 10, 2014, from https://nces.ed.gov/programs/coe/indicator_cva.asp.

National Center for Education Statistics. (2014, January). *Status dropout rates.* Retrieved January 5, 2014, from https://nces.ed.gov/programs/coe/indica tor_coj.asp.

National Center for Universal Design for Learning. (2013, March). *A tale of four districts: UDL implementation—Bartholomew Consolidated School Corporation (BCSC).* Retrieved March 25, 2014, from http://www.udlcenter.org/imple mentation/fourdistricts/bartholomew.

National Education Association of the United States. (1894). Committee of Ten on Secondary School Studies. *Report of the Committee of Ten on secondary school studies: With the reports of the conferences arranged by the committee.* Pub. for the National Education Association by the American Book Co.

Nellie Mae Foundation. (2014). *Strategy and initiatives.* Retrieved December 30, 2013, from http://www.nmefoundation.org/about-us/strategy-and-initiatives.

Newell, R., Ryzin, V., & Meier, D. (2009). *Assessing what really matters in schools.* Lanham, MD: Rowman & Littlefield.

Noyes, J., & Garland, K. (2008, September ). Computer- vs. paper-based tasks: Are they equivalent? *Ergonomics, 51,* 1352–1375. Retrieved January 10, 2014, from http://www.twosides.info:8080/content/rsPDF_382.pdf.

Pink, D. (2009). *Drive.* New York: Riverhead Books.

Reggio Kids. (2014). *The Reggio approach.* Retrieved January 20, 2014, from http://www.reggiokids.com/the_reggio_approach.html.

Rickabaugh, J. (2012, February 27). *Jim Rickabaugh on CESA #1 Institute.* Retrieved July 22, 2014, from http://www.personalizelearning.com/2012/02/jim-ricka baugh-on-institute-cesa-1.html.

Rose, D., & Gravel, J. (2012). *Curricular opportunities in the digital age.* Retrieved February 5, 2013, from http://www.studentsatthecenter.org/sites/scl.dldev .com/files/Curricular%20Opportunities%20Digital%20Age.pdf.

Rose, T. (2013, June 19). *The myth of average: Todd Rose TEDxSonomaCounty.* Retrieved July 30, 2013, from http://youtu.be/4eBmyttcfU4.

Sahlberg, P. (2011). *Finnish lessons.* New York: Teachers College Press.

Schwartz, K. (2014, February 3). *Teaching strategies math and inquiry: The importance of letting students stumble.* Retrieved February 4, 2014, from http://blogs.kqed. org/mindshift/2014/02/math-and-inquiry-the-importance-of-letting-students-stumble.

Science Leadership Academy. (2014). *About SLA.* Retrieved May 1, 2014, from http://www.scienceleadership.org.

Scott, C. (2010). The enduring appeal of 'learning styles.' *The Australian Journal of Education, 54,* 5–17. Retrieved October 14, 2013, from http://search.informit .com.au/documentSummary;dn=087128755217364;res=IELHSS.

Shaw, L. (2013). *Montessori: The missing voice in the education reform debate.* Retrieved May 1, 2014, from www.montessori.org.

Sincero, S. M. (2011, July 16). *Social development theory.* Retrieved July 16, 2014, from https://explorable.com/social-development-theory.

Sizer, T. (2004). *Horace's compromise: The dilemma of the American highschool.* New York: Houghton Mifflin.

Sloan Consortium. (2005, May). Blended learning: Sleeping giant. *Sloan-C View,* 4(5). Retrieved August 8, 2013, from http://sloanconsortium.org/publica tions/view/v4n5/coverv4n5.htm.

Staker, H., & Horn, M. (2012, May). *Classifying K-12 blended learning.* Retrieved November 12, 2013, from http://www.innosightinstitute.org/innosight/wp-content/uploads/2012/05/Classifying-K-12-blended-learning2.pdf.

Sturgis, C. (2013). *What is competency-based learning?* Retrieved May 10, 2013, from https://sites.google.com/site/competencybasedpathways.

Sturgis, C., Patrick, S., & Pittenger, L. (2011). *It's not a matter of time: Highlights from the 2011 Competency-Based Learning Summit.* Retrieved September 2, 2013, from http://www.inacol.org/cms/wp-content/uploads/2012/09/iNACOL_Its_Not_A_Matter_of_Time_full_report.pdf.

Sudbury Valley School. (2013). *The Sudbury model.* Retrieved December 28, 2013, from http://www.sudval.com/01_abou_01.html.

Thomas, J. (2000). *A review of the research on project-based learning.* Retrieved November 23, 2013, from http://www.bie.org/research/study/review_of_project_based_learning_2000.

Tomlinson, C. (2012). *What is differentiation?* Retrieved July 17, 2014, from http://differentiationcentral.com/what-is-differentiated-instruction.html.

Toshalis, E., & Nakkula, M. (2013). *Motivation, engagement and student voice.* Retrieved June 10, 2013, from http://www.studentsatthecenter.org/topics/motivation-engagement-and-student-voice.

Trucano, M. (2011, December 2). *School computer labs: A bad idea?* Retrieved September 10, 2013, from http://blogs.worldbank.org/edutech/computer-labs.

Truss, D. (2013, December 23). *Kids talk about learning.* Retrieved July 22, 2014, from http://www.personalizelearning.com/2013/12/kids-talk-about-learning-at-inquiry-hub.html.

Tucker, M. (2012). Sahlberg's vision: Balancing teacher capacity and national education goals. *Education Week.* Retrieved from http://blogs.edweek.org/edweek/top_performers/2012/05/sahlbergs_vision_balancing_teacher_capacity_and_national_education_goals.html.

U.S. Census Bureau. (2009). *Educational attainment: Five key data releases from the U.S. Census Bureau.* Retrieved July 22, 2014, from http://www.census.gov/newsroom/cspan/educ._

United States Department of Education. (2010). *National education technology plan.* Retrieved January 22, 2012, from www.ed.gov/technology/draft-netp- 2010/individualized-personalized-differentiated-instruction.

Verona Area School District. (2014). *Welcome to VASD.* Retrieved May 1, 2014, from http://www.verona.k12.wi.us.

Vittra Schools. (2013). *Telefonplan—Learning spaces.* Retrieved December 30, 2013, from http://vittra.se/english/Schools/StockholmSouth/Telefonplan/LearningSpaces.aspx.

Vygotsky, L. S. (1962). *Thought and language.* Cambridge, MA: MIT Press.

Walker, K. (2012). *Play matters: Investigative learning for preschool to grade 2* (2nd ed.). Camberwell, Australia: ACER Press.

Washor, E. (2014, April 8). *Personalization and student engagement.* Retrieved July 22, 2014, from http://www.personalizelearning.com/2014/04/what-do-you-mean-by-personalization.html.

Waterhouse, L. (2006). Multiple Intelligences, the Mozart effect, and emotional intelligence: A critical review. *Educational Psychology, 41,* 207–225. Retrieved October 10, 2013, from http://graduatestudenthelp.com/LynnWaterhouse .pdf.

Watkins, C. (2006). Personalised classroom learning. *INSI Research Matters, 29.* Retrieved August 10, 2012, from https://www.academia.edu/7185028/ Personalised_Classroom_Learning.

Watkins, C. (2009). Learners in the driving seat. *School LeadershipToday, 1*(2), 28–31. Retrieved February 10, 2013, from https://www.academia.edu/7184990/ Learners_in_the_driving_seat.

Watkins, C. (2010). Learning, performance and improvement. *INSI Research Matters, 34.* Retrieved May 10, 2013, from https://www.academia .edu/2309010/Learning_Performance_and_Improvement.

Watkins, C. (2011). *Learning: A sense-maker's guide.* Retrieved April 2, 2013, from https://www.academia.edu/547778/Learning_a_sense-makers_guide.

Weimer, M. (2002). *Learner centered teaching: Five key changes to practice.* New York: Jossey-Bass.

Welch, L., & Richardson, W. (2013, October 23). *Architects of their learning.* Retrieved July 22, 2014, from http://www.personalizelearning.com/2013/10/archi tects-of-their-learning-km-explore.html.

*What is the history of the K-12 education system?* (2013). Retrieved January 10, 2014, from http://www.wisegeek.org/what-is-the-history-of-the-k-12-education- system.htm.

Wilborn, G. (2012, May 28). *Personalized learning at Colorado Springs D11.* Retrieved July 22, 2014, from http://www.personalizelearning.com/2012/05/personal ized-learning-colorado-springs.html.

Willingham, D. (2005, June). Ask the cognitive scientist: Do visual, auditory, and kinesthetic learners need visual, auditory, and kinesthetic instruction? *American Educator.* Retrieved January 20, 2014, from http://www.aft.org/ newspubs/periodicals/ae/summer2005/willingham.cfm.

Yowell, C. (2013). *Reimagining the experience of education.* Retrieved September 10, 2013, from http://connectedlearning.tv/connie-yowell-reimagining-experi ence-education.

Zimmerman, B. J. (1990). Self-regulated learning and academic achievement: An overview. *Educational Psychologist, 25*(1).

# Index

Page numbers followed by *f* or *t* indicate figures or tables, respectively.

A SAGE Company

Corwin is committed to improving education for all learners by publishing books and other professional development resources for those serving the field of PreK–12 education. By providing practical, hands-on materials, Corwin continues to carry out the promise of its motto: **"Helping Educators Do Their Work Better."**